Volume 18

Advances in
Librarianship

Volume 18

Advances in
Librarianship

Edited by

Irene P. Godden

University Libraries
Colorado State University
Fort Collins, Colorado

ACADEMIC PRESS
San Diego New York Boston London Sydney Tokyo Toronto

This book is printed on acid-free paper. ∞

Academic Press, Inc.
A Division of Harcourt Brace & Company
525 B Street, Suite 1900, San Diego, California 92101-4495

United Kingdom Edition published by
Academic Press Limited
24-28 Oval Road, London NW1 7DX

International Standard Serial Number: 0065-2830

International Standard Book Number: 0-12-024618-X

PRINTED IN THE UNITED STATES OF AMERICA
94   95   96   97   98   99   BC   9   8   7   6   5   4   3   2   1

Contents

Contributors   ix
Preface   xi

Library and Information Science: Its Content and Scope
Pertti Vakkari

    I. Introduction   1
   II. The Relationship between Library Science and
       Information Science   6
  III. The Relation of Information Science to Other Sciences   12
  IV. Central Conceptualizations of Information Science   24
   V. Conclusion: Orientation Strategies as Integrators of the
      Broadening Field   47
      References   51

Students and the Information Search Process: Zones of Intervention for Librarians
Carol Collier Kuhlthau

     I. Introduction   57
    II. Information Seeking as a Constructive Process   58
   III. Model of the Information Search Process   58
   IV. Common Patterns in the Process of Information Seeking   61
    V. Misunderstanding of Search Tasks   62
   VI. Principle of Uncertainty for Library Services   62
  VII. Concept of Diagnosing Zones of Intervention   63
 VIII. Five Zones of Intervention   64
   IX. Levels of Mediation   65
    X. Levels of Education   66
   XI. Counselors' Role in Information Search Process   66
  XII. Process Intervention Strategies   67
 XIII. Conclusion   71
      References   72

Reshaping Academic Library Reference Service: A Review of Issues, Trends, and Possibilities
Chris Ferguson

   I. Introduction   73
  II. Anatomy of a Crisis   74
 III. Reshaping Reference Service   87
  IV. The Future of Reference   96
   V. Conclusion   102
      References   103

The Information Needs of Children
Virginia A. Walter

   I. Introduction   111
  II. What Is Known about the Information Needs
      of Children?   112
 III. Research on Children's Information Needs in
      Southern California   115
  IV. Implications   126
   V. Conclusion   127
      References   128

Information Management Systems Planning: A Process for Health Science Libraries and Institutions
Elizabeth K. Eaton

    I. Introduction and Background   131
   II. Information Technology in the Health Sciences—
       Historical Perspectives   133
  III. The National Library of Medicine's IAIMS Program   138
   IV. First Four IAIMS Sites   141
    V. 1986 IAIMS Awards and Common Elements   143
   VI. Tufts University IAIMS Planning Grant   145
  VII. Defining Success   152
 VIII. Conclusion   155
       References   156

Public Library Funding: Issues, Trends, and Resources
Brian A. Reynolds

   I. History   161
  II. Funding Formats   163

III. Cost Control   166
IV. Entrepreneurship   170
 V. Fees and Fundraising   176
VI. Political Action   180
VII. Conclusion   185
     References   186

Romania and United States Library Connections
Opritsa D. Popa and Sandra J. Lamprecht

  I. Overview of Romanian Librarianship to 1989: A Legacy
      of Despair   189
 II. Crisis and Transition   195
III. In Search of New Paradigms: Romania's Libraries and
      U.S. Models   199
IV. U.S. Librarians in Romania   206
 V. The Road Ahead   209
     References   212

Indoor Air Quality: Planning and Managing Library Buildings
Carmel C. Bush and Halcyon R. Enssle

  I. Introduction   215
 II. Planning for New Buildings   220
III. Planning for Existing Buildings   227
IV. Establishing a Baseline   230
 V. Summary   230
     References   234

Index   237

Contributors

Numbers in parentheses indicate the pages on which the authors' contributions begin.

Carmel C. Bush (215), Morgan Library, Colorado State University, Fort Collins, Colorado 80523

Elizabeth K. Eaton (131), Health Sciences Library, Tufts University, Boston, Massachusetts 02111

Halcyon R. Enssle (215), Morgan Library, Colorado State University, Fort Collins, Colorado 80523

Chris Ferguson (73), Thomas and Dorothy Leavey Library, University of Southern California, Los Angeles, California 90089-0182

Carol Collier Kuhlthau (57), School of Communication, Information and Library Studies, Rutgers University, New Brunswick, New Jersey 08903

Sandra J. Lamprecht (189), Shields Library, University of California, Davis, California 95616

Opritsa D. Popa (189), Shields Library, University of California, Davis, California 95616

Brian A. Reynolds (159), San Luis Obispo City-County Library, San Luis Obispo, California 93403-8107

Pertti Vakkari (1), Department of Information Studies, University of Tampere, 33101 Tampere, Finland

Virginia A. Walter (111), Graduate School of Library and Information Science, University of California, Los Angeles, California 90024

Preface

A speaker at a recent professional conference, responding to the theme of the future of libraries, asked, "Will libraries be the gas stations or the road kill on the information highway?" Another and perhaps less provocative way to phrase this question would be to ask what the foundation of the profession of librarianship is, and then to try to determine what values from our long history we may want to incorporate into the foundation for building the future. To what will we hold constant in a time of transformation?

Vakkari, in his review article, "Library and Information Science: Its Content and Scope," provides a thoughtful and eminently readable history of the changing definitions of the field of library/information science, gives a working definition of the broader frame of information science as a field of research, and suggests orientation strategies for the future. He offers the dominant theme for this volume by supporting the definition of information science as a cognitive science that facilitates the effective communication of desired information between human generator and user, which is developed in its many variant applications in the articles that follow.

Kuhlthau summarizes recent studies of information-seeking behavior as a constructive process, introduces the concept of diagnosing possible zones of intervention, defines levels of mediation, and suggests a model that includes specific roles for librarians, as well as delineated strategies for productive intervention. Librarians and other information professionals involved in the design of reference and instruction programs will find her well-supported ideas both stimulating and useful.

In a fortuitous companion piece to Kuhlthau, Ferguson has written a comprehensive, timely, and balanced article on the subject of reshaping reference services, which should find a wide readership among the many librarians who are presently involved in reviewing this current key service and who are trying to decide what intervention aspects need to be retained, what needs to change, and what values should determine the decision.

One important audience in the information transfer process that is rarely studied is children, who, while they are heavy library users in both public and school libraries, are not necessarily provided with the information they critically need to thrive. Walter, after reviewing the field, addresses this deficiency with the results of a study that tried to determine the information needs of children in a specific target population. Implications for library practice and further research are given.

Addressing the core issue of information transfer from the system planning view, Eaton gives a detailed description of the planning process for an information system in a health science library and describes the benefits.

Successful information transfer depends on many things, and results vary. Resources are essential, and Reynolds gives a concise overview of the history and currently successful strategies of obtaining funding for public libraries, while Popa and Lamprecht describe the cooperative relationship between librarians and library organizations of Romania and the United States.

Managing the library buildings that house both people and physical objects, with accompanying health and preservation concerns, are areas often either overlooked or left to facility management engineers with little understanding of the special needs of buildings that house extensive and solid stack areas packed with fragile and often dusty paper items. This neglect has often resolved in air quality that is dangerous to people and books, as well as to sensitive computer equipment. Bush and Enssle supplement the literature with detailed recommended plans for managing both new and existing buildings.

Irene P. Godden

Library and Information Science:
Its Content and Scope

Pertti Vakkari
Department of Information Studies
University of Tampere
33101 Tampere
Finland

I. Introduction

Augustine was right. When thinking about a certain thing like time, you know what it is, but when you try to express it, it disappears. The same applies to library and information science. Usually you do not think what it is, and when you do, you are able to form a vague idea about it without being able to inform others what it is. To define universals is always an effort. Scholars have written libraries about the definitional problems of universals. However, most members of our scientific community are Augustines of our time, so seldom can one find well-articulated ideas about library and information science.

The silence is understandable. In general, researchers are interested in matters directly contributing to their tasks and duties. Functioning, practical ideas and solutions concerning the research projects are the currency of the everyday life of a researcher. Discussion about the nature, scope, and common central concepts of the field of research in question is not seen as relevant to those problems. Library and information science? So what? asks the researcher.

There are at least two positive answers. First, discussion about the scope and content of a young field of research is forming the identity of its scientific community. Central means for the social institutionalization of a specialty is its internal organization and boundary definition (Vakkari, 1992; Whitley, 1974). Exchange of opinions, even disputes, about the nature and limits of the field are constructing identity and thus bases for its social cohesion.

Second, conceptions of the structure and scope of a discipline are always social constructs that include certain objects within that domain and exclude others. Depending on the level of articulation, the outline of a discipline dictates what the central objects of inquiry are, how they should be conceptualized, what the most important problems are and how they should be studied, as well as what kind of solutions are fruitful. Although the articulation is usually general, it guides the solutions of researchers in their specific projects. This general frame is the toolbox from which they pick them, without necessarily knowing they are doing so.

From now on I shall use the term information science for our field of research. The word *library* is excluded, because, as will be shown later, it is not conceptually economic to use a linguistic expression that does not have a content. Information science conceptually contains the necessary elements for the universe of discourse of our field, including librarianship. However, when citing a text, I have used the writer's expression.

In the following pages, the question of whether information science is a discipline or a field of research is left open. I use both terms as synonyms referring to a field of research as distinguished from a field of professional activity. The quest is for integrating and unifying features for it presented in the literature.

In order to be able to discuss the definitions of information science, one should in principle have one's own definition of it. As Schrader (1986) has put it, the rationale for selecting instances of a phenomenon must precede the selection activity. The paradox lies in the fact that one should have a criterion (i.e., definition of the field) in order to be able to select relevant literature containing the discussion of its nature. However, the problem is not as severe in the case of selecting writings about the definitions and descriptions of the field as in selecting writings for analyzing the empirical features of the research in the field. In the first case, nearly all texts expressed that their concern was metaanalysis of our field of research. When one is reflecting certain features of a discipline in general, a common habit is to name it. Writers do not leave it as a secret.

Identifying metatheoretical writings has not been a problem. From them I have chosen the most typical or detailed presentations about the central dimension and features of information science. I have restricted the review to the discussions published in the 1980s and early 1990s. I have included, however, some central writings from the end of the 1970s because they have contributed significantly to the conceptions in the following decade. Another restriction is geographic. Although the aim is to identify the most important writings, language barrier is a limiting factor. I have concentrated on contributions published mainly in Anglo-American literature, to some extent taking into account discussions in the German language area and in the Nordic countries. There is of course variation among culturally different countries about the conception of information science. It would be misleading to generalize the findings of the review beyond the scope presented. I believe, however, that I am not wide of the mark if I claim that the most general differentiation between the library institution-oriented conception and a wider conception of our field is known everywhere.

The presentation is structured as follows. First, I introduce some conceptual tools from the sociology and philosophy of science. The characteristics of a research field introduced by Bunge (1982) augment the analysis of the nature of information science. Wagner (1984; Wagner and Berger, 1985) made a distinction between different kinds of theoretical activity in sociology. It is shown that the same distinction is applicable to the analysis of our field of research. The actual analysis starts with the question about the relation between library science and information science. After that, the relations of our field of research to others will be tackled on the bases of empirical and theoretical analyses. Finally, some central metatheoretical ideas of information science will be reviewed. The central findings and trends in discussion together with a recommendation to form theoretical research programs in information science are presented in conclusion.

A. Characteristics of a Research Field

Mario Bunge (1982) characterizes criteria to demarcate science from pseudoscience. These characteristics do not help to differentiate information science from other cognitive fields or to decide if it is a science or a field of research. Its scientific status can be decided only by using Bunge's criteria indirectly. However, Bunge's criteria enable one to take a closer look at the scientific orientation of our field. Frederick Suppe (1985) also refers to similar categories when discussing the conception of science in the contemporary philosophy of science.

Bunge (1982) characterizes a cognitive field as a sector of human activity aiming at gaining, diffusing, or utilizing knowledge of some kind, whether this knowledge is true or false. The family of cognitive fields can be partitioned into two disjoint subsets: the subset of research fields and that of belief fields. Belief fields include religions, political ideologies, and pseudosciences, and research fields include humanities, basic and applied sciences, and technology (including medicine and law). What characterizes a research field is active research or inquiry of some sort (i.e., the formulation and solution of problems, the invention of new hypotheses or techniques).

For the definition of a particular science Bunge (1982) introduces eight criteria. (1) The general outlook of philosophical background G. It consists of an ontology, epistemology, and the ethos of the free search for truth. (2) The formal background F is a collection of up-to-date logical and mathematical theories. (3) The domain or universe of discourse D is composed exclusively of real entities. (4) The specific background B is a collection of up-to-date and reasonably well-confirmed data, hypotheses, and theories obtained in other fields of inquiry relevant to that particular field. (5) The problematics P consists exclusively of cognitive problems concerning the nature of the Ds as well as problems concerning other components of the particular field. (6) The fund of knowledge K is a collection of up-to-date and testable theories, hypotheses, and data compatible with those in B and obtained in the particular field at previous times. (7) The objectives or goals O include discovering or using laws of the Ds, systematizing (into theories) hypotheses about D, and refining methods in M. (8) The methods in M consists exclusively of scrutable and justifiable procedures.

Any cognitive field that satisfies these conditions will be said to be a science. Although this definition fits mainly the natural sciences, it can also be applied to analyzing other types of sciences, including information science. The aim is not to decide if our field of research is a science or not but to use these categories as tools for analyzing the nature of information science.

It is not fruitful to use all the listed categories in the analysis. A civilized reader can immediately conclude that there hardly exists any collection of logical or mathematical theories within information science. Although one could accept Bradford's, Lotka's, or Zipf's laws as mathematical theories, they do not form a sufficiently formal background for information science. Moreover, a detailed analysis of the fund of knowledge within our field is not possible. Discussing the nature of a field of research is not a question of single theories or hypotheses, so-called unit theories. One has to scrutinize the theoretical constructs on the level of the whole discipline (i.e., efforts to describe the discipline as a totality). These attempts can be called orienting strategies or metatheoretical frameworks (Wagner and Berger, 1985).

In the analysis the problems of the general outlook of information science and its domain will be discussed together. In the literature on the nature of our field the ontological and epistemological commitments are usually mixed and treated with the problems concerning the universe of discourse typical for information science. Usually it is hard to distill clear ontological or episte- mological conceptions of our field. They are implicit in the discussion con- cerning the domain (i.e., what are the central objects of inquiry in the disci- pline). It is no wonder because the way we shape the basic phenomena and conceptualize them directs our conceptions of the entities most important to our field. A stand on the nature of the field dictates the objects to be scruti- nized. If we think, for example, that the main focus of our discipline are libraries and information service institutions, we postulate in a crude ontologi- cal sense that those are the central existing entities within our domain. They would form the base for the construction of the discipline.

The specific background is related to the degree to which we are using concepts and results from other relevant fields of inquiry in our discipline.

According to Bunge (1982), a pseudoscience learns little or nothing from other cognitive fields. Information science is often claimed to be an interdisciplinary field of research, which borrows its theories and methods from others. The accuracy of this assertion is discussed when analyzing connections among information science and other disciplines argued in the literature.

The objectives and problematics of a cognitive field are interwoven. The goals of a field of research are mainly cognitive including the finding of laws and regularities and the understanding and prediction of facts in terms of regularities. The problematics of a science are also in line with its goals consisting exclusively of cognitive problems (Bunge, 1982). The main objective of a science is to add to its research literature so that the scientific community can use it as the base for future research. Practical objectives as well as practical problematics are typical for fields other than that of scientific inquiry. If science tries mainly to conceptualize and understand its object of interest, nonscience in this respect attempts foremost to find solutions to practical problems in everyday life. A differentiation between cognitive and practical objectives and goals also demarcates a field of inquiry from a field of practical activity. It implies that the methods used in science are scientific methods, not methods of operation in some practical field.

B. Types of Theoretical Activity

Discourse on the nature and scope of a field of research is metatheoretical activity. It is a discussion about theory; about what concepts it should include, how these concepts should be linked, and how theory should be studied. According to Wagner and Berger (1985), similar to Kuhn's paradigms, theories of this sort provide guidelines or strategies for understanding social phenomena and suggest proper orientation of the theorist to these phenomena. They are called orientation strategies.

An orientation strategy may include the development of ontological and epistemological arguments concerning the subject matter of the discipline in question, the nature of the reality studied by the discipline, and the values and goals of inquiry. It may also involve the articulation of the conceptual foundation employed in the description and analysis of studied phenomena. Finally, it is likely to incorporate the formulation of directives for the selection of theoretical problems of investigation and for the construction and evaluation of proposed problem solutions (Wagner and Berger, 1985).

Wagner and Berger (1985) claim that there is little growth at the level of orientation strategy. New strategies such as ethnomethodology seldom replace older strategies; more often they add to the list of metatheoretical options that are available in (sociological) analysis. Part of the reason for the rigidity both within and between strategies is that the differences between strategies are, in general, fundamental. Basically, the claims of an orienting strategy are directives. They are statements about values (e.g., the value of function as a conceptual tool; in information science, the value of cognitive structure) not statements about facts (e.g., the specific function performed by a particular institutional structure—for present purposes—the specific function performed by a certain cognitive structure). Such prescriptive arguments are largely nonempirical, and conflicts between them are often unresolvable.

To theorize at all, one must assume some kind of metatheoretical framework. It specifies what problems are worth investigating, what concepts and methods are useful in constructing theories, and what solutions are legitimate to consider. It is obvious that an orientation strategy provides the discipline with specific lenses to focus on certain aspects of the reality to investigate. It gives shape to the domain of investigation of the discipline.

Orientation strategies are basically systems of values guiding theoretical and empirical work at the level of unit theories and theoretical research programs. A unit theory is concerned with the actual presentation and evaluation of theoretical statements. A theoretical research program consists of sets of interrelated theories. One of the most important effects of orientation strategies is on the determination of what ideas are the core of the program. The core ideas of a program are those that are most central and most important in its account of social phenomena. Consequently, these ideas are the ones most likely to be dictated directly by the strategy (Wagner, 1984).

When applied to the analysis of the nature of information science Wagner and Berger's approach suggests which orienting strategies characteristic to information science should be looked for. It means that one has to look for different ways to articulate information science at the level of the discipline. The articulations function as directives as to how to conceptualize the basic phenomena of interest to the field. It directs the attention of the scientific community to certain features and aspects of the domain. It also suggests the most fruitful problems within the field and the legitimate solutions for them. Their approach also shows that different orientation stategies are mutually exclusive and thus lead to different research programs and unit theories.

II. The Relationship between Library Science and Information Science

The relationship between library science and information science has long been of interest to the professional and academic community. There has been uncertainty about their relationship. There are two basic conceptions concerning their relationship. First, they can be regarded as two separate disciplines with some common interest. However, they might be seen as identical so that they form a single whole. A variant of the latter is to see one as a part of the other. The following presents arguments for and against the identity and separateness conceptions of our field of research.

A. Library Science and Information Science as Distinct Fields

Historically it is undeniable that library science was born before information science or its predecessor, documentation. In the early nineteenth century Martin Schrettinger in his famous *Bibliothek-Wissenschaft* (1809–1828) defined library science as the summary of all theoretical guidelines necessary for the purposeful organization of a library. Schrettinger's book presents the principles of librarianship in axiomatic form. The definition concretely shows that the focus of the examination is to ensure swift and sure access to documents in the library. Although Schrettinger's book can be said to have corresponded to the science ideal of the time, it nevertheless dealt with principles of librarianship (i.e., professional matters) (Vakkari, 1986).

Documentation is the predecessor of information science. The term was introduced by the founders of the International Bibliographic Institute, Otlet and La Fontaine. The successor of the institute was the International Federation for Information and Documentation (FID). Documentation refers to the creation, transmission, collection, classification, and use of documents; documents may be broadly defined as recorded knowledge in any format (Rayward, 1983). According to Schrader (1984), this description of documentation as distinct from librarianship or library science was merely the first in a long line of efforts in the literature to tease apart the concepts differentiating the two perceived domains of scholarly study.

Historically the difference between library science and documentation crystallizes in the notion that the object of library science is to provide access to graphic records in libraries whereas documentation facilitates the access to documents in any formats independent of the institution. Library science is linked with a certain type of document and institution but documentation focuses its attention on all kinds of documents and the institutions that transmit them. The common feature is their aim to facilitate access to information.

The notion of library science and information science as two separate disciplines is of historical origin. Although the idea has had to give way to the notion that the two form a single whole, it still has its adherents. An authoritative advocate of the idea of separateness is Tefko Saracevic.

Saracevic (1992) defines librarianship as devoted to the organization, preservation, and use of human graphic records. He quotes Shera when stating that the aim of the library is to maximize the utility of graphic records for the benefit of society. For Saracevic (1992) information science is a field devoted to scientific inquiry and professional practice addressing the problems of effective communication of knowledge and knowledge records among humans in the context of social, institutional, and/or individual uses of and needs for information.

Although Saracevic (1992) sees a strong common ground between library science and information science, he suggests there are stronger arguments for demarcating them. The common basis is in the shared social role and in their general concern with the problems of effective utilization of graphic records. But he also finds significant differences; they are (1) the selection of problems addressed and the way they were defined, (2) theoretical questions asked and frameworks established, (3) the nature and degree of experimentation and empirical development and the resulting practical knowledge-competencies derived, (4) the tools and approaches used, and (5) the nature and strength of interdisciplinary relations established and the dependence of the progress and evolution on interdisciplinary approaches. All these differences warrant for Saracevic the conclusion that librarianship and information science are two different fields in a strong interdisciplinary relation rather than the same field or one as a special case of the other.

The points Saracevic makes are interesting. It is seldom that writers explicate so clearly the criteria they are using when demarcating between the two fields. However, as he does not elaborate the arguments, they remain mere assertions. The criteria do not imply the claimed demarcation between library science and information science. It would be as legitimate to assert the unity of those fields on the basis of the criteria used. One also believes that his definition of library science is reducible to his definition of information science.

B. Information Science as Unifying Concept

A close reading shows that the difference between librarianship and documentation is not as great as has been claimed. In his classic *Documentation*, Bradford (1948) defines documentation as the art of collecting, classifying, and making readily accessible the records of all kinds of intellectual activity. He adds that documentation is no more than one aspect of the larger art of librarianship; as a special aspect it also needs special study. The type of material forms the point of distinction for Bradford. Books are for libraries, other materials are for documentation. What is crucial is that documentation is a species of librarianship. The grand old man of library science, Shera, for his part, considers that the social purpose of the library is to bring the human mind and the graphic record together . . . "The hard core of librarianship remains basically as it has always been . . . mastery of the substantive content of graphic records" (Wright, 1987, pp. 144–145). Although there are differences in the terminology, the common features of the definitions are obvious.

There are different ways to see the relationship between librarianship and information science as a unified discipline. Maybe the most radical version is argued by Gernot Wersig (1992). First, he makes an ontological knockout by denying the existence of library science. According to Wersig, there is little proof that specific kinds of organizations provide a sound basis for a scientific or academic discipline. As long as there are no disciplines such as hospital science or jailhouse science, the concept of library science is not very convincing. Wersig does not, however, deny that the problems of such institutions may be solved by scientific approaches or that these approaches would not benefit from the education and training of professionals for the institutions. These approaches might be grouped together in bodies of knowledge or learned institutions, but this would form a field of study rather than an academic discipline.

His other argument is a logical paradox. Even if Wersig (1992) was convinced that there were good reasons to speak of library science and that there were good reasons to speak of information science, he would still deny that the two form a conjunctive pair. The only way to make this reasonable would be to consider information science to be a field of study concerned with information organizations that are not libraries. This implies that either libraries are not information organizations, in which case it remains questionable whether they should be coupled with information organizations at all, or they are information organizations and then information science would be the proper generic term.

Only Wersig's second argument concerns the relationship between library science and information science. He claims that the proper generic term for our discipline is information science. His argument is valid on the condition that we accept that libraries are not information organizations qualitatively so different from other information institutions that they could form a basis for a discipline. It seems that Wersig is not denying the possibility of handling problems of librarianship within the field of information science. Like many other writers he sees libraries as information organizations inter alia, providing access to information for the benefit of users.

Peter Ingwersen (1992a) also uses information science as a generic term and sees library science as special R&D activity within information science. Library science, in his opinion, is concerned with the information processes that take place in libraries. As such, it becomes a special case where, for instance, information retrieval is called reference work and information management is named library management. In order to avoid unnecessary fragmentation into functional-locational sciences, Ingwersen (1992b) suggests that library science is information science research carried out in library and similar information service environments. Otherwise it would be as logical to have an online-information service science in the future. His idea is to use information science as a generic term and outline it as a broader field of research. Within that, discipline problems concerning librarianship form a special applied field of research. One could also state that libraries are a field of application for information science research.

Previous analyses concerning the relationship between library science and information science did not deal in detail with the content or fields of either. Patrick Wilson doubts the sense of such a division and outlines an alternative, which he calls research and development on bibliography. Wilson (1983) uses the phrase bibliographic sector for the assemblage of institutions and organizations that collectively take the output of the publishing industry and try to make it accessible for public use. The bibliographic R&D centers on the problems of the bibliographic sector and focuses mainly on the problems of libraries and bibliography-producing agencies, to the exclusion of book trade. Wilson (1983) divides it into six categories. The first includes work aimed at improving the means of storage, manipulation, transmission, and display of bibliographic information, based on the application of information technology. The second includes work aimed at improving techniques for creating the bibliographic information to be manipulated, stored, transferred, and displayed. The third field is devoted to studying some of the characteristics of the literature that constitute the input to the bibliographic sector and the use of that literature. The last three categories can be briefly described as consisting of studies of the bibliographic sector itself as it has been, as it is now, and as it ought to be in the future. The categories refer to historical, state-of-the-art, and policy studies.

Wilson's basic argument is that if his categorization is accepted, it is impossible to differentiate between library science and information science. If the branch of information science can be identified by its subject matter, it must, according to Wilson (1983), be the subject matter of categories two or three or both. But the work done in these categories is done both by people calling themselves information scientists and people calling themselves librarians. Content representation is a major practical and theoretical concern for librarians. Thus, information science cannot be distinguished from library science by its special subject matter. Wilson claims that no methodological or topical criterion will provide a clear division between work done by those who think of themselves as librarians and those who think of themselves as information scientists.

Wilson (1983) admits that we cannot use what people call themselves as a criterion for definition. We can simply define information science by reference to specified subject matter and methods. If we interpret Wilson's argument to mean that he is trying to show that it is impossible to draw clear-cut boundaries between library science and information science, I think his argument is valid. Wilson's (1983) conclusion is that the bibliographical R&D community is not composed of two groups, information scientists and library scientists. It is a single but wildly heterogeneous group. Its work is similarly motley in character. Wilson is claiming that it is impossible and probably fruitless to define our field as library science or information science; he suggests that there may be better ways to describe and characterize it. Schrader (1984) and Lancaster (1984) have also argued against the possibility of separating information science from the field of librarianship.

A less radical view is that the library institution forms a paradigmatic model for our discipline. According to Ford (1990) our field has expanded beyond the traditional context of library as an institution. Its domain must include an understanding of how information is (and might be) recorded, stored, preserved, and retrieved to meet the needs of individuals and society. The domain should be broadly defined but also include the library as an institution that has historically been a center of activity for information recording, storage, preservation, and retrieval. As the domain evolves and expands, an institutional model provides focus and concrete illustrations of how the domain in its theoretical aspects can be applied and used in the political, economic, and social environment.

This model can be called a generalized library-based model for information science. The strategy is to generalize the information process that takes place in library context and to use it for modeling information processes in other contexts that are of interest to (library and) information science. The model is realistic in the sense that it represents the most accepted approach to our field of study (Ford, 1990). The model has also been discussed by Miksa (1992).

Unlike the foregoing, the views of Wersig, Ingwersen, and Wilson represent a relatively radical way of perceiving information science. Their starting point is the notion that it forms a whole and dividing it into library science and information science would not be fruitful. Other subdivisions are more appropriate. However, they do not want to exclude librarianship from information science's objects of inquiry. It is one of the many objects of interest. It can be regarded as an applied field of research in information science, as seen by Ingwersen. A significant feature of their view is also the fact that the subject of information science is not tied up with any particular information organization. It can be claimed, consequently, that the transition from library science to information science has broadened the scope of our discipline. One could also ask, if a conceptual differentiation between the two fields is impossible, what is the expression library science used for?

III. The Relation of Information Science to Other Sciences

One of the characteristics of a particular science as outlined by Bunge (1982) is a specific background, which is a collection of up-to-date and reasonably well-confirmed data, hypotheses, and theories obtained in other fields of inquiry relevant to that particular science. In order to fulfill the criteria a cognitive field has to use, to a certain extent, methods, concepts, and results from other fields of research. This implies that a field of research has to learn from other cognitive fields and to contribute to the development of other fields of inquiry. In isolation the field of research is in danger of losing its scientific character and turning into a pseudoscience.

The extent to which a particular science profits by the achievements of another science is an empirical question. It can be defined by comparing research done in the respective fields, the concepts and methods used, and the results gained. Nevertheless, a large part of the discussion on the relation between information science and other disciplines does not use empirical but theoretical arguments. One question has been which branch of sciences it belongs to—whether it is a natural or a social science. Where the concepts and results most fruitful in promoting library and information science might be found is also of interest. These writings can be characterized as metatheoretical. As a strategic orientation, their perspective and aim are to describe the object of inquiry of information science in relation to other disciplines (cf. Wagner, 1984). From the approaches and solutions peculiar to these fields, it is possible to derive directives about how the object of inquiry of our discipline or the problems of one of its subfields should be conceptualized and analyzed. The directives are usually theoretic-methodological in nature, dealing with the outlining and conceptualizing of a field and its problems; they do not give detailed advice on the application of certain theories or methods. The directives indicate the direction where the concrete solutions should be sought.

In the following, I first examine the metatheoretical discussion about information science's relation to other disciplines and after that present empirical analyses on the relation of our discipline to other fields of study.

A. The Natural Sciences

There have been attempts to place library and information sciences (LIS) on many central branches of science with firmer or looser arguments. It is not uncommon to use no arguments at all. The most common alternatives have been to interpret it as a natural science, social science, or a part of humanities.

The idea that information science is a natural science or in any case contains elements of it has two main roots at least. According to Paisley (1990) some of the foremost research in the discipline results from natural sciences. This refers to the contributions of such disciplines in two senses: first, as a source of paradigms and methods for research and, second, as the ultimate test of whether information science is evolving into a discipline. Thus, researchers apply the parent science's concepts, procedures, and methods when they arrive at a new field, in outlining it, and to their own research as well. They do not necessarily regard LIS as a natural science but nevertheless transfer some features of the natural scientific paradigm to the research of the discipline. Tradition ties down their conceptions of the fruitful formulation of a problem, legitimate methods, and acceptable solutions. In the research practice LIS is constructed according to a natural scientific model.

Another reason for the emphasis on the natural or rather the technical scientific side has to do with the use of information technology, computers, and theories related to them, such as Shannon and Viewer's theory of signal transmission, within the field of library and information science (Saracevic, 1992; Warner, 1990). As Saracevic (1992, p. 6) puts it: "Information science is inexorably connected to information technology. A technological imperative hangs over information science." The fact that computers and data processing have become common especially in information retrieval has led to the application of methods and theories from computer science in the research of the field. In this case we move somewhere between the two disciplines.

Probably no one has seriously claimed that LIS is a natural science. Instead natural and technical scientific approaches and methods can be found in library and information science. However, Brown's (1987, p. 102) statement is still valid: "While statements asserting the essentially scientific nature of information science abound in the literature, detailed consideration of what such a claim implies and arguments in support of it are substantially less ubiquitous." In the following I examine the metatheoretical discussion on the natural and engineering scientific features in library and information science.

The only article discussing library and information science's relation to natural sciences and knowledge engineering is by Harmon (1990). In order to bring LIS into relation with the fields she studies, she defines information science as follows: "Information science centers on the development of principles, laws, models, and theories that predict or explain information phenomena associated with natural artificial systems. Such systems include e.g., cells, molecules, organs, organisms, computers, organizations, communities, and atmospheric systems" (Harmon, 1990, p. 32). The definition is formed in such a way as to be compatible with the natural sciences. In her definition she includes elements of biological and physical systems that one finds hard to imagine having anything to do with the systems and information phenomena that are studied in information science. As she does not specify how, for example, cells, molecules, organs, or atmospheric systems relate to the information phenomena, which are interesting from the library and information science point of view, the definition does not function. Neither does she try to outline which concepts, methods, or results of natural sciences could be of use in the research carried on in our discipline. Perhaps there are none, because Harmon (1990) ends up stating that attempts to model information science after single, monolithic, and well-circumscribed natural science disciplines appears to be inappropriate.

A more detailed analysis on the natural scientific nature of information science, especially its cognitive side, has been presented by Bernd Frohmann (1992a, 1992b). Referring to the writings of B. C. Brookes he claims that Brookes' theoretical intentions are expressed through a discourse about information in the voice of natural science. Frohmann (1992b) founds his claim on Brookes' way of defining theory and his concepts. According to Brookes (1975) a theory has to possess (1) a unique subject area, (2) a set of basic concepts, (3) a set of fundamental laws, and (4) an explanatory theory. This means according to Frohmann (1992a) that Brookes sets the theory firmly within a natural scientific paradigm. He does not found his claim on arguments or by citing literature. Nevertheless it cannot be concluded without further qualification that these four criteria represent a conception of theory peculiar to the natural scientific paradigm. The natural scientific character could only be assessed by a thorough analysis of each criterion and explication of the conception of theory in natural sciences (cf. Outhwaite, 1983). In this case, the natural scientific nature of information science remains unproven.

When analyzing Brookes' concepts Frohmann does not view them as a part of a theoretical construction but as separate rhetorical tools. Taking the concepts out of their context brings the danger of their meaning not being precisely understood. The fact that certain terms refer to natural objects does not necessarily mean that the theory's conception of the phenomena it examines would be natural scientific by nature. It cannot be ascertained by presenting phrases; the structure of the theory needs to be analyzed. Although in his earlier writings Brookes (1975, 1977) often refers to such objects, in his series of articles on the foundation of information science (Brookes, 1980), such references are scarce. Brookes (1980) even states that information science is a social science.

Frohmann (1992b) is right about Brookes' arguments not functioning as a reportage of scientific research but as a constitution of a certain kind of information science. It is by no means his results of empirical research that Brookes represents; he does metatheoretical analysis with the purpose of creating a strategic orientation as a basis for information science. Frohmann in his analysis does not explicate his conception of natural science, and so the extent to which the orientation Brookes offers is natural scientific remains unsettled. It seems likely that Brookes' directives for information science contain natural scientific features but not to the extent claimed by Frohmann. Thus the claims concerning the natural scientific features of the cognitive trends in information studies remain unsubstantiated.

The fact that the use of data processing has become more common, in information retrieval (IR) especially, has brought concepts and methods from computer science to information studies. Correspondingly, the results of IR research in information science have benefited computer science. There are so many common features that from a computer science point of view it might have been logical to combine the information retrieval, representation, and management elements from information science with the software and artificial intelligence sides of computer science (Ingwersen, 1992b). Saracevic (1992) has also stressed their interconnections by listing a number of areas (e.g., expert systems, intelligent interfaces, and human–computer interaction) within computer science useful for information science.

No one has seriously argued that information studies belongs to natural sciences, although the migrants of science have brought, often implicitly, natural scientific approaches and concepts to the research done in the discipline. However, computer science has explicitly contributed to IR research in particular. Methods of computer science are necessary, although not sufficient, in its problem solving.

B. The Humanities

Library and information science is deeply rooted in the humanities. The early research in the field was mainly done with history or the history of ideas as a starting point, and for a long time this remained the case. The situation was strengthened by the notion of the (academic) librarian as a scholar who had to master the totality of sciences, however superficially. The humanities formed the foundation, although the mastery of other sciences was also sought (Vakkari, 1991). Philosophy, too, as contributive to the organizing of knowledge and creating of classification systems, has been close to library and information science. Especially after the World War II the work done in libraries and information services has become more complicated and computerized, and this has undermined the historical trend. The number of scholars doing research on book and library history has decreased considerably.

Humanities can be understood in two ways at least, as arts or as a specific kind of knowledge. In the literature the relation of information studies and humanities has been analyzed in the latter sense only. Judging by the small number of studies, information studies has not been seen as belonging to the humanities but as being either natural or social science by nature.

Margaret Stieg (1990) examines the relation by using the concept humanities for that distinct knowledge that is humanistic, concerned with human values and expressions of the spirit of humans. For Stieg, information science seems to be a science. It implies that the relationship between information science and the humanities is a microcosm of the relationship between science and humanities. However, she bridges the cultural gap between science and humanities by stating that the humanities taken in this sense permeate all knowledge, and all knowledge is science properly understood (Stieg, 1990). The solution is clever but not very informative; it is not helpful in defining the relation.

When scrutinizing in more detail the effect of humanities on information science, Stieg (1990) emphasizes its significance in dealing with questions of principle—in the first place the meaning and ethic of activities. It is a question of stating the reasons for the sense and objectives of activities, such as the purpose of service, or of solving the ethical problems of the discipline. This would mean mainly discussing the (moral) philosophical problems of the field. Stieg does not present any clear conclusions concerning the specific contributions of the humanities to information science. Although she mentions the possible contribution of linguistics, she does not present the implications for the cognitive development of the field.

C. The Social Sciences

Although many studies (Belkin, 1978; Ingwersen, 1992a; Neill, 1992; Warner, 1990; Wersig, 1992; Wilson, 1984) refer to information science as a social science, its social scientific features or the relation to social sciences has seldom been explicated. It has been thought self-evident that it belongs to social sciences. Warner (1990) argues that this is justified by a recognition that the established domains of information science are social, not natural. Information transactions typically involve interactions of individuals with individuals or with socially constructed information systems, within a social framework. Methodologies for investigation modeled on the physical sciences and technology, either by explicit derivation or as an accepted inheritance, are therefore radically misplaced and have not been productive, claims Warner. They are then inappropriate to the social nature of the activities studied by information science and have failed to yield adequate concepts of information and information behavior or a satisfying model of information man. Neill (1992) also doubts the suitability of research methods borrowed from the natural sciences in information science.

Although not arguing it directly, Belkin (1978) also seems to classify information science within social sciences when he states that it is especially concerned with information in the context of human communication and that human communication in general and information in particular must be studied in terms of social objectives and group dynamics, among other social variables. In a more recent article Belkin (1990), when shaping the relevant phenomenon of study for information science from the cognitive viewpoint, considers its scope as the human communication system, in which texts play a key role, and individuals within that system in their interactions with texts (or information) and with one another in relation to such texts. Ingwersen (1992b) shares with Belkin and Warner the conception of information science as a social science when he states that the transfer of recorded knowledge involves transactions and communication of meaning among humans and among humans and systems containing conceptual structures. Tom Wilson (1984) also places information science indirectly with social sciences when he scrutinizes the nature of human information behavior.

If it is typical for the social sciences to study interaction among individuals and groups, and if we define the phenomena of interest to information science in the spirit of Belkin, Ingwersen, Warner, and Wilson as communicative interaction of individuals with each other, texts in the broad sense of semiotics (Belkin and Robers, 1976), and systems containing texts and their surrogates, the implication is that LIS is a social science.

1. Information Science and Communication Studies

Many writers sharing the opinion that information science is a social science relate it to communication sciences (Borgman and Schement, 1990). The point of departure when shaping the phenomena of interest for LIS is that it is a question about human communication. And human communication is the common focus of all communication sciences, including information science (Paisley, 1990). The writers may specify it in different ways, but the basic idea is human communication of information between its generator and its user with the help of systems or facilitating structures. The ways in which this idea has been expanded is discussed later when taking a closer look at the content of information science.

Ingwersen (1992b) takes the view that one of the two major trends in information science is a move toward communication. The relationship was reinforced during the 1980s under the influences of a more user-oriented research view and the studies of cognitive sciences. As a consequence, some schools of communication and library and information science did merge during the mid-1980s. He believes that the allegiance mainly suits the studies addressing behavior and interaction of the human elements of transfer of recorded knowledge. Saracevic (1992) also stresses the shared interest between information science and communication studies in human communication. He calls for attention to the idea that information as phenomenon and communication as a process need to be studied together.

As many seem to think that communication science and information science are closely related and have a lot to give to each other, I will examine their relation in the light of the analyses of Borgman and Schement (1990) and Ruben (1992). I will pay special attention to Ruben's ideas, because they shed light on essential sides of the characteristics of information science.

2. Signs of Convergence?

Borgman and Schement (1990) have observed links between communication studies and information science. They share common research topics, common researchers, and have formal organizational links. Their point of departure is that this sporadic evidence indicates the possibility of a trend toward convergence of subject matter and institutional structures. They ask how such convergence might appear, suggest several models, and discuss the nature of the evidence necessary to validate them.

The models of convergence are paradigm shift model, crossover model, overlapping fields model, and common theory model. The first supposes that after a paradigm shift within both fields, the fields might be moving together into a merged field. According to the crossover model the convergence of information science and communication studies may not be a case of whole fields converging or diverging but rather a migration of individual researchers over time between the two fields. The researchers move with their cognitive capital and invest it in the other field, enriching it with new ideas, problems, and concepts (Borgman and Schement, 1990).

The overlapping fields model implies that the fields may not be converging as such but simply overlapping. While the two fields may have a number of research areas in common, each has other areas that are distinctly its own. The model suggests that no fundamental change is occurring in the relationship of information science and communication studies. Rather, there has always been an overlap between the fields (Borgman and Schement, 1990). The common theory model suggests that although the two fields may be separate at the level of academic department, the individual researcher, and even at the specific research topic, each field draws its more general theories from a common body of knowledge. In fact, the theories may be applied different ways, using different research methods and terminology, thus maintaining a semblance of separateness (Borgman and Schement, 1990).

Although the fields have held problems of knowledge gap, diffusion of innovations, information seeking behavior, information policy, invisible colleges, and scientific communication in common for some time, the common questions do not equal paradigm or theory convergence. In fact, Borgman and Schement (1990) cannot validate any of the models of convergence on the basis of the empirical evidence. It seems, however, that the overlapping and crossover models are most valid in explaining what is happening in the relations of these two fields. As the writers mention, there are several examples of scholars working in both fields including Berelson, Paisley, and Dervin. They also show many common problem fields, although there exists no commonly held paradigm or general theory.

Information science and communication research share many common areas of study. In theory one could define communication research without difficulties in such a way that it would include most parts of information science. It is a theoretical and cognitive problem. However, disciplines are constructed not only on the basis of their cognitive features, how they define their phenomena of interest, and basic problems, but also by their social structures. The social institutionalization or research fields, founding institutions, research posts, doctoral programs, scientific associations, and journals, are means to construct and create identity for a scientific specialty (Whitley, 1974). The social structure creates a need for a division of labor between the newcomer and older fields of research. It leads to the differentiation in research topics and problem formulations. All have to reclaim their field in order to dig their own hole.

William Paisley (1990) especially has criticized both information studies and communication research for digging their own holes too eagerly without seeing important common research areas emerging with the new information technology. He claims that information science dwells on information storage and retrieval, devoting much less attention to the process by which information is communicated and used and to social costs and benefits of knowledge. A similar criticism of information studies is also expressed by Halloran (1983). Paisley (1990) claims that the narrow focus has two adverse consequences: First, studies are weakened by these arbitrary limits, and second, researchers in each field, looking across the fence at their neighbors' work, find it too parochial to be of interest.

Paisley (1990) suggests that research efforts have to be directed at an area that flourishes on the borders of communication and information science with little input from researchers in this field. New business, professional, and public information systems are being developed and adopted in large numbers. Those that are not library-based or do not lend themselves to study within a retrieval framework have not received as much attention from information scientists as standard bibliographic systems. Paisley also argues that office automation, paperless information systems, and networking are related topics that belong within information science. Moreover he demands research efforts on problems of expert systems and human-computer interface issues, which have been largely left in the hands of computer scientists and engineers. Problems of creation of knowledge and publication are also given too little attention by information science.

Although the topics listed by Paisley have attracted more interest since their presentation in 1987, his message is still valid. More research effort is needed in these areas, which are becoming more important within information studies, especially with the digitalization of information. However, Paisley does not argue his claims for broadening the field of information studies the way he does from any conceptual frame of reference. Why must we accept these fields of research and problems as legitimate interests of study within our discipline? It seems that his conception of information science as a branch of communication sciences and its aim to facilitate the communication of information are functioning as integrative elements in his view of our field.

3. Information Studies and Communication Studies: A Comparison of Frames

Ruben (1990, 1992) takes the view that both scholarly push and market pull are forcing information studies and communication research toward each other. Both areas of study are concerned, according to him, with the activities involved in the creation, organization, transmission, storage, management, and use of information. Ruben sees also a strong generic relationship between library studies and communication. Particularly among scholars of mass communication, the basic focus is on institutions whose primary function is the selection, organization, and distribution of information for consumption by large, anonymous, and heterogeneous market groups. These activities are as basic to the mission of libraries as they are to the mass media.

One can accept his claim that library and information service institutions can functionally be viewed as a part of communication institutions. Although there are differences in the way library and information science and communication institutions are selecting, organizing, and distributing information, they are, however, converging in consequence of the opportunities given by the new information technology. Mass media, publishers, newpapers, or TV are changing nonrecurrent messages from units to be transmitted into information storages. They try to process the documents they have created into as flexible a format as possible and then store them for future use. They diversify their information products for different target groups more precisely than before. One can get a newspaper or TV programs matched to one's interest profile. For the traditional mass media institutions the digitalization of information and data transfer technology brings new functions, which are characteristic of libraries and information services. Thus the objects of inquiry and the way to conceptualize them converge to some extent.

In order to scrutinize closer the relationship between the two fields, Ruben (1992) analyzes fundamental paradigmatic differences and similarities between them. Table I provides a summary of this comparison.

Ruben (1992) suggests that the fundamental theoretical focii of communication theory are the construction of meaning and the nature of human message- (or information-) related behavior. For information studies, comparable emphasis typically is placed on the transmission of information, involving services, systems, and institutions that facilitate this goal.

From the perspective of communication studies, Ruben (1992) argues that information is not, per se, transmitted between or retrieved by individuals when they interact. Rather human interaction involves the ongoing creation of meaning by interactants through a process that influences—and is influenced by—participation in relationships, groups, organizations, cultures, and societies. Meaning construction is manifest in thoughts and emotions; the relationship between the meanings a particular information provider intends to transmit and those particular recipients derive is seen as complex, multifaceted, and difficult to predict and control. The information studies perspective,

Table I   Communication and Information Studies: A Comparison of Paradigms[a]

Dimension	Communication studies paradigm	Information studies paradigm
Primary theoretical focus	Construction of meaning	Information transmission
Primary research focus	Interaction and behavior	Documents and systems
Codes/channels emphasized	Interpersonal verbal Interpersonal nonverbal Mediated verbal Mediated nonverbal	Mediated verbal Mediated visual
System/network perspective emphasized	Formality varies, purposefulness varies	Formal, managed, purposeful
Some functions, uses, outcomes examined	Personal growth Relationship development News and entertainment Organizational processes Socialization Cultural development	Information use Problem solving Information organization Retrieval appropriateness Information system and services effectiveness

[a] Source: Ruben, B. (1992). The communication-information relationship in system-theoretic perspective. *Journal of the American Society of Information Science* **43**, 19.

according to Ruben, frequently takes a more instrumental view of the nature and dynamics of interaction between information providers (and/or systems) and recipients—emphasizing the retrieval, transmission, and use of information by a logical and rational user who has a need to solve particular problems or fill knowledge gaps.

When comparing the central research focus or context, Ruben (1992) claims that in communication studies the theoretical concern with the construction of meaning typically leads to an operational interest in interaction and behavior—between individuals, within and among relationships, groups, organizations, societies, and internationally—and in varying contexts and circumstances. In information studies the operational emphasis is more generally on documents (information) and systems—particularly libraries—and their interface with users.

When comparing channels or code, Ruben (1992) notes that communication studies typically examines face-to-face (interpersonal) channels, as well as interaction that is technologically mediated. Focus may be on verbal and/or nonverbal codes (visual, tactile, auditory, and to a far lesser extent olfactory and gustatory). In information studies, priority is given to mediated channels (primarily mass mediation, e.g., books, CD-ROM, microfiche, or computer), utilizing verbal (print) and graphic (illustrations, graphic, or images) channels, and emphasizing visual codes.

From a systems-network perspective Ruben (1992) also identifies differences. Where information studies emphasize managed, formal systems in which information transfer is a guiding purpose, communication studies are as likely to examine systems that are not formally structured and where interaction is not necessarily undertaken with information transfer goals in mind—such as casual conversations between strangers or mass communication entertainment.

Consistent with the perspectives described previously by Ruben (1992), he takes the view that information studies emphasize outcome measures and assessment, the effectiveness of the information transmission function, the appropriateness of information storage and retrieval, task completion or problem solving, or the utility and value of systems and services for organizing or disseminating information and for user problem solving. Communication studies examines a range of intended and unintended outcomes and consequences of interaction, including personal growth, relationship development, news and entertainment, organizational development, socialization, and cultural development, along with consequences having to do with information used in conjunction with task-related activities.

Although Ruben admits that it can be problematic dichotomizing what may be more accurately represented as a continuum, it seems that he has caught some important and typical features of information studies by contrasting it with the characteristics of communication research. Traditionally information has been conceptualized in information studies as a thing (Buckland, 1991). The term information is used attributively for objects, such as data and documents that are referred to as information because they are regarded as informative. The cognitive turn in information studies has laid more emphasis on the conceptual structures in documents and in the minds of people, thus changing the focus toward meaning articulation. The slow perspective change from systems to people in information seeking studies has also gained room for the sense-making of humans in different situations (cf. Dervin, 1992). Although information science is becoming more aware that construction of meaning and conceptual structures are also its primary theoretical focus, differences will still remain. The main focus in sense-making and construction of meaning in information studies is not usually the interaction of individuals but the interaction among recorded knowledge, text, its surrogates, and a human being. Despite the fact that the differences are primarily theoretical and research focii are converging, differences in the other aspects, such as channels, systems perspective, and functions examined, remain.

D. Empirical Relations of Information Science and Other Disciplines

The preceding analysis was based on the theoretical arguments on the relation between information studies and other fields of research. According to these arguments, information studies has a lot of interconnections with other fields of research. Most of the discussion has been on the metatheoretical level directing research in information studies to useful and fruitful fields. An interesting question is to what extent our discipline is really using conceptual and methodological tools that other fields have developed. Their actual use by information science is one criterion of its scientific nature (cf. Bunge, 1982). It is also important to be able to contribute to the development of adjacent fields of research. Some results from the few existing empirical studies on the relations of information science to other disciplines follow.

In his cocitation analysis on the relationship of information science to social sciences, Small's (1981) findings were that although information studies was not completely separate from social sciences, it was fairly isolated. Small (1981) concludes that information science certainly is not the central discipline, with strong linkages to diverse fields, that many would like it to be.

The results by Paisley (1990) and Borgman and Rice (1992) about the relationship between information science and communication studies are similar. Paisley showed that the central journals in these disciplines in 1980 do not refer to the articles published in the adjacent field. The study by Borgman and Rice (1992) asked whether the disciplines of information science and communication are converging, as indicated by a bibliometric study of all core journals for both disciplines in the *Social Sciences Citation Index* for the period 1977 to 1987. Results show very little convergence between these disciplines, at least on the basis of cross-disciplinary journal citation patterns, although the number of journals involved has increased slightly over time. A few journals are mainly responsible for the cross-disciplinary citing, and they are primarily information science journals citing communication journals.

Linguistics has received attention in the literature of information science, indicating that a possible relationship exists between the two fields. Amy Warner (1991), in her citation analysis, has shown that information science literature cited linguistic theory very little. It seems that linguistic theory has not been widely exploited by information science researchers.

However, the export of ideas from information science to other fields has not been very successful. Cronin and Pearson (1990) have shown that some major figures in information studies did not receive many citations from other fields. Their conclusion was that information studies does not have a great deal to offer cognate disciplines.

Although one has to bear in mind the restriction of citation analyses, it seems on the basis of these few examples that the metatheoretical claims about the multidisciplinary nature of information studies are not valid. It is isolated from other disciplines and does not use their concepts, methods, or results in its studies. Although one believes that the picture of information studies is more colored by the contributions from other fields, it would be fruitful for the field to use more the ideas and results created in other disciplines. As Bunge (1982) stated, a pseudoscience learns little or nothing from the development of other cognitive fields.

IV. Central Conceptualizations of Information Science

Some central outlines recently drawn and the discussion about them are treated in greater detail here. The examination is introduced with Alvin Schrader's (1986) analysis of the various conceptualizations of information science. He concludes that the field has to be defined on the basis of its social function. Paisley's (1990) idea of a policy frame of reference for defining the scope of information science is an attempt to base the cognitive field on the social institutionalization of the profession. This idea is connected to a broader view of information science as a design science. Then an outline of two paradigms for library and information science as a design science (Miksa, 1992) is presented: library as a social institution and information movement in a system of human communication. As an heir to the latter, the cognitive view of information studies is presented.

Most ideas presented are theoretical constructs. There are some empirical analyses of the research output of the field including attempts to classify the subject matter of information science (Atkins, 1988; Järvelin and Vakkari, 1990, 1992; Peritz, 1981). The classification schemes created are not usually backed with a well-argued theoretical analysis of the content of the field. Possibly the most systematic division of information science into subfields is presented in Järvelin and Vakkari (1990).

A. Definitional Elements Used

Schrader (1986) has analyzed various conceptualizations of information science to determine to what extent the professional community possesses a common and unified understanding of its domain. He has identified five major elements in the literature published mainly before 1980 that serve as analytic foci. These elements are the name used to designate the domain, the nature or kind of domain, the content of the domain, the focus of the domain, and the function of the domain. For our purposes the most important features are the last four.

Schrader (1986) found a long list of heterogeneous descriptions about the nature of the domain. The descriptions varied from professional practice to a scientific discipline. It was not clear to the writers if the domain is a question of professional activity, scientific activity, or a combination of both. If information science was considered a scientific activity, there was no consensus about the nature of this activity. The range of the conceptions varied from a metascience to a field of study. The claims reveal, according to Schrader, confusion and ambiguity among writers and therefore a lack of consensus. The common weakness has also been the fact that the descriptions have not been elaborated.

Schrader (1986) shows that the content of the domain has been identified as a wide variety of things. The most common is information, but knowledge and data have also been mentioned frequently. Schrader argues that almost all writers about the domain have described its content as information or as recorded information. This uniformity, however, does not extend beyond the use of the term information. Schrader's claim seems to imply that the basic concept of information science has not been defined explicitly and that there is a lack of consensus as to its content, although the seekers are looking at it from the same point of view. His conclusion is that the conceptual chaos in the literature has inhibited conceptual evolution.

Three principal categories of the domain focus have been found in the literature by Schrader (1986). These are an emphasis on objects, human beings, or both objects and human beings. He criticizes the definitions of information science that focus exclusively on objects—to make information accessible, to retrieve information, to manage information—because they do not recognize the social nature of the action being expressed. The focus of these definitions is on the artifacts of human thought, on the manipulation of objects without specification of why or for whom. Schrader (1986) finds equally incomplete the definitions that focus exclusively on people. Generally, these definitions consist of functions that seek to influence, change, transform, or manipulate human thought and behavior. Functioning with respect to objects or artifacts is ignored. One could say that these definitions stress the augmentation of human activity without referring to any means. Schrader is right when he stresses that the function of enlightenment or informing is too broad to be claimed as unique to any one domain. He concludes that since the domain of information science constitutes more than the study of information it must be recognized that both objects and people are involved.

Schrader (1986) has developed a typology of generic definitions of information science on the basis of generic functions that are purported to characterize this domain. He states that the function of an endeavor determines the form and content of the endeavor. He seems to think that the function of a domain determines its content and shape. Schrader is referring to domain as an area of practical activity. The point of departure is that the functional definition of a domain of practical activity can be generalized as a definition of a domain of scientific activity. The functions found by Schrader (1986) are to make accessible, to retrieve, to transfer, to process, to counsel, to link, to create . . . transfer, to create . . . use, to use (to facilitate the use), to mechanize, and to study.

Schrader (1986) does not find the ways in which these functions have been described useful as a definition of the domain of information science. He argues that the minimum criteria for an adequate conception of its domain is the specification of inquiry into a clearly identified social function, one that treats in some fashion a specified universe of objects for a specified universe of uses by human beings. By proposing the basing of the definition of the domain for information science on its social function, Schrader is fixing our field of research on the firm basis of a practical activity. This way of defining has long roots in the history of information science, at least from the times of Schrettinger. As shown, the recent attempts are also indirectly constructed on the same basis. The only difference seems to be in definitions of the practice for the field of study of information science. The problem is how we should draw the boundaries of the field of practice for information science.

B. A Design Science within a Policy Frame

One of the most representative views of the nature of information studies based on the social function of the field is expressed by Paisley (1990). From this perspective the discipline is seen as a servant of the professional practice. Paisley (1990) calls it policy frame of reference. Within it the institutional context of information science includes training for librarianship, training for information science research, managing information resources and providing services, and developing new information systems and products. Within the institutional context, argues Paisley, the charter of information science is to produce knowledge that will guide the information institutions in fulfilling their concepts. Such research informs policy, implements policy, and evaluates its results.

Although there are other contexts (e.g., epistemological) for the discipline, Paisley (1990) believes that most members of the scientific community of LIS share the policy frame. Within this frame information science as a field of research is legitimized by its contribution to the field of practice. It implies that its domain, main objects and concepts, fundamental problems, and fruitful solutions are basically articulated by the needs of the professional community.

This mode of thinking about the nature of science can be called behavioralism (Vakkari, 1989). In behavioralism scientific problems are always practical problems of decision making. Correspondingly, scientific results are recommendations for action related to these problems. According to behavioralism, scientists can always be seen either as decision makers or their counselors. The science does not have stable results of a theoretical nature. Its aim is not to contribute to the theoretical body of scientific knowledge but to produce recommendations for professional practice.

A contrasting concept, according to which the primary purpose of science is knowledge, is called cognitivism (Vakkari, 1989). Research is seen as systematic pursuit of new knowledge; the scientist is not primarily a counselor but a seeker of truth. The scientist attempts to contribute to the total body of scientific knowledge. Cognitivism does not deny, however, that science also forms the basis of practical action. Accepted theories and hypotheses form the basis of rational decision making and action. The point of departure for cognitivism is that the aims of science include both the theoretical pursuit of truth and the search for applicable knowledge.

As many major figures of our scientific community have argued, there is an intimate connection between research and professional practice within our field. This reflects a conception of the applied nature of the discipline. As an applied science, information studies might validly be characterized as a design science. A design science helps to create an artificial world of concrete

and abstract artifacts. According to Herbert Simon (1982), design sciences
are technical and social sciences of engineering, which are concerned with
the way things should be in order to accomplish certain goals. They have
emerged when some profession that requires skills has moved from rules of
thumb that are based on trial and error to instructions based on scientific
method. A design science tells us how to proceed in order to accomplish our
goals. Its results come in the form of technical norms: If we want to enhance
the precision of a search from a large textual database, we need to diminish
the size of the retrieved set, or, If we want the collection to match the clients'
expectations more closely, we must observe their information needs. In general form technical norms express an objective A and a belief B about the
state of the world, as well as a means X. They can be formulated as follows:
If you want A and believe that you are in situation B, you must do X.
Technical norms are thus statements that have value concepts expressing
objectives in the conditional part and normative concepts in the conclusion
(Niiniluoto, 1985). Sciences generating technical norms are called design
sciences. As a design science, information studies could be characterized as
pursuit of new knowledge that aims at enhancing the facilitation of communication of desired information between human generator and use (cf. Belkin,
1977) or the fluency of information process in relevant contexts.

The connection between A and X in situation B originates from the fact
that X is either the necessary, sufficient, or probable cause of A. Thus the
results of a design science are concerned with the relation of A and X in
situation B. The more complex the system or a situation B, the harder it is
to know whether the procedure X will lead to result A. This is why an
increasing number of disciplines have started to examine the relation between
means and goals systematically; with the help of the scientific method.

Although the objectives and situations of the profession often direct
the research done in information studies at least implicitly, as underlying
assumptions, not all the research is applied by nature. A design science has
its instrumental and descriptive sides. Establishing technical norms requires
familiarity with the regularities of the profession. This view points to the
liberal cognitive view of science, which unites theoretical and practical
goals.

The fact that professional skills are increasingly based on science does
not mean that the profession is becoming a science. We can still distinguish
among a profession, professional activities, professional skills, and the science
created to enhance these skills. This difference should be kept in mind so
that information science is not called scientific inquiry and professional practice or a person working in an information service unit an information scientist.

C. Institution and Information Movement Paradigms

Schrader gives a sinister picture of attempts to define information science. Francis Miksa (1992), however, has been able to distill from the definitional harvest two paradigms of library and information science. The term *paradigm* is used by Miksa (1992) for a set of ideas that represent what is considered to be the central phenomenon of the LIS field and serves as a framework for the field's systematic knowledge and research. The two paradigms elicited do not, according to Miksa, preclude the existence of still other concurrent paradigms. The two are singled out because they appear to him to be the most widely held paradigmatic models in the field—more widely appealed to and more dominant than any others.

The first paradigm consists of a group of ideas related to the library viewed as a social institution. Its roots are in the work of scholars at the Graduate Library School of the University of Chicago during the 1920s and 1930s, who developed it using research ideas and methodology from sociology and education. Miksa (1992) believes that this paradigm still commands a notable influence throughout the field, especially in proving a significant body of the language that library practitioners typically use to describe their work. It is also related to the main background assumptions used in much current research upon which LIS agency administration and planning is based.

The focus of the paradigm is the library. It is viewed according to Miksa (1992) as a social institution and a well-defined and unique social organization. The library's most important function is identified with its collection of documents and its facilities. It exists primarily to make possible for a given public the use of its collection. The public generally initiates the use, usually coming to the library facilities to gain access to them. Several subsidiary tasks, such as acquiring, organizing, and physically arranging and housing the materials collected and also providing appropriate tools and personal assistance at the point of retrieval and use not only facilitate this basic function but also provide a framework for the education of practitioners and for much of the field's specific research.

This view of the library, claims Miksa (1992), includes a view of the cultural and social change that provides a broader context and rationale for why the library should have become an important and distinct element of society. In this view social and cultural change is facilitated when individuals take in or use organized social knowledge relevant to the conduct of their lives—when, in short, social knowledge contained in documents held by the library is effectually transferred to them. The chief method of transfer is reading. Although the most important result of transfer is the education and socialization of individuals, the same process also facilitates solutions to personal and social problems and the production of new knowledge. In this paradigm, argues Miksa (1992), the library is viewed as an extremely significant social organization among all the institutions involved with cultural and social change. All in all the library is characterized in terms of its social institutional properties and functions, and it has also been placed in a large social context.

The second paradigm has focused on the process of information movement that forms a system of human communication, a process modeled generally in the terms of the flow of information between two points through a channel while incorporating feedback for control, as the central phenomenon of the LIS field. Its beginnings have been in mathematical communication theory, which has served as a model for information transfer system in the field.

This paradigm has, according to Miksa (1992), not only contributed the word *information* to the name of the field but also supplied an entirely new set of terms by which LIS practitioners might characterize their activity. It also underlies much current research in information retrieval and bibliometrics, although its basic concepts often function as background assumptions. Miksa (1992) sees that the paradigm has especially focused on the information movement that occurs in a system where knowledge representing objects (documents) is sought and retrieved in response to the inquiries initiated by the individuals. It includes a wide range of particular concerns that surround or consist of elements in a more specific process. Miksa (1992) gives as examples the creation and growth of documents in society, their organization and retrieval or the organization and retrieval of their surrogates, and the use made of them.

Within the realm of LIS, argues Miksa (1992), this kind of generalized information system model has not only been applied as a model of the basic document retrieval process of LIS agencies but has also been used to characterize the LIS agencies in general and to model information movement within environments not specific to LIS. The latter include, for example, information flow in public and private agencies or among the members of a discipline, profession, or specialist group. One could interpret Miksa in such a way that the information movement paradigm has supplied the field with a new model for the basic function of the library—the document retrieval system. The library conceived as a document retrieval system can serve as a model for other similar systems in a different context. The document retrieval model can thus be generalized to all relevant cases for interest to the field. Thus the second paradigm implies a much wider conception of the domain of LIS than the first. It includes not only library as an information system but also all other agencies conceived as information systems in which knowledge representing objects or their surrogates is sought and retrieved in response to human information needs. When the first frame emphasizes the social role of the library, the latter is concerned with the communicative mechanism of the information systems like the library.

Miksa (1992) found three key changes in the fundamental concepts of our field provided by the flow paradigm. They are the idea of controllable information flow, the idea of information as a divisible and measurable unit, and the idea of information movement having both physical and semantic realms of meaning. The first two and the first part of the third idea seem to refer to information as a commodity or as a thing, as Buckland (1992) puts it. They imply a technological conception of information as a controlled, measured, and nicely packed commodity that can be sent and received in bundles. However, the interest has switched from the purely physical realm to the semantic one. Miksa (1992) takes the view that this shift has brought about the current redirection of interest in LIS information retrieval research toward themes that have arisen within the context of artificial intelligence and general cognitive studies.

Each paradigm, having come into being at different times and in different intellectual contexts, has viewed different phenomena as being central to the LIS field. Miksa (1992) shows some central limitations of the paradigms. The first overemphasizes the role of library in the social process. The second has a general lack of social perspective connected with conceptualizing information movement as a linear process and information use as an instrumental activity. Because of these limitations Miksa (1992) sees that a single combination of them as suggested in the name of the field—library (first paradigm) and information (second paradigm) science—is not adequate. He calls for a more essential approach to overcome the limitations of the models.

D. The Cognitive View of Information Science

Where Miksa finds signs of reorientation within the information movement paradigm toward cognitive themes driven by semantic problems, Saracevic (1990) sees a more manifest change. He argues for a major shift in the research paradigm for the field as a whole. The original research agenda for information science formulated in the 1950s and 1960s, labeled by him as a systems viewpoint, concentrated on effective information retrieval on the applied side and on the nature of information in Shannon's sense on the basic side. From the end of the 1970s onward a growing number of researchers have become convinced that the systems viewpoint is no more progressive (cf. Ingwersen, 1992b). Saracevic believes that they have advocated a problem orientation toward knowledge structures in terms of Brookes (1975) and Belkin (1977) or toward users and uses (Dervin, 1977; Dervin and Nilan, 1986) or in

Ingwersen's (1987) terms toward cognitive aspects. The label cognitive viewpoint became established as its name—the opposite of the systems viewpoint. The cognitive viewpoint is in a formative stage according to Saracevic (1990), even though Belkin (1990) has already described some of its research contributions.

Saracevic (1990) summarizes the development as follows: The paradigm shift to the cognitive viewpoint has reoriented research away from systems to emphasize questions about knowledge structures, human–computer interaction, information seeking, and human information behavior in general, with the underlying assumption that a better understanding in these areas will contribute to the design of better information systems and of critical components oriented toward users, such as intelligent interfaces.

The paradigm in information science seems to be shifting within the information movement frame from the systems view to the cognitive view. It has been characterized by a change of the focus from information systems to humans. Taking individuals as the point of departure in research has implied a concentration on the meaning of information, its semantic and pragmatic aspects. The main problem is how people give meaning to information in the context of its use and seeking, and what the implications to information systems design are. This has led to the study of conceptual structures and their change as well as individual sense-making in information seeking, retrieval, and use. The concentration on subjects instead of objects (systems) could also make it legitimate to call this paradigm user-oriented.

1. The Cognitive Viewpoint

The cognitive viewpoint of information science is a metatheoretical approach, which has some theoretical implications. As a metatheory it is discussion about theory, what concepts it should include and how those concepts should be linked. Similar to Kuhn's paradigms, theories of this sort provide guidelines or strategies for understanding social phenomena and suggest the proper orientation of the theorist to these phenomena. Wagner and Berger call them (1985) orientation strategies. An orientation strategy may include ontological and epistemological arguments about the subject matter of the discipline and the articulation of conceptual foundations employed in the description and analysis of the phenomena of interest. It includes also formulation of directives for the selection of theoretical problems for investigation. Wagner and Berger (1985) remind us that the claims of an orientating strategy are directives. They are statements about values, not about facts. Such prescriptive arguments are thus largely nonempirical.

If we follow Saracevic (1990) by putting under the umbrella of the cognitive viewpoint information retrieval studies orientated researchers like

Belkin and use and user studies oriented researchers like Dervin, it is difficult to find any well-formulated metatheoretical viewpoint that could form a common paradigm in a strict sense. What seems to unify those who are striving for a new approach is an interest in the subjects (users) and their way of categorizing and processing information in information use and seeking situations. The general approach and problems might be similar but the conceptual frames seem to differ, I would call these different approaches subject (user) oriented and reserve the cognitive viewpoint for that approach best formulated by Belkin (1978, 1990) and contributed to by Ingwersen (1992a).

Belkin (1990) has briefly described the cognitive viewpoint as an orientation strategy and a research program leading to empirical support. He stresses its features as an orientation strategy by stating that it suggests what information science should study and how it should be studied. He also points out that many of its ideas, which have been expressed in abstract terms, have led to theoretical, experimental, and practical advances. Thus he suggests that the orientation strategy also has theoretical contributions in terms of at least a loose research program (i.e., a set of interrelated theories).

The genesis of the cognitive view in information science is traced by Belkin (1990) from several publications in the mid-1970s. What is crucial for the view is the idea that at both ends of the communication systems of interest for information science cognitive processes occur. The implication is that those processes and what they entail are significant for the field. The essence of the approach is the idea of human perception, cognition, and structures of knowledge. Its advocates refer usually to the paradigmatic definition of the cognitive view given by De May (1977): Any processing of information, whether perceptual or symbolic, is mediated by a system of categories or concepts that, for the information-processing device, are the models of his/her world.

The essence of the cognitive viewpoint is, according to Belkin (1990), that it explicitly considers that the states of knowledge, beliefs, and so on of human beings (or information-processing devices) mediate (or interact with) that which they receive, perceive, or produce. The point is that our action and thinking are bound by our conceptual structure. This is parallel to the idea in philosophy of science that observations are theory-laden, that we see and interpret the world through our concepts and frames of reference.

This conception is a significant part of the foundation of cognitive science, and it has also been used in other disciplines. In information science, Belkin (1990) points out, the approach has led to consideration of the phenomena and situations of relevance in terms of representations of knowledge, intentions, beliefs, texts, and of interactions among such representations. He admits that the viewpoint does not specify precisely what the relevant phenomena of study might be, but provides, however, a fairly strong framework to make such a decision. For information science, it has typically meant considering its scope as being concerned with some sort of human communication system, in which texts play a key role, and with individuals within that system in their interactions with texts (or information), and with one another in relation to such texts.

2. The Fundamental Equation

The features described earlier form an orientation strategy for information science by the cognitive approach. Belkin is one of its foremost figures. Before we analyze in more detail his conception, I shall introduce Bertram Brookes' contribution to the orientation strategy of the cognitive viewpoint in information science. He was one of the major founding figures of the cognitive view.

The motivation of Brookes' efforts to develop a theory for information science was his doubt about the existence of theoretical information science. He has discerned bits of theory scattered around the world like a peddler's bread. In order to create its theoretical foundations he builds on the ontology of Karl Popper.

Brookes' (1980) point of departure is that of all social sciences, information science is intimately concerned with the interactions between mental and physical processes or between subjective and objective modes of thought. To understand this relation he seeks tools from the conceptual arsenal of Popper. His ontology consists of three spheres of reality. World 1 is furnished with physical objects, events, and processes in the time and space, matter and energy, organic and inorganic nature. World 2 consists of human mental states, mental events, the psyche. To World 3 belong artifacts and abstractions created by human social activity, culture, and society. For instance, stars, stones, the human body, and books as physical entities are members of World 1, perceptions, feelings, and thoughts of human beings and higher animals members of World 2, and works of·art, theories, associations, and concepts belong to World 3.

For Brookes (1980), World 2 is the sphere of subjective human knowledge and World 3 the sphere of objective knowledge. The latter consists of products of the human mind as recorded in languages, the arts, the sciences, and the technologies. Especially World 3, Brookes (1980) feels, should commend itself to the scientific community of information science because, for the first time, it makes available to their professional activities a rationale that can be expressed in other than purely practical terms. He suggests that the theoretical task of information science is to study the interactions between Worlds 2 and 3, to describe and explain them and so to help to organize knowledge rather than documents for more effective use. In adopting the interaction between

Worlds 2 and 3 as our field of study we could lay claim to a territory no other discipline has already claimed. The last claim, however, is not valid, because many others, like communication science, reception studies in arts and literature, economics, and sociology, are digging in that area. Brookes has reduced World 3 too much by taking into acount only the recordings of human thoughts.

Brookes comes closer to the cognitive viewpoint when laying foundations for information science by presenting its fundamental equation (Brookes, 1975). He (Brookes, 1980) defines knowledge as a structure of concepts linked by their relations and information as a small part of such a structure. The knowledge structure may be objective or subjective. Brookes has formulated the fundamental equation as follows:

$$K[S] + \Delta I = K[S + \Delta S]$$

It states in a general way that the knowledge structure $K[S]$ is changed to the new modified structure $K[S + \Delta S]$ by the information ΔI, the ΔS indicating the effect of the modification. Brookes (1977) points out that this equation implies that information modifies what is denoted by $K[S]$, which is a knowledge structure, that knowledge and information have the same dimensions, and that information is structured in the same way as knowledge.

The equation is expressed in general terms. As such it does not define the content or scope of information science. The equation refers to the growth of knowledge in many ways (e.g., in terms of theory growth or learning or knowledge use by individuals). At least until now information science has hardly contributed to the knowledge of these problem areas. One can doubt if there exists ΔI from information science that would have modified the conceptual structure $K[S]$ concerning these problems. The information science community has not studied learning, use of information, or growth of theories, but how information, usually documents, have been acquired for different uses. The problem is that Brookes has not contextualized and elaborated his equation to be specific enough for the needs of information science. However, he stresses that we have to consider the objective and subjective cognitive structures and processes that lead to the growth of knowledge in order to be able to organize knowledge and not only its carriers (documents) for more effective use (cf. Brookes, 1980). In fact the last part of his sentence refers to the context of information science. It is within this context where the frame and basic concepts of information science should be defined.

Brookes (1975) is aware of the general nature of his equation: It does not solve the problems of information science but rather poses them. He therefore states that the interpretation of the equation is the basic research task of information science. He suggests that the appropriate way to interpret the equation is to consider the interaction between people and objective knowledge as recorded in the published literature in order to discover more about subjective knowledge structures.

An adherent of cognitive viewpoint, Ingwersen (1992c), has developed the equation. He interprets the model to include the generation and reception of information in such a way that a state of knowledge (knowledge structure) is transformed. Ingwersen takes into account the reception of potential information (pI) by the individual from which the information (ΔI) will be distilled and he also scrutinizes on the basis of the new conceptual structure the creation of new infomation (pI'), which is potential to other recipients. He also introduces Belkin's (1978) anomalous states of knowledge concept to enrich the interpretation of the equation. After treatment by Ingwersen the model is

$$pI \; -> \; \Delta I + K[S] \; -> \; K[S + \Delta S] \; -> \; pI'$$

It states that of potential information pI the information ΔI is perceived. ΔI is mediated by the actual knowledge state (including the problem space and state of uncertainty) K[S], transforming the state of knowledge into a new state K[K + ΔS] with the effect ΔS. The modified state of knowledge may generate new information pI', with potential for other recipients. Although Ingwersen has enriched the equation with new concepts, it does not cast more light on the domain of information science than Brookes' model. It is also too general for the purpose of exact definition. In order to be more useful the model should be contextualized more precisely to the information seeking and use situations by individuals.

3. The Fundamental Problem

When analyzing the proposed concepts of information for information science Belkin (1978) points out that most of the definitions lack the necessary context. They are isolated definitions without relations to other central concepts in the field. They have been pursuits for ultimate definition of the phenomenon disregarding the usefulness of the concept for the research and definitions of our cognitive field. Belkin (1978) suggests an opposite approach. Since the aim is to find an information concept that will be suitable and useful for information science, one has to begin by considering the context and needs of information science, isolating from them a minimum set of requirements for the concept. Belkin believes that without a conceptual frame the definition is not useful for the aims of the discipline.

One of the most common premises of recent philosophy of science is that the meaning of a concept is theory-dependent (cf. Tuomela, 1973). Although a definition is required, its theoretical frame, other concepts, and their relations give added content to the concept. Not only *definiens* but also the whole theoretical context is signifying the definiendum. This implies that in order to be useful a concept has to fit into a theoretical frame of reference.

Belkin's (1978) point of departure for the outline of the context of information science is the goal of scientific activity, which is to produce useful knowledge in solving problems associated with the objects of study. He suggests that the formulation of the problem information science wishes to solve is of basic significance. It is through the establishment of the problem that the precise area of systematic, scientific investigation can be specified and the assumptions governing that activity developed. In that way he is at the same time pursuing an appropriate outlining of information science. We can call this the fundamental problem for information science. Belkin (1978) takes the problem to be facilitating the effective communication of desired information between human generator and user.

Belkin's definition is similar to primitive concepts in definitions. They have to be taken as given, because an attempt to define all the concepts leads to *reductio ad absurdum*. Similarly, Belkin does not give any grounds for his choice. However, leaving the founding problem of a field of research without justification is questionable. When the whole conceptual construction of information science is meant to be based on this foundation, one would like to know how valid it is.

In the literature referring to Belkin's formulation, no doubts about this starting point have been raised. There are at least two reasons. First, it includes a commonly shared and implicitly accepted vision of the basic function of library and information services. Facilitating access to information is commonly held to be the task of those services. Buckland (1992) states that access can be regarded as a unifying concept for the whole field and that all the provision and use of retrieval-based information services are concerned with access to information. It seems that Belkin's conception of information science, at least on a foundational level, can be placed under the information movement paradigm by Miksa. For Miksa (1992) the paradigm focuses on the information movement that occurs in a system where knowledge representing objects are sought and retrieved in response to inquiries initiated by the individuals.

Second, the wide silent acceptance of the founding problem can be attributed to Belkin's elaborations on it. It is not the problem as such but its explications that might have acquired most understanding for it.

One can also claim that Belkin's formulation is not a problem but a task formulation. Facilitation of effective communication of desired information between human generator and user is not an aim of a field of research, it is an aim of a field of practice. The acceptance of this formulation implies a design science conception of information science. Actually Belkin is declaring that the purpose of information service community is the foundation for information science. This is not surprising, because we are always bound by tradition. There are hardly any attempts at defining the field that are not based on practical premises. However, one has to underline that the roots of the explication of the problem by Belkin are not in the profession but in the cognitive sciences. He only takes this formulation for a starting point in order to find context for his elaborations.

As a first step to interpret his problem Belkin (1978) draws from it five concerns for information science:

1. Information in human, cognitive communication systems
2. The relationship between information and generator
3. The relationship between information and user
4. The idea of desired information
5. The effectiveness of information and the effectiveness of information transfer

With these five concerns Belkin is shaping dimensions of the phenomena of interest for information science. With the help of certain criteria he can now formulate requirements for the concept of information for information science. His argument is: If we are interested in phenomena like this, the information concept should be like that. Thus, the requirements are at the same time specifications of his conception of information science. According to Belkin (1978) the concept (1) must refer to information within the context of purposeful, meaningful communication, (2) should account for information as a social communication process among human beings, (3) should account for information that is requested or desired, (4) should account for the effect of information on the recipient, (5) must account for the relationship between information and state of knowledge (of generator and recipient), and (6) should account for the varying effects of messages presented in different ways.

Belkin (1978) gives a structural definition of information based on information retrieval or, as he states, on the recipient-controlled communication system. The definition is given from a cognitive viewpoint. Belkin first introduces an auxiliary concept, text, which is a collection of signs purposefully structured by the sender with the intention of changing the conceptual structure of a recipient. Then he proposes that the information associated with a text is the generator's modified (by purpose, intent, knowledge of recipient's state of knowledge) conceptual structure that underlies the surface structure (e.g., language) of that text. This definition is subsequently elaborated by Ingwersen (1992a, 1992b).

The idea behind this conception is that the generator of a text shapes his/her conceptual structure on some topic in order to communicate it. The structure is converted by linguistic rules into a communicable structure, the text, which becomes a part of the corpus of texts to which potential recipients have access. The recipient instigates the communication system by recognizing an anomaly in her/his state of knowledge, this recognition being akin to the partition of the generator's state of knowledge that identifies the conceptual structure to be communicated. The recipient then converts this anomalous state of knowledge (ASK) into some communicable structure (e.g., a request), which is used to retrieve from the corpus of texts some texts that might be appropriate for resolving the anomaly.

This classical description by Belkin (1978) actually represents the hard core of the object of information science seen from the cognitive viewpoint. It is concerned with the description of conceptual structures of texts, their generators and users, and how to match the descriptions of the two latter groups in order to retrieve relevant texts to the users. Although this is the paradigmatic case, one has to admit that the adherents of the cognitive viewpoint have broadened the scope of their interest at least to the field of information seeking studies (cf. Belkin, 1989). However, the main target of the research from this viewpoint has been problems of information retrieval.

If we apply Occam's razor, which states that one should not use more concepts than is necessary, to the fundamental problem by Belkin, one might wonder what the role of the generator in this scheme is. It is not enough for the purposes of information science to scrutinize the relations between information (texts) and user (Kärki, 1993). A person with ASK is seeking information, not the generator of the information, in order to resolve the anomaly. It is also obvious that we can describe the conceptual structure of the text without referring to its generator. And although in many cases the user of the information is simultaneously a generator of a new text, it does not imply the necessity of that concept. What is left for information science is the facilitation of effective interaction between desired information and its user or, more traditionally, facilitation of access to desired information.

Belkin does not elaborate his conception of information science further, because his concept is specific enough to enable him to define the concept of information for the discipline. His strategy has been to refer to some of the most important dimensions and phenomena of interest to information science to facilitate his definition of this crucial concept. There are at least two important features in it. By using the phrase desired information he is fixing the point of view of information science with that of the subject (user). The question is about the information a person needs for use. There is a move from system to user. Second, he suggests that information science has to do with the internal states of knowledge of the generator and recipient of information. In order to be able to facilitate the communication of desired information between its generator and user within retrieval-based information systems information science has to concern itself with the conceptual structures of generator, information, and user. Belkin's emphasis on the mental states of humans has directed the interest of information science to new ontological domains (cf. Bunge, 1982). The objects and phenomena of the World 2 by Popper have not been a serious concern of information science before. The cognitive viewpoint is opening a perspective on it. The objects in World 3 by Popper have also not been conceptualized earlier as conceptual structures by information scientists before the representative of this viewpoint. The view is filling the domain of information studies with new objects and relations.

4. The Subfields of Information Science

Ingwersen (1992a, 1992b) has also developed the conception of information science from the cognitive viewpoint, taking Belkin's fundamental problem as a starting point. According to him (Ingwersen 1992a) the statement implies the study of the user's reasons for acquiring information, recorded in systems of various kinds, the process of providing desired information to users qualitatively, and the process of use and further generation of information. Information science is dealing with all kinds of users and all means of recording.

Based on Belkin's five areas of concern Ingwersen (1992a) outlines the dimensions of information science in greater detail. The first area deals mainly with formal and informal transfer of information, for instance, scientific communication or information flow within institutions. The second seeks to understand the generation and development of information needs within society, among specific groups of people or individually. It is the nature of and reasons for desired information that is the focus of attention, those reasons being problem solving or fulfillment of cultural, emotional, or factual goals. The third area studies methods and technologies that may improve performance and quality of information in information systems. Further, this area is concerned with the development of theories and ways to ease the transfer processes of information between generators and users. It is closely linked to the fourth area of concern, which deals with generated knowledge and forms of its analysis and representation in (text) information systems. The problems of indexing and classification as well as of measurements and distribution of R&D production belong to it. Finally, the fifth major area of study has its focus on the relevance, use, and value of information.

The five areas described are presented in Figure 1. Ingwersen (1992a) feels that it forms a framework to describe subfields of information science and illustrates his claim by naming some of them with the help of the figure. Numbers in brackets refer to the five areas described earlier. Informetrics (i.e., quantitative study of processes of written communication, such as bibliometrics) is mainly concerned with Areas 1 and 4. Information management, including evaluation and quality of textual and other media-based information retrieval systems, is basically concerned with Areas 3 and 4. Information (retrieval) systems design belongs to Areas 3, 4, and 5. Information retrieval interaction is concerned with the study of information processes in Areas 2, 3, and 4. One could add that information need and use studies deal with

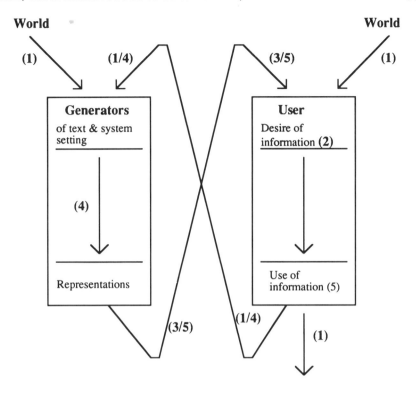

text = text, graphics, pictures, sound

Fig. 1   Major areas of study in information science. (Source: Ingwersen 1992c)

Areas 2 and 5. The figure gives an interesting frame to name and shape the subfields of information science.

5. Cognitive Fruits of the View

On the basis of empirical studies, Belkin (1990) has concluded that taking the cognitive viewpoint of information science can lead to highly beneficial results in a variety of areas of interest to information science. For him it seems reasonable to suggest that other areas, which have not yet been considered from this point of view, might benefit from it. He believes also that this evidence suggests that the cognitive viewpoint might serve as a means for integration, relating work in various areas of information science to one another, and therefore provide the structure for a unified and effective information science.

Belkin thus claims that the cognitive viewpoint in information science can form an integrative frame for its research. As an orientation strategy it has stressed the significance of studying conceptual structures both of documents and of human beings and their interaction when searching for desired information. In that way it has directed members of the scientific community of information science to certain theoretical problems. However, one could claim that the basic problem, or better, the basic interest of the viewpoint to facilitate the communication of desired information between human generator and user is the classical one in our field. This point of departure is not new, but the way the phenomena has been conceptualized is pioneering. Its attempts to redefine information and cognitive processes by human beings have been innovative and lead clearly to new and promising results. The approach has turned the interest of our field from inside the walls of the library into the heads of our clients. It has been a reaction against the naive empirical research concentrating on the human being as a complex of external characteristics and of information as a thing (i.e., physical objects like data or documents) (cf. Buckland, 1991).

One of the most important features of the cognitive viewpoint is its ability to connect the concept of information and thus the results of our field of research to the other fields of research. Its use of the structural information concept and interest in the cognitive structures is shared by many fields of cognitive sciences. It means that this conception of information science has a specific background that is a collection of up-to-date and reasonably well-confirmed results obtained in other fields of inquiry relevant to the field (cf. Bunge, 1982). This helps information science utilize results, concepts, and methods from other fields of research as well as contribute to their development.

The cognitive approach is not a uniform movement. Although it has features of a metatheory, it has not created a theoretical research program to cover most of the field. If a theoretical research program is understood as a set of interrelated theories, together with research relevant to evaluating them (Wagner and Berger, 1985), only information retrieval research, using Belkin's ASK model conceptualized in terms of cognitive view, could be labeled as a research program. Research activity in different areas of information science using this approach has not yet been able to show explicit connections between the theoretical constructs they are using in explaining their objects of study. The research efforts are scattered and theoretical work to unify conceptually the research results in different areas of study is waiting to be tackled. However, one might expect that the cognitive viewpoint is the primary challenger for this work because of its more developed conceptual frame. It provides tools for integrating many parts of the field under the same conceptual scheme. In that way it could lead to the conceptual evolution in our field as claimed by Schrader (1986).

6. Critique of the Cognitive Viewpoint

The viewpoint has gained success, yet there is also some well-founded criticism against it. The best summary of its alleged weaknesses is given by Frohmann (1992a, 1992b) in his discourse analysis of the cognitive viewpoint. He claims that its theoretical model for information science is sought from the natural sciences. This argument has been discussed earlier in this article. Further, Frohmann (1992b) blames the cognitive approach for theoretical imperialism. This means that it presents itself not as a local theory of specific problems but as a total theory for information science. Thus, he has observed its nature as an orienting strategy. He is correctly pointing out that some of its claims are not based on empirical results. What he does not mention is that it is a common strategy within the scientific community. He is mixing the different types of theoretical activity, the formulation of an orientation strategy with the formulation and testing of specific unit theories (cf. Wagner and Berger, 1985). Both have their legitimate role in research. The cognitive viewpoint like other orienting strategies presents directives and theoretical problems for future research. The results of the concluding research program are crucial when assessing the fruitfulness of an orientating strategy.

Frohmann (1992a) also blames the cognitive viewpoint for referentiality and reification of images, internalization of representations, radical individualism and erasure of social dimension of theory, insistence upon knowledge, constitution of the information scientist as an expert in image negotiation, and instrumental reason, ruled by efficiency, standardization, predictability, and determination of effects. One of the main features of this criticism is that the viewpoint does not include the social dimension in its theories but concentrates solely on the mental structures of users. Frohmann (1992b) feels that information becomes an alteration inside the minds of social atoms, that information seeking becomes expertly guided individual image repair, and that information sought becomes an image located within large-scale depositories of representations of an objective world. He claims that the volatile mass of phenomena of possible interest within information processes is reduced by the cognitive viewpoint to few key referring expressions, whose function is to construct a manageable set of stable figures and key structures as investigational objects of an objective world. Among the most important of these are image, model, picture, knowledge structure, and knowledge store. Frohmann is correct in many respects. The point is, however, that the aim of a science is to reduce and construct its fundamental phenomena of interest with the help of a few powerful basic concepts. Merely stating this fact is not very illuminating. What is needed are assessments of the way the conceptualization has been done. This observation by Frohmann can be reduced to his criticism about the individualized mentalistic and asocial character of theoretization in the cognitive viewpoint.

Possibly the most important point in the criticism by Frohmann is the notion of the radical individualism and erasure of the social dimension in the theories of the cognitive viewpoint. He has not been alone in his criticism. Paisley (1989) and Miksa (1992) have also argued against the narrow social perspective of the approach with little or no serious attention to the social aspects of the information processes, either in terms of the social context of individual users or the social context of the system itself. Rudd (1983) has warned information scientists not to lean too much on Popper's model of three worlds because his definition of World 3 does not take into account the social context of information. The social conditions and social effects of the facilitating structures for information have not been tackled by the cognitive viewpoint due to its methodological individualism (on methodological individualism: Nagel, 1961, Chapter 14).

The tension between social and individual dimension in social science theoretization is not new. It reflects in general the dualism between structuralistic and social action theories analyzed by Giddens (1981). Basic concepts of social sciences like structure and action defy attempts to integrate them in a well-balanced theory. As Savolainen (1992) puts it, there is no reason to believe that the case of information science would be easier in this respect. One could say that there are few attempts at that kind of theoretical work by the information scientists in general and from the cognitive viewpoint in particular. Only one of the researchers critized by Frohmann, Brenda Dervin (Dervin and Clark, 1991), has tried to bridge the gap between individual action and social structure perspectives. Her attempts have so far had limited results. However, for the cognitive point of view the integration of social structures in its theories should be a challenge.

E. Other Attempts to Shape the Domain

Here some minor ways to shape the task and content of information science are discussed. The tiny hermeneutical tracks within our field are traced and the postmodern view of information science by Wersig (1992) is presented.

There have been some minor phenomenological and hermeneutical attempts to discuss the nature and domain of information science. The interest is recent, going back to the end of the 1980s. Possibly the first attempt to use hermeneutics in the problems of information science was a study by Rafael Capurro (1986) on the foundations of the hermeneutics of Fachinformation (subject information). Daniel Benediktsson (1989) and Ivar Hoel (1992) have argued for the fruitful use of hermeneutics in information science research. Both describe some basic hermeneutical concepts on a general level without connecting them firmly to the analysis of information science. Capurro (1992) has attempted to characterize information science on the basis of a hermeneutical analysis. He suggests a pragmatic foundation for information science. Information means in his conception the possibility of sharing thematically a common world within specific forms of life. Information is not substantial but a dimension of human existence. With the term *information* Capurro refers to the shared background information, preunderstanding, which enables us to interact and communicate with each other. It is not a relationship between a knowing subject and a known object but rather an effect produced by a set of concepts that makes it possible to think certain facts or states of affairs and not others (cf. Outhwhaite, 1983). Information is shared by members of a form of life or of an interpretative audience. As a common background it is not meaningful to talk about information as something that can be transmitted or retrieved. It is like the air you breathe.

Defined in this way information becomes, according to Capurro (1992), a rhetoric category; information science can be considered as a subdiscipline of rhetoric. As such it includes a formal-methodological, as well as a cultural-historical perspective.

Although sharing the same interest in documents and text as hermeneutics, Houser (1986) does not attempt to shape the domain with the help of its tools. He claims that the domain of information science consists of documents. According to him, recorded social discourse published in the documents is central to it. This definition can be accepted with reservations. It is obvious that information science is interested in documents of different kinds, but the conception does not specify the relation of documents to other phenomena of interest for information science. It does not tell from what angle to scrutinize the documents. It also forgets that there are many informal features of information that are of interest to information science.

Wersig (1992) argues for a new type of science, which is needed to solve the problems of our postmodern society. He believes that the engineering objective of the previous documentation and its successor did not adequately qualify it as a recognized discipline (Wersig, 1991). But according to him, there is an emerging need for a scientific approach to the problem of actors dealing with knowledge under conditions of a change in the role of knowledge. This change is further supported by the phenomenon of informatization.

Wersig (1992) articulates the basic formula for information science as information is knowledge to action. It means that rational behavior needs knowledge. The knowledge has to be transformed into something that supports a specific action within a specific situation. This implies that the main objective of information science is people confused by the situation of knowledge usage. The aim of information science is, according to Wersig, to help actors to cope with their information problems, which are becoming more confusing in the postmodern society.

If information science responds to this challenge of societal changes, it would be established (together with some others like ecology) as a prototype of new or postmodern science. Postmodern science is not, Wersig (1992) proposes, like classical science, driven by the search for a complete understanding of how the world works but by the need to develop strategies to solve in particular the problems raised by classical sciences and technologies. Its outcome would not be statements about the nature of things but strategies to deal with problems. This calls for the development of internal problem perspectives and structuring the field from that internal perspective.

This description of and goal for information science resembles that of design science. Its aim is to help us to reach our goals by producing information relevant to attaining them. Wersig does not discuss in detail what kind of information his postmodern science would produce. If he includes the formulation of goals for the strategies to the burden of postmodern science, the classical conception of science, including design science, hardly fits his conception. If it seeks information as means of reaching the goals, his proposal is similar to design science. It, too, is producing technical norms for action as described earlier.

In order to face this new theoretical situation, Wersig (1992) proposes three approaches: First, the development of basic models by redefinition of broad scientific concepts (e.g., system leading to the concept of actor, communication leading to the concept of complexity reduction). This means that the first step in theory building for information science is to take relevant broad concepts already in existence, evaluate them, and reformulate them for the purposes of the discipline. Second, Wersig proposes a scientific reformulation of interconcepts (i.e., concepts that are so common that they have not yet been scientifically worked out, for example, knowledge and image). They are called interconcepts because they interrelate a set of traditional disciplines without being understood to be transdisciplinary. Finally, the aim of information science is the interweaving of models and interconcepts. Wersig (1992) hopes that this theoretical work will lead to knotting together the different interconcepts and models to be found in different disciplines. This protonetwork of basic concepts of information science could be made more comprehensive with the concepts from other areas. The perspective to that practical activity should be the problem of knowledge usage under postmodern conditions of informatization.

The program outlined is partly problematic because the meaning of a concept is heavily theory-dependent. In order to be able to interweave different concepts and especially different bits of conceptual nets one has to be able to confirm that the bits fit together. The reformulation of a concept away from its context usually means that it has been separated from the original network. Although the concept fits with the new theory, the remaining part of the old one remains unattached. In order to combine theories one has to work with entire networks.

V. Conclusion: Orientation Strategies as Integrators of the Broadening Field

Generally the researchers of a given discipline are not interested in the meta-theoretical questions of that discipline. They are content if they can define the concepts they require in their own research. They believe that there is no need to contemplate how the wider conceptual network used in other research has been arrived at and through which the whole discipline could be understood. The scant nature of the debate there has been on this in information science circles reflects the general view prevailing in the scientific community. The small body of literature addressing this aspect does, however, include some profound and constructive analyses of the nature of information science.

There are at least two justifications for self-scrutiny. On the one hand, it is of assistance in gaining an understanding of how the field of study has developed and what may fall within its scope. This yields an overview of what has been researched and how. On the other hand, such a picture may assume the character of an orientation strategy. By defining the basic concepts and demonstrating the area of reality opening up to research and further by showing how this research should be approached, the orientation strategy frequently leads to theoretical research programs in which the directives of this strategy are implemented, operationalized, and tried out empirically. Self-scrutiny within the discipline is of appreciable aid to researchers in the field because it provides tools with which to work and guidance in the choice of certain problems. Although self-scrutiny may not always result in the formation of an orientation strategy, theoretical attempts at definition invariably have the effect of showing the way in which the discipline is to move. They are an attempt to conceptualize the field in a certain way, to the exclusion of other conceptions.

Information science has been characterized from the outset as being purpose-minded. Although its name has been changed through documentation from library science to information science, its raison d'etre has always rested on the support it provides for certain practical activity. It is dominated by a long, consistent progression from Schrettiger via Bradford to Belkin. The purpose to which information science is pledged is to facilitate access to desired information. Information research came into being and flourished on the sustenance provided by this principle, from which it will continue to hold its mandate in the future. It is design science, whose mission it is to provide, with help from research, the guidelines through which access to information can be enhanced. It includes both a descriptive and a facilitating component.

Information science has also broadened its scope over the years to information facilitating contexts other than libraries. This has caused both terminological and conceptual confusion. The basic question has been how to designate and conceptualize our field of research. One of its culminations is the dilemma about the relation between library science and information science. The most validly argumented view in the literature is that the question makes no difference. It is incorrectly formulated. As Ingwersen (1992b), Wilson (1983), and Wersig (1992) have argued, information science forms a totality, which is not fruitful in theory or practice to divide into library science and information science. Other subdivisions are more suitable for research and also practical purposes, as Ingwersen and Wilson have proposed. However, this conception does not imply that problems of librarianship would be excluded from information science. It is one of its field of application. If we cannot conceptually differentiate library science from information science, the corresponding linguistic distinction is unnecessary. Thus, library science is a linguistic expression without content. As such its use is meaningless.

Information science has usually been characterized as a social science. A social science typically studies interaction between individuals and groups. As such information science studies the communicative interaction of individuals and groups with each other, texts in a semiotic sense, and systems containing texts and their surrogates. Proposals for a natural scientific nature of information science are seldom found in the literature. When they exist, the conclusion is that information science is not a natural science. The only justified claim is that emigrants from the natural sciences have brought some elements of their mother discipline and applied it to information science. However, this does not transform it into a natural science.

A central feature of a science is that it takes and uses results of other disciplines as well as contributes to the development of adjacent fields (cf. Bunge, 1982). There is much theoretical discussion about the relations of information science to other fields of research. The importance of borrowing conceptual and methodological tools from other disciplines has been generally acknowledged. It is seen as a central means to advance the development of information science. Cognitive sciences, psychology, computer science, linguistics, and communication have been the most commonly mentioned as sources of contribution. In theoretical discussion, however, it has seldom been shown explicitly what theories, concepts, or methods from other disciplines could be used in the problems of information science. There are some exceptions. Belkin and Roberts (1976; Belkin, 1978), for example, have argued for applying conceptual tools of cognitive science to define the concept of information for information science. On a disciplinary level it is difficult to argue in detail for using some tools from other disciplines without insight for what purposes to use them. It requires an orientation strategy, an articulated vision about the basic problems, subject matter and fruitful solutions for the discipline (cf. Wagner and Berger, 1985). If you do not have one, you can only refer to the importance of borrowing from others, but you cannot tell what to borrow.

The theoretical claims of the usefulness of the results of other sciences and the multidisciplinary nature of information science is not supported by empirical findings. The few inquiries about the matter show that our field of research is uncommunicative. It is isolated from other disciplines not using their concepts, methods, or results in its own studies. If the scientific import is minimal the export of ideas from information science seems to be still more modest. Although it is probable that the picture is not as dark as described, it needs more shades from other fields. Active contact with and use of literature from other disciplines is required.

The scope of information science has broadened significantly. The change could be depicted with the help of Miksa's (1992) conception of the two paradigms of information science. One could claim that library as a social institution paradigm has been forced to give way to the paradigm of information movement. It seems that the focus of the discipline has shifted from the library and information service institution to a broader conceptualization of the field. The dominant paradigm can be described as focusing on the information movement that occurs in a system where knowledge-representing objects are sought and retrieved in response to the inquiries initiated by individuals. This retrieval system model can be applied in different contexts to identify the phenomena of interest for information science. The model is generalizable beyond the walls of libraries and information service institutions to all relevant cases for the field. It is broader in its scope than the traditional library and information institution model.

The most advanced variant of the information movement paradigm is the cognitive view of information science best articulated by Belkin. His formulation about the fundamental problem of information science to facilitate the effective communication of desired information between human generator and user, forms the legitimation and also the foundation for information science. It defines the scope of the field. It functions as the context for defining the basic concepts of information science. The cognitive view has two important contributions to the paradigm of information science. It has shifted the focus from information system to its user (subject) by emphasizing the concept of desired information. However, in order to be able to facilitate the access to desired information the discipline has to be concerned with the conceptual structures of information, its generator, and its user. The latter is the view of the orientation strategy of the cognitive viewpoint, which is inspired by the ideas of cognitive sciences. The approach is broader in its scope than that of the information movement paradigm by Miksa. It also includes means facilitating access to information in addition to retrieval-based systems. It has enriched our field of research proposing new objects for its domain, introducing fresh problematics, and has thus accumulated its fund of knowledge. This broadening perspective is not due solely to the cognitive view. One could say that it is the continuation of the trend that has tried to widen the domain of information science beyond the walls of the library and information service institutions.

The trends emerging from the literature in the last decade described by many writers (e.g., Ingwersen, 1992b; Saracevic, 1992) can be crystallized as a shift from object to subject. The specific trends are operationalizations of this change. The central change is the idea of subjects actively constructing meaning in the situations they are facing. Subjects are seen not as passive receivers of information but actors deriving their own sense from it. The act of becoming informed is interaction between the conceptual structure of the text and conceptual structure of the subject depending on the intention of the subject. By implication the conceptualization of information shifted from understanding it as a thing to a conceptual structure (cf. Buckland, 1991). The other aspects of this change move the point of view from systems to users and from technology to humans. This has meant also increased under-standing of information use as an integral part of information seeking.

The cognitive viewpoint or emphasis on subject has been the major force for reorientation. However, it has not made a total breakthrough in the field. There is still at least the library (including information services) as a social institution paradigm, which continues to receive, if in declining amounts, backing from some parts of the profession. Its weakness is that it cannot produce an articulated and well-formed conceptualization of its central ideas. The inadequate articulation of its central conceptions as an orientation strat-egy is also the crucial weakness of the information resources management movement, which could function as a challenger of the cognitive view. The promise of the movement is that it is interested in both individual information use and its organizational and social context. It connects them by looking for ways to augment information use and seeking in different contexts in order to support the objectives of an organization. That it has not articulated itself as an orientation strategy is due to the fact that it has developed an ideology but no basic concepts for the field. It has defined the central problem of information resources management but not its basic concepts.

It seems that the cognitive view has taken the role of the leading orienta-tion strategy in our field of research. Its most challenging task is to try to overcome its methodological individualism by enriching its theoretization with concepts of social structure. Although all of us are making sense in our own situations, the sense-making is social and collective in that the concepts and senses we are using are not individual, they are products of a shared culture. They are social constructs. In order to make sense we must have access to repositories of socially constructed meaning structures (i.e., texts in a semiotic sense) whether in written or spoken form. These repositories are manifested and maintained in many ways. Different institutions and organizations are maintaining and reproducing them. Individuals make sense in different situations and reform their conceptual structures in order to overcome anomalies using the common meanings maintained by these institutions. The very decision to choose among different sources by individuals is socially conditioned, and the way they understand the message is directed by the shared meanings provided them in their contexts. Both the individual information use and the institutional information access context are socially conditioned. It seems that the social constructionistic approach developed recently in the social sciences could add social aspects to the cognitive view, especially when they share a common interest in conceptual structures.

Much of the theorizing about our field of research is too general and does not contribute to the formation of orientation strategies that could provide a starting point for theoretical research programs. They could help to integrate the different parts of the broadening field of information science. One can claim in line with Wagner and Berger (1985) that theoretical research programs offer the most probable way to increasing our knowledge about the phenomenon we are interested in. Research programs are by definition social constructs with shared meanings. To fulfill a program requires concerted efforts by individual researchers and research groups. In order to make more theoretical progress with empirical results we need more researchers who are ready to share common tasks and concepts (i.e., meanings). It requires more cooperation between research groups. Finally, it also requires genuine theoretical work in order to integrate theories into broader and more precise frameworks. Usually crucial progress in science is conceptual innovations. This would also be the promising way to start the export of ideas from information science to the other fields of inquiry.

References

Atkins, S. (1988). Subject trends in library and information science research 1975–1984. *Library Trends* **36,** 633–658.
Belkin, N. (1978). Information concept for information science. *Journal of Documentation* **34,** 55–85.
Belkin, N. (1990). The cognitive viewpoint in information science. *Journal of Information Science* **16,** 11–16.

Belkin, N., and Roberts, S. (1976). Information science and the phenomenon of information. *Journal of the American Society for Information Science* **26**, 197–204.

Benediktsson, D. (1989). Hermeneutics: Dimensions toward LIS thinking. *Library and Information Science Research* **11**, 210–234.

Borgman, C., and Rice, R. (1992). The convergence of information science and communication: A bibliometric analysis. *Journal of the American Society for Information Science* **43**, 397–411.

Borgman, C., and Schement, J. (1992). Information science and communication research. In *Information Science: The Interdisciplinary Context* (M. Pemberton and A. Prentice, eds.), pp. 42–59. Neal-Schuman, New York and London.

Bradford, S. (1948). *Documentation*. Washington, DC.

Brookes, B. C. (1975). The fundamental equation of information science. In *Problems of Information Science*. VINITI, Moscow.

Brookes, B. C. (1977). The development of cognitive viewpoint in information science. In *International Workshop on the Cognitive Viewpoint*. (M. De Mey, ed.), University of Ghent, Ghent.

Brookes, B. C. (1980). The foundations of information science. Part 1. Philosophical aspects. *Journal of Information Science* **2**, 125–133.

Brown, A. (1987). *Toward Theoretical Information Science: Information and the Concept of Information*. (University of Sheffield, Department of Information Studies Occasional Publication Series 5) Sheffield, England.

Buckland, M. (1991). *Information and Information Systems*. Praeger, New York.

Buckland, M. (1992). Information as thing. *Journal of the American Society for Information Science* **42**, 351–360.

Bunge, M. (1982). Demarcating science from pseudoscience. *Fundamenta Scientia* **3**, 369–388.

Capurro, R. (1986). *Hermeneutik der Fachinformation*. Alber, Freiburg.

Capurro, R. (1992). What is information science for? In *Conceptions of Library and Information Science* (P. Vakkari and B. Cronin, eds.), pp. 82–96. Taylor Graham, London and Los Angeles.

Cronin, B., and Pearson, S. (1990). The export of ideas from information science. *Journal of Information Science* **16**, 381–391.

De Mey, M., ed. (1977). *International Workshop on the Cognitive Viewpoint*. University of Ghent, Ghent.

Dervin, B. (1977). Useful theory for the librarianship: Communication not information. *Drexel Library Quarterly* **13**, 16–32.

Dervin, B. (1992). From the mind's eye of the "user." In *Qualitative Research in Information Management* (J. Glazier and R. Powell, eds.), pp. 61–84. Libraries Unlimited, Colorado.

Dervin, B., and Clark, K. (1991). Communication and democracy: A mandate for procedural invention. In *Communication and Democracy* (S. Splichal and J. Wasko, eds.), Ablex, Norwood, New Jersey.

Dervin, B., and Nilan, D. (1986). Information needs and uses. In *Annual Review of Information Science and Technology*, Vol. 21 (M. Williams, ed.), pp. 3–33. Knowledge Industry Publications, White Plains, New York.

Ford, B. (1990). The library as locus. In *Information Science: The Interdisciplinary Context* (M. Pemberton and A. Prentice, eds.), pp. 115–131. Neal-Schuman, New York and London.

Frohmann, B. (1992a). Knowledge and power in library and information science: Toward a discourse analysis of the cognitive viewpoint. In *Conceptions of Library and Information Science* (P. Vakkari and B. Cronin, eds.), pp. 135–148. Taylor Graham, London and Los Angeles.

Frohmann, B. (1992b). The power of images: A discourse analysis of the cognitive viewpoint. *Journal of Documentation* **48**, 365–386.

Giddens, A. (1981). Agency, institution, and time-space analysis. In *Advances in Social Theory and Methodology* (K. Knorr-Cetina and A. Cicourel, eds.), pp. 161–174. Routledge & Kegan Paul, Boston.

Halloran, J. (1983). Information and communication: information is the answer, but what is the question? *Journal of Information Science* **7**, 159–167.

Harmon, G. (1990). Relationship with the natural sciences and knowledge engineering. In *Information Science: The Interdisciplinary Context* (M. Pemberton and A. Prentice, eds.), pp. 25–41. Neal-Schuman, New York and London.

Hoel, I. (1992). Information science and hermeneutics. In *Conceptions of Library and Information Science* (P. Vakkari and B. Cronin, eds.), pp. 82–96. Taylor Graham, London and Los Angeles.

Houser, L. (1986). Documents: The domain of library and information science. *Library and Information Science Research* **8**, 163–188.

Ingwersen, P. (1987). Toward a new research paradigm in information retrieval. In *Knowledge Engineering: Expert Systems and Engineering* (I. Wormell, ed.), pp. 150–168. Taylor Graham, London.

Ingwersen, P. (1992a). Conceptions of information science. In *Conceptions of Library and Information Science* (P. Vakkari and B. Cronin, eds.), pp. 299–312. Taylor Graham, London and Los Angeles.

Ingwersen, P. (1992b). Information and information science in context. *Libri* **42**, 99–135.

Ingwersen, P. (1992c). *Information Retrieval Interaction*. Taylor Graham, London.

Järvelin, K., and Vakkari, P. (1990). Content analysis of research articles in library and information science. *Library and Information Science Research* **12**, 395–421.

Järvelin, K., and Vakkari, P. (1992). The evolution of library and information science 1965–1985. A content analysis of journal articles. In *Conceptions of Library and Information Science* (P. Vakkari and B. Cronin, eds.), pp. 109–125. Taylor Graham, London and Los Angeles.

Kärki, R. (1993). *Characteristics of Information Studies and Sociology of Science and Study of Scientific Communication as Their Common Field of Interest.* Licentiate theses, Department of Information Studies, University of Tampere (in Finnish).

Lancaster, F. (1984). Implications for library and information science education. *Library Trends* **32**, 337–347.

Miksa, F. (1992). Library and information science: Two paradigms. In *Conceptions of Library and Information Science* (P. Vakkari and B. Cronin, eds.), pp. 229–252. Graham Taylor, London and Los Angeles.

Nagel, E. (1961). *The Structure of Science.* Routledge & Kegan Paul, London.

Neill, S. (1992). *Dilemmas in the Study of Information.* Greenwood, Westport, Connecticut.

Niiniluoto, I. (1985). Progress in the applied sciences. In *History and Progress of Sciences* (E. Kaukonen, J. Manninen, and V. Verronen, eds.), pp. 169–192. Academy of Finland, Helsinki (in Finnish).

Outhwaite, W. (1983). *Concept Formation in Social Sciences.* Routledge & Kegan Paul, London.

Paisley, W. (1990). Information science as a multidiscipline. In *Information Science: The Interdisciplinary Context* (M. Pemberton and A. Prentice, eds.), pp. 3–24. Neal-Schuman, New York and London.

Peritz, B. (1981). The methods of library science research: Some results from a bibliometric survey. *Library Research* **2**, 251–268.

Rayward, W. B. (1983). Library and information sciences. Disciplinary differentiation, competition, and convergence. In *The Study of Information* (F. Machlup and U. Mansfield, eds.), pp. 343–363. Wiley, New York.

Ruben, B. (1990). Redefining the boundaries of graduate education. In *Information Science: The Interdisciplinary Context* (M. Pemberton and A. Prentice, eds.), pp. 70–83. Neal-Schuman, New York and London.

Ruben, B. (1992). The communication-information relationship in system-theoretic perspective. *Journal of the American Society for Information Science* **43**, 15–27.

Rudd, D. (1983). Do we really need World III? Information science with or without Popper. *Journal of Information Science* **7**, 99–105.

Saracevic, T. (1990). *Information Science Revisited*. Rutgers University, School of Communication, Information & Library Studies. Research Report Series 90-24. Rutgers, New York.

Saracevic, T. (1992). Information science: Origin, evolution and relations. In *Conceptions of Library and Information Science* (P. Vakkari and B. Cronin, eds.), pp. 5–27. Graham Taylor, London and Los Angeles.

Savolainen, R. (1992). The sense-making theory—An alternative to intermediary-centered approaches in library and information science? In *Conceptions of Library and Information Science* (P. Vakkari and B. Cronin, eds.), pp. 149–164. Graham Taylor, London and Los Angeles.

Schrader, A. (1984). In search of a name: Information science and its conceptual antecedents. *Library and Information Science Research* **6**, 227–271.

Schrader, A. (1986). The domain of information science: Problems in conceptualization and in consensus building. *Information Services & Use* **6**, 169–205.

Schrettinger, M. (1808–1829). *Versuch eines Vollständiges Lehrbuchs der Bibliothek-Wissenschaft I–III*. München.

Simon, H. (1982). The Sciences of the Artificial. (2d ed.) The MIT Press, Cambridge, MA.

Small, H. (1981). The relationship of information science to the social sciences: A cocitation analysis. *Information Processing and Management* **17**, 39–50.

Stieg, M. (1990). Information science and humanities. In *Information Science: The Interdisciplinary Context* (M. Pemberton and A. Prentice, eds.), pp. 60–69. Neal-Schuman, New York and London.

Suppe, F. (1985). Toward an adequate information science. In *Toward Foundations of Information Science* (L. Heilprin, ed.), pp. 7–27. Knowledge Industry Publications, White Plains, New York.

Tuomela, R. (1973). *Theoretical Concepts*. Springer, Wien.

Vakkari, P. (1986). Roots of library science in historia literaria. *Wolfenbütteler Notizen zur Buchgeschichte* **11**, 72–81.

Vakkari, P. (1989). The role of research in library and information education. *International Journal of Information and Library Research* **1**, 185–196.

Vakkari, P. (1991). Reading, knowledge of books, and libraries as a basis for the conception of scholarship in eighteenth-century Germany. *Libraries and Culture* **26**, 66–86.

Vakkari, P. (1992). Opening the horizon of expectations. In *Conceptions of Library and Information Science* (P. Vakkari and B. Cronin, eds.), pp. 1–4. Graham Taylor, London and Los Angeles.

Wagner, D. (1984). *The Growth of Sociological Theories*. Sage, Beverly Hills.

Wagner, D., and Berger, J. (1985). Do sociological theories grow? *American Journal of Sociology* **90**, 697–728.

Warner, A. (1991). Quantitative and qualitative assessments of the impact of linguistic theory on information science. *Journal of the American Society for Information Science* **42**, 64–71.

Warner, J. (1990). Semiotics, information science, documents and computers. *Journal of Documentation* **46**, 16–32.

Wersig, G. (1991). Informationswissenschaft in der Bundesrepublik Deutschland—Gegenwärtige Stand und Perspektiven. *Informatik* **37**, 126–129.

Wersig, G. (1992). Information science and theory: A weaver bird's perspective. In *Conceptions of Library and Information Science* (P. Vakkari and B. Cronin, eds.), pp. 201–217. Graham Taylor, London & Los Angeles.

Whitley, R. (1974). Cognitive and social institutionalization of scientific specialties and research areas. In *Social Processes of Scientific Development* (R. Whitley, ed.), pp. 69–95. London.

Wilson, P. (1983). Bibliographical R&D. In *The Study of Information* (F. Machlup and U. Mansfield, eds.), pp. 389–398. Wiley, New York.

Wilson, T. (1984). The cognitive approach to information behavior and use. *Social Science Information Studies* **4,** 197–204.

Wright, H. (1987). Shera as a bridge between librarianship and information science. *Journal of Library History* **22,** 137–156.

Students and the Information Search Process: Zones of Intervention for Librarians

Carol Collier Kuhlthau
School of Communication, Information and Library Studies
Rutgers University
New Brunswick, New Jersey 08903

I. Introduction

Librarians have a long and distinguished tradition of services assisting students to find information for research assignments in a variety of courses and in various disciplines. In one sense, these services are interventions for improving access and learning. *Interventions*, as I use the term, refer specifically to those situations in which librarians directly interact with students who are in the process of information seeking or expect to be in the near future.

There are two basic library services in which the professional librarian is involved in such intervention: reference and bibliographic instruction. Reference is mediation with the student to help in the location and use of sources and information. We might think of mediation as occurring on different levels, from a simple response to a specific question to getting involved in a student's extended search process. Bibliographic instruction is education for learning tools, sources, and concepts of information and strategies for locating and using tools and sources. Bibliographic instruction, also, may be described as occurring on different levels, from general introductory sessions to instruction on identifying and interpreting information to consultation on an evolving problem.

All services of the library are directly related to students' information seeking behavior. Recent studies of the information search process of secondary students and undergraduates reveal a complex, constructive process of learning from a variety of sources (Kuhlthau, 1989). These studies indicate important directions for services in reference and bibliographic instruction.

II. Information Seeking as a Constructive Process

In order to appreciate the dynamic nature of the information search process it is helpful to look to the literature describing constructive processes (Bruner, 1986; Dewey, 1933; Kelly, 1963). Two basic themes run through the theory of construction. One is that we construct our unique personal worlds, and the other is that construction involves the total person incorporating thinking, feeling, and acting in a dynamic process of learning. The constructive process is not a comfortable, smooth transition but rather an odyssey of unsettling and sometimes threatening experiences.

George Kelly's personal construct theory (1963) is particularly useful for identifying common patterns in construction. Kelly describes a constructive process as evolving through a series of phases that involve the emotions as well as the intellect. At the first encounter with a new experience or idea, the typical person is confused and anxious. This state of uncertainty increases until the person reaches a threshold of choice where the quest to find meaning is either abandoned or a hypothesis is formed that moves the process along to confirm or reject the new construct (Bannister, 1977).

This view of construction provided a frame of reference for a series of studies on the information search process (Kuhlthau, 1991). The hypothesis for these studies was that an information search is a process of construction that involves the whole person.

A series of five studies was conducted of students' perspective of information seeking in libraries. The first study addressed the general problem of learning more about the student's experience in the search process. The underlying question was whether students' experiences in the information search process resembles the phases in the process of construction depicted by Kelly. A qualitative study of a group of high school seniors in an extensive information seeking task over an extended period of time provided the opportunity to analyze and investigate the full range of the constructive process rather than single incidents of information seeking (Kuhlthau, 1988a).

III. Model of the Information Search Process

The findings were reported in a model of the information search process depicting common patterns of tasks, feelings, thoughts, and actions in six stages: initiation, selection, exploration, formulation, collection, and presentation.

A. Stage 1: Initiation

The search process begins with the announcement of the research assignment, which frequently causes students to express feelings of uncertainty and apprehension. Their thoughts center on contemplating the assignment and comprehending their task. They recall prior experiences with similar assignments and begin to explore the boundaries of possible topics to select. They may talk to each other about the assignment and browse the library collection.

B. Stage 2: Selection

In the second stage of the search process students select topics to research. They frequently feel uncertain until they have made their choices and then express a brief elation after their selection. Their thoughts involve weighing possible topics against the criteria of personal interest, the assignment requirement, the information available, and the time allotted for the project. They predict possible outcomes of their choices and select the topic that they consider to have the most potential for success. Their actions include continuing to talk to other people, in particular their teacher, classmates, and family; making a preliminary search of the library; and using reference sources to gain an overview of topics under consideration.

C. Stage 3: Exploration

The third stage, when students explore information to learn about their topics, is often the most difficult. As they seek information, they are likely to become increasingly confused by the inconsistency and incompatibility they encounter among different sources and with their own preconceived notions. Feelings of doubt concerning their topics are prevalent, as well as doubt in their ability to do the assignment well and in the library to have the information they need. In exploratory thinking, efforts and attention need to concentrate on learning about the general topic and on seeking an appropriate focus. The students' actions involve locating information and evaluating relevance, reading to become informed, and reflecting on new information. Taking notes should consist of listing interesting facts and ideas rather than copying long passages from texts. Tolerating uncertainty while intentionally seeking a focus is helpful for students during the exploration stage.

D. Stage 4: Formulation

The fourth stage, when students form a focus from information on the general topic, is the critical point in the search process. The focus is a personal perspective, an angle or hypothesis, that is developed from reading and reflecting on information gathered about a general topic. As a focus is formed, feelings shift from confusion and doubt to optimism and confidence. When students do not form a focus during the search process they often experience difficulty throughout the remainder of the assignment that may result in writing blocks.

E. Stage 5: Collection

In the fifth stage, students collect information on their focused view of the topic rather than on all aspects of the topic in general. Although they realize the considerable amount of work ahead at this point they have more confidence, a sense of direction, and frequently experience an increased interest in their projects. The focus serves as a controlling idea for gathering information and directing the search. Students find it helpful to seek information to define and extend their focused topics, taking detailed notes only on that which pertains to their chosen focus and not on the topic in general. In this stage, a comprehensive search of the library collection and use of a wide range of sources is helpful.

F. Stage 6: Preparation

The sixth stage of the search process prepares students to write. As closure approaches, they draw the search to an end, frequently noting diminishing relevance and increasing redundancy in the sources of information they encounter. They express feelings of relief, as well as satisfaction and occasionally disappointment, depending on the success of their search. Strategies that students find helpful are to return to the library for a final search before beginning to write and to outline in order to organize their ideas for writing.

This model of the information search process became the hypothesis for further studies to verify and refine the concept of construction proposed. Two longitudinal studies and two studies of larger, more diverse populations of library users were conducted. The findings of these studies provided verification of the model, which may be summarized in this way (Kuhlthau, Turock, George & Belvin, 1990). The information search process is a complex process of construction in which students progress from uncertainty to understanding. Uncertainty, confusion, and frustration are associated with vague, unclear thoughts about a topic or problem. As thoughts become more clearly focused, students report increased confidence and feeling more sure, satisfied, and relieved.

IV. Common Patterns in the Process of Information Seeking

In the studies four important patterns were noted in the students' information search process. First, there were distinct changes in thoughts and confidence during the information search process. Students' comments at two points in the search illustrate this change. Before the formulation stage one student said, "I was worried that I couldn't do a good job because I didn't know what I was doing." After the formulation stage the same student stated that, "I felt pretty happy about it. I was beginning to find recurrent themes." Another student described a similar experience. Before formulation the student commented, "I was confused, lost, because I like to know that things are in order." After formulation the student said, "I was a lot more relieved because I had a goal. Once you know what you are looking for, it's so much easier to go about what you are doing." Students commonly feel more confident after formulation when they have a sense of direction and a clearer understanding of their task. After the formulation stage they are usually able to conduct their research more independently than in earlier stages of the search process.

Second, rather than a gradual increase in confidence from the beginning of the search to the end there was a noticeable dip in confidence during the third stage of the information search process, exploration. The exploration stage was found to be the most difficult for students. At this point they were most likely to change their topics, expressed more confusion and frustration, and were less engaged in their project than in later stages of the search process.

Third, the task of formulating a focus was often misunderstood. The formulation involved in the search process required more than narrowing a topic. Rather students were required to formulate their personal perspective of the problem or topic. Students who had not formulated a focused perspective during the search process described great difficulty writing the research paper. One student commented that,

> I had a general idea not a specific focus, but an idea. As I was writing, I didn't know what my focus was. When I was finished, I didn't know what my focus was. My teacher says she doesn't know what my focus was. I don't think I ever acquired a focus. It was an impossible paper to write. I would just sit there and say, "I'm stuck." There was no outline because there was no focus and there was nothing to complete. If I learned anything from that paper it is, you have to have a focus. You have to have something to center on. You can't just have a topic. You should have an idea when you start. I had a topic but I didn't know what I wanted to do with it. I figured that when I did my research it would focus in. But I didn't let it. I kept saying, "this is interesting and this is interesting and I'll just smush it altogether." It didn't work out.

Fourth, interest in the topic commonly increased after formulation. At the beginning of the assignment, students' main motivation was external. The teacher's requirements provided the primary impetus for approaching the task. After formulation when students had constructed their own understandings of the topic under investigation and had formed their own perspective of certain aspects of the problem, they became more interested and intellectually engaged. By the end of the project many students were motivated by internal, personal interest.

V. Misunderstanding of Search Tasks

Although the studies reveal the information search process to be a dynamic constructive process, students rarely understood that the library might play an important role in each of the stages of the process. When questioned about their search task at each of the stages, students' perception of task differed considerably from those described in the model in the stages of the information search process. The appropriate task for each stage according to the model is listed here.

1. Initiation: to recognize information need
2. Selection: to identify general topic
3. Exploration: to investigate information on general topic
4. Formulation: to formulate focused perspective
5. Collection: to gather information pertaining to focus
6. Presentation: to complete information search

In each stage of the search process, students responded that their task was to gather information and to complete information search, thus indicating that they did not identify the more exploratory and formulative tasks as being a legitimate part of the search process. There was evidence of a lack of tolerance for the early exploratory stages leading to formulation and few strategies for accomplishing the tasks of those early stages. Negative terms were used to describe their action in the early stages, such as *procrastination*, *lazy*, and *disinterested*. Rarely did students acknowledge the need for time to read and reflect in order to formulate a focus to move the search ahead.

VI. Principle of Uncertainty for Library Services

These studies indicated an important dichotomy in library services. On the one hand, librarianship is based on a principle of certainty and order, what I have called the bibliographic paradigm (Kuhlthau, 1993). In it sophisticated systems for collecting, classifying, organizing, and retrieving texts or information have been developed that may be matched to specific queries in an efficient and orderly manner.

On the other hand, many of the important information needs of students that arise within the context of academic life cannot be expressed in a single, precisely formulated question. On the contrary, uncertainty and confusion characterize most information problems, particularly in the early stages. Therefore, a conflict arises when library services developed under the bibliographic paradigm are used to match the uncertainty and disorder of the varied information needs of students in a dynamic learning environment.

The studies of the student's perspective of the process of information seeking dictate the necessity of recognizing a principle of uncertainty for library services (Kuhlthau, 1993b). An uncertainty principle would acknowledge feelings of anxiety and lack of confidence and recognize the uncertainty, confusion, and frustration associated with vague, unclear thoughts about a problem or topic. An uncertainty principle would acknowledge the complex constructive process of moving from uncertainty to understanding.

VII. Concept of Diagnosing Zones of Intervention

Within this context of uncertainty in the information search process and the need for more exploratory strategies particularly in the early stages, the concept of a zone of intervention was developed. The zone of intervention is modeled on Vygotsky's (1978) notion of a zone of proximal development in teaching and learning. Vygotsky, whose work has had profound influence on learning theory, developed the concept of identifying an area or zone in which intervention would be most useful to a learner. This concept provides a way for understanding intervention into the constructive process of another person. Identifying when intervention is needed and determining what intervention is helpful calls for diagnostic skills. Intervention when an individual is self-sufficient is unnecessary, as well as intrusive and annoying. Intervention when individuals cannot proceed on their own or can proceed only with great difficulty is enabling and enriching. When a person can do with assistance what he or she cannot do alone is the zone of intervention.

Intervention based on a principle of certainty and order, that is, intervention in the bibliographic paradigm, concentrates on matching a person's query with the library collection. Intervention based on an uncertainty principle encompasses the holistic experience of using information from the perspective of the individual student. Such intervention addresses a full range of information needs within the dynamic stage of the information search process including initiating, selecting, exploring, formulating, as well as gathering and collecting.

This is not to suggest that librarians be involved in every stage of the information search process of every student. On the contrary, the concept of a zone of intervention presumes that there is a way to determine when it is important to intervene and when intervention is unnecessary. The critical question is what is the zone of intervention that is helpful to an individual in his or her information seeking process. The concept of a zone of intervention calls for diagnosing research problems and developing appropriate interventions.

VIII. Five Zones of Intervention

Students' arrive at the library with different states of knowledge and at different points in the information search process. These states of knowledge and stages of process require a range of intervention. In my view, interventions with students may be thought of as occurring in five zones, as shown in Table I.

In zone 1 (Z1) the problem is self-diagnosed and a search is self-conducted. In zone 2 (Z2) through zone 5 (Z5) the problem is diagnosed through an interview to elicit a problem statement and background information. A problem statement or a request for information or a particular resource by the student usually initiates the interview. The librarian should seek background information on the problem in at least four areas: task, interest, time, and availability.

Examples of questions to gain background in these categories might be: What is the nature of the overall task that initiated the information search? What is the task of the particular stage of the search process the student is experiencing? What aspects of the overall task are of particular interest to the individual student? What are the time constraints of the task and the information search process? What information is readily accessible and what is the extent and depth of the information available? These interrelated considerations create a complex set of contexts and choices for each individual student to address.

Using the expanded theoretical framework that incorporates the uncertainty principle with traditional frameworks of organization and order, the librarian determines the zone of intervention that is indicated. The student's situation is identified as a product problem or a process problem. A product problem may be addressed with a source of information, often within the library collection. A process problem, however, is more complex and needs to be addressed in a holistic, ongoing way. A process problem places the student in one of the stages in the constructive process of seeking meaning.

When a problem is identified as a product problem Z2 through Z4 intervention is indicated. Z2 intervention requires the right source. Z3 intervention requires some relevant sources and Z4 requires a sequence of relevant sources. However, when a problem is identified as a process problem Z5 intervention is indicated. Z5 requires dialogue between the librarian and student leading to exploration, formulation, construction, learning, and application.

IX. Levels of Mediation

The concept of zones of intervention determined by the nature of the student's problem and the stage of the student's process leads to the identification of levels of mediation and education as shown in Table I. Reference service may be differentiated in five levels of mediation. The first level is the organizer. The organizer is essential for providing access to a collection of resources but requires no direct intervention. The organizer provides the organized collection for a self-service search that corresponds to Z1 intervention.

The second level of mediation is the locator responding to Z2 intervention. The locator offers ready reference intervention. A single fact or single source search is conducted in response to a specific query requiring a specific answer or source.

The third level of mediation is the identifier, which responds to Z3 intervention. The identifier provides standard reference intervention. A topic or question is presented by the student in a brief interview. A subject search is conducted resulting in the identification of a group of relevant sources recommended in no particular order.

The fourth level of mediation is the advisor, which responds to Z4 intervention. The advisor provides pattern intervention. A problem is presented by the student and negotiation of an approach results in the identifica-

Table I Intervention Diagnostic Chart

Zones of intervention	Levels of mediation	Levels of education	Intervention
Z1	Organizer	Organizer	Self service
Z2	Locator	Lecturer	Single source
Z3	Identifier	Instructor	Group of sources
Z4	Advisor	Tutor	Sequence of sources
Z5	Counselor	Counselor	Process intervention

tion of a group of sources recommended in a particular order for use. A subject search is conducted identifying a sequence of relevant sources.

The fifth level of mediation is the counselor responding to Z5 intervention. Z5 is the only level that goes beyond a source orientation to address the constructive process of learning from a variety of sources. The counselor provides process intervention. A problem is identified through a dialogue that leads to a strategy, sources, sequence, and continuing redefinition in the information search process. The holistic learning experience of the user is an integral part of the mediation.

X. Levels of Education

In a similar way, bibliographic instruction may be described on five levels of education that parallel those of mediation and also correspond to the five zones of intervention. On the first level, the organizer provides the organized collection for self-service use but offers no instruction at Z1 intervention.

On the second level responding to Z2 intervention, the lecturer provides orienting instruction. Orientation is offered consisting of a single-session overview of services, policies, facility, and collection. Orientation is general and not addressed to a specific problem, question, or assignment.

The third level of education is the instructor that responds to Z3 intervention by providing single-source, course-related instruction. A variety of independent sessions are offered to instruct on one type of source to address a specific problem related to a course assignment at point of need. Instructional sessions are separate, not interrelated or connected.

The fourth level of education is the tutor, which responds to Z4 intervention by providing strategy, course-integrated instruction. A series of sessions are offered to instruct on the use of a group of sources and to recommend a sequence for using the sources to address a specific problem integrated with a course assignment.

The fifth level of education is the counselor responding to Z5 intervention by providing process instruction. Instruction at this level incorporates holistic interaction over time through guidance in identifying and interpreting information to address an evolving problem. The counselor merges the role of educator and mediator in ongoing process intervention.

XI. Counselors' Role in Information
Search Process

Libraries have developed extensive services to respond to intervention into Z2 through Z4. Product or source intervention of the locator/lecturer, the identifier/instructor, and the advisor/tutor are well established and quite effective in many cases, although perhaps not articulated in this way. While there is always room for improvement and innovation, librarians can take pride in the accomplishments of interventions into these zones.

Process intervention in Z5, however, is in desperate need of development. Although the notion of an information counselor is not new, the identification of the counselor as the provider of intervention in the constructive process of information seeking is an innovative way of viewing library services (Dosa, 1978; Debons, 1975).

Longitudinal studies of undergraduates indicate a critical need for process intervention (Kuhlthau, 1988b,c). One of the college graduates who had been exposed to the process approach to information skills in high school noted that he was better prepared for college research assignments than other students. He describes a need for Z5 intervention in this way.

> I had more exposure to research papers than most high school students. By working with you I learned not to panic if it doesn't all fall in together the first day you walk into the library. I had a lot of friends in college who were panicked at doing a research paper. I'll welcome a research paper any day regardless of the subject. To tell you the truth I haven't come across any of my peers who think like that, not a one. When my roommate's research paper was due last semester, I helped him with it. He doesn't even know what he is afraid of. Maybe of not finding the one article that is going to make his paper? I'll worry about a paper because things don't fall into place but it's not the kind of thing I lose sleep over. I've learned to accept that this is the way it works. Tomorrow I'll read this over and some parts will fall into place and some still won't. If not I'll talk to the professor. The mind doesn't take everything and put it into order automatically and that's it. Understanding that is the biggest help.

The counselor's role in Z5 intervention is firmly grounded in an uncertainty principle. An important aspect of the counselor's role is to create an engaging learning environment. Innovative ways of guiding and coaching students through the early stages of exploration and formulation need to be developed. Mediation and education can be built around strategies of collaborating, continuing, charting, conversing, and composing.

XII. Process Intervention Strategies

A. Collaborating

The information search process need not be thought of as an isolated, competitive undertaking but may be considered a cooperative venture with the librarian as a collaborator. When the librarian takes on a collaborative role as an interested participant in the project, process intervention is the natural result.

Peers may also serve as collaborators. A team approach to library research more closely matches tasks outside the academic environment. Collaborative techniques such as brainstorming, delegating, networking, and integrating are productive activities for information seeking and develop abilities valued in the workplace. Interventions that promote collaboration in the process of information seeking build skills and understandings that transfer to other situations of information need.

B. Continuing

Continuing intervention addresses evolving information problems rather than queries that can be answered in a single incident with one source. The process of information seeking involves construction in which the student actively pursues understanding and meaning from the information encountered over a period of time. The process is commonly experienced in a series of thoughts and feelings that shift from vague to anxious to clear and confident as the search progresses. Continuing intervention responds to students' complex, dynamic learning process in Z5.

Process intervention that continues throughout the full duration of the information search process not only guides students in one specific research assignment but also establishes transferable process skills. Students are led to view information seeking as a constructive process and to know that exploration and formulation are essential tasks for bringing order to uncertainty through personal understanding. Continuing intervention also addresses the concept of enough. An important understanding for addressing continuing, complex problems is a notion of what is enough information for closure and presentation. What is enough was a relatively simple notion when a person could gather all there was to know on a topic. The concept of enough is quite a different matter in the present-day information environment. Understanding what is enough is essential for making sense of information around us. Enough relates to seeking meaning in a quantity of information by determining what one needs to know and by formulating a perspective on which to build. The information search process treats the concept of enough as what is enough to make sense for oneself.

The concept of enough may be applied to the tasks in each of the stages of the information search process. Continuing intervention enables students to decide what is enough to recognize an information need, to explore a general topic, to formulate a specific focus, to gather information pertaining to the specific focus, to prepare to share what has been learned, or to solve a problem.

Continuing intervention supports students throughout the information search process and guides them in using information for learning in each stage of the process.

C. Conversing

Conversation gives the counselor an opportunity to listen to the student and to recommend appropriate strategies for working through the particular stage in the process that the student is experiencing. Diagnosis of the student's stage is important since formulation of a focused perspective is the turning point in the search. The counselor recommends different strategies before and after the formulation of a focus. Prior to formulation, a more invitational approach to searching is recommended; there might be exploratory reading and reflecting in order to better understand the problem. Following formulation, a more focused approach of documenting and organizing in order to solve the problem is recommended.

In the early stages, counselors guide students away from overly indicative conversations that narrow the inquiry without exploring the broader prospects. After a focused perspective has been formed, counselors guard against overly invitational conversations that promote gathering general information rather than limiting the search to concentrate information pertinent to the focused perspective. Counseling in the stages of the search process guide students through the entire sequence of starting, exploring, focusing, gathering, and closing.

Caution should be used in discussing the stages of the search process not to belabor the issue beyond the point of being helpful to the student. Merely acknowledging the presence of confusion and uncertainty at the beginning and recommending strategies for proceeding is usually sufficient to get a person started. It is important, however, to suggest that some ongoing assistance may be helpful and to offer an invitation to schedule sessions or meeting for counseling throughout the process.

Conversations encourage students to discuss ideas in the information encountered as the information search progresses aiding them to form their own perspective of a topic. Counselors may encourage dialogue by drawing from the student's dynamic process through invitational, exploratory questioning. The following questions are examples of those that may initiate and sustain conversations with students. What ideas seem particularly important to you? What questions do you have? What problems are emerging? What is the focus of your thinking? What are the guiding ideas for your search? Where are the gaps in your thinking? What does not fit with what you already know? What inconsistencies do you notice in the information you have encountered?

Counselors can discuss the sequence of stages in the process with students and come to some agreement on the stage the student is in. Conversation provides an opportunity for the counselor to acknowledge feelings commonly associated with the particular stage that the student is experiencing. For example, if a selection or exploration stage is identified the counselor may say, "You are probably feeling somewhat uncertain and a bit anxious at this point. Most people do." When a collection stage is identified, the counselor's comments would be directed toward the student's personal perspective and particular area of interest. Charting and composing interventions are an excellent basis for conversing with students.

D. Charting

Charting intervention is effective for visually presenting a large amount of information in a compact way. It is particularly helpful for guiding students in formulating ideas and for presenting the complete information search process to them.

One particular charting intervention has been consistently effective for making students aware of the stages in the information search process and for helping them to understand what to expect in each stage. A chart of the model of the information search process is used to illustrate the tasks, feelings, thoughts, and actions that are commonly experienced in each of the six stages (Kuhlthau, 1994).

For most students a critical zone of intervention is the stage of exploration, after a general area or topic has been selected but before a personal perspective has been formed. By using a chart of the six stages of the information search process, the counselor may identify the student's stage in the process, acknowledge the student's feelings, explain the task before him or her, and recommend appropriate strategies. Strategies recommended in the exploration stage may be quite different from those recommended in the collection stage. For example, students in the exploration stage may be advised to read for general themes and to list ideas, whereas students in the collection stage may be advised to read for details and take copious notes.

Conceptual mapping techniques may be applied to charting intervention for presenting and visualizing emerging ideas. Conceptual maps organize ideas and show connections between disparate concepts, similar to outlining but with more visual elements. A simple conceptual map might begin with a circle or box containing the general topic or main idea. Surrounding circles or boxes may be added to show related concepts, with lines and arrows connecting the elements in a meaningful display. The visual, nonlinear aspect of conceptual mapping fosters the creative process of connecting ideas and organizing information as a search progresses.

Charting intervention is a creative way to demonstrate common patterns in the information search process, to foster formulation, and to organize ideas for presentation.

E. Composing

Composing promotes thinking and formulation in the search process. Journal writing has been found to be an excellent way to encourage composing, to advance formulation, and to track an individual's constructive process. Counselors may recommend that students keep research journals in which they record ideas, questions, and connections as they progress through their search. Writing in a research journal is much more comprehensive than jotting notes on notecards or in a notebook. A journal may be started when the project is first initiated and be kept until the presentation is made. However, the purpose of the journal changes as the search progresses. Students are instructed to set aside some time each day or every few days to write about their problem or topic. Instructions might be stated in the following manner:

> In early stages when you are deciding on what topic to choose, write to clarify or define possible choices. Write about conversations you have about your topic. As you proceed in the process write your reactions to your readings as well as your thoughts and questions about your topic. Be sure to record all incidents where you made an important decision or discovery. Include the development of a central theme, a point of view or focus in your thinking. Record any deadend of a path or change in the problem or topic which prompted a new approach.

The main objective of composing during the search process is to serve as a tool for formulating thoughts and developing constructs. Counselors may also recommend free writing as a means of assisting formulation. Students may be encouraged to write about the focus of their topics or problem at several different points in the search process. These pieces of writing promote private reflection, which can help students to make connections and inferences in the information they encountered and to see gaps that need further investigation. When these writings are shared with the counselor they can form a basis for deep understanding of the student's evolving information problem.

Composing is commonly the outcome or product of the information search process. Students are assigned a research or term paper to be written. Composing interventions, however, apply writing throughout the information search process as a means for fostering formulation of ideas on an evolving problem from the information encountered in an extensive search process.

XIII. Conclusion

Consideration of how library services change in the information age lead to the identification of vital new roles for librarians in the process of information seeking. There has been much talk of the wonders of the information society with technologies for increasing and rapid access to information but librarians need to address the real concerns of an individual seeking meaning in this information-rich environment. Students need a clear understanding of the constructive process of information seeking and should develop strategies for learning from a variety of sources.

Librarians in the information age are called to diagnose zones of intervention when students benefit from counseling in the information search process. They need to develop process interventions to guide students in seeking meaning from information for deep understanding.

Acknowledgment

Portions of this paper were presented in the Beta Phi Mu 1992 Annual Distinguished Lecture at the University of Michigan, School of Information and Library Studies.

References

Bannister, D., ed. (1977). *New Perspectives in Personal Construct Theory*. Academic Press, London.

Bruner, J. (1986). *Actual Minds, Possible Worlds*. Harvard University Press, Cambridge, Massachusetts.

Debons, A. (1975). An educational program for the information counselor. In *Proceedings of the 38th ASIS Annual Meeting*, pp. 63–64. Knowledge Industry Publications, White Plains, New York.

Dewey, J. (1933). *How We Think*. Heath and Company, Lexington, Massachusetts.

Dosa, M. (1978). Information counseling and policies. *Reference Librarian* **17**, 7–21.

Kelly, G. (1963). *A Theory of Personality: The Psychology of Personal Constructs*. W. W. Norton and Company, New York.

Kuhlthau, C. (1988a). Developing a model of the library search process: Investigation of cognitive and affective aspects. *Reference Quarterly* **28**, 232–242.

Kuhlthau, C. (1988b). Perceptions of the information search process in libraries: A study of changes from high school through college. *Information Processing and Management* **24**, 419–427.

Kuhlthau, C. (1988c). Longitudinal case studies of the information search process of users in libraries. *Library and Information Science Research* **10**, 251–304.

Kuhlthau, C. (1989). Information search process: A summary of research and implications for school library media programs. *School Library Media Quarterly* **18**, 19–25.

Kuhlthau, C. (1991). Inside the search process: Information seeking from the user's perspective. *Journal of the American Society for Information Science* **42**, 361–371.

Kuhlthau, C. (1993a). *Seeking Meaning: A Process Approach to Library and Information Services*. Ablex, Norwood, New Jersey.

Kuhlthau, C. (1993b). A principle of uncertainty for library and information science. *Journal of Documentation* **49**, 339–355.

Kuhlthau, C. (1994). *Teaching the Library Research Process* (2d ed.). Scarecrow Press, Metuchen, New Jersey.

Kuhlthau, C., Turock, B., George, M., and Belvin, R. (1990). Validating a model of the search process: A comparison of academic, public and school library users. *Library and Information Science Research* **12**, 5–32.

Vygotsky, L. (1978). *Mind in Society: The Development of Higher Psychological Processes*. Harvard University Press, Cambridge, Massachusetts.

Reshaping Academic Library Reference Service: A Review of Issues, Trends, and Possibilities

Chris Ferguson
Thomas and Dorothy Leavey Library
University of Southern California
Los Angeles, California 90089-0182

I. Introduction

Local, state, and federal governments restructure haltingly, higher education lumbers toward major upheaval, and academic libraries evolve toward a new paradigm that has yet to be defined clearly. Under these circumstances, it should be no surprise that the impact of relentless technological change, fiscal paroxysm, and organizational instability have wreaked havoc in the reference services community. In the last decade cognitive overload and low morale have become common place, stress and burnout have emerged as a major professional issue, a serious question of reference service quality has surfaced, and a disparate series of organizational and operational changes have been or are being effected in the name of reform.

Yet reference providers are in fact getting the job done in ways and to extents unimaginable only a few years ago.

> The smoothness with which today's library staff have assimilated nationally networked cataloging, online searching, online local catalogs, microcomputers, local networking, compact discs, and the wide variety of other systems based on digitized information, while at the same time quietly schooling their patrons in the use of these systems, is a largely unrecognized miracle in American higher education over the past decade and a half. (Govan, 1991, p. 33)

Even so, many difficult service and resource allocation choices must be made, and a confusion of purpose and direction among reference providers inhibits adoption of theoretical frameworks that could inform responses to the many pressures on contemporary reference service.

In the following pages some of the manifestations of the present turmoil in academic library reference service will be explored, examining where and

ADVANCES IN LIBRARIANSHIP, VOL. 18
Copyright © 1994 by Academic Press, Inc.
All rights of reproduction in any form reserved.

how command of the reference desk has been lost and what may be required to regain control. After surveying the leading external influences on contemporary reference, some of the many efforts to reshape reference service will be examined. Unless reference providers become more aware of service alternatives that accommodate both recent and anticipated changes among academic user groups and the scholarly communication system, reference service is doomed to respond with too little, too late; the literature of academic library public service will remain particularist and idiosyncratic.

II. Anatomy of a Crisis

A. Overviews

Turmoil at the reference desk is not a new phenomenon in the annals of librarianship, nor has the vocabulary of crisis in this arena changed appreciably in two decades. The notion of crisis as a framing concept is common (Hernon and McClure, 1987b; Miller, 1984; Rettig, 1984; Vavrek, 1974), though authors often employ the term differently. Variations on this theme include malaise as a dimension of crisis (Miller, 1984), loss of control (Goodyear, 1985), obsolescence (Miller and Rettig, 1985), and conceptual disarray (Campbell, 1992).

One of the more evocative general assessments of the current state of reference service is advanced by a university librarian who has not worked extensively as a reference provider. Campbell (1992) is unable to ascertain just what reference providers do, how much they do it, how much they should do it, or how well they do it. Reference service, he concludes, is "virtually in conceptual disarray" (p. 29). This state of disarray is further evidenced by continuing controversies over bibliographic instruction, the place of the reference desk in the reference-information construct, levels of service vis-à-vis categories of users, the professional status of reference providers, and the overall philosophy of delivery versus facilitation.

Following an admittedly crude analysis of types of reference questions and advancement of the goal of developing computer-based resources to answer 75% of them, Campbell (1992) offers a model of reference service where access engineers engage in knowledge cartography (mapping information sources), consumer analysis, and access engineering (transferring information upon demand from its source directly to the user). From this operational model Campbell derives a new economic model for reference service, whereby substantial and increasing investment is made in access engineering as the need to support technical services decreases.

Responses to Campbell's observations and proposals were swift and strong. Postings on the listserv LIBREF in October and November 1992, for example, faulted Campbell's lack of experience as a reference provider, rejected his terminology as pretentious and the concepts behind them as essentially what reference providers already do routinely, and suggested that his focus on technology overlooks the patron. Very little of a positive nature was posted during the protracted discussion, and several key parts of Campbell's arguments were not discussed.

The uneven and largely self-serving content of the LIBREF responses as a whole may be a function of the medium or they may be indicative of a problem in reference service today, as are recurring discussions on the same listserv regarding what we call reference providers (librarians, information specialists, access engineers, etc.). In the absence of a strong and shared conceptual framework, many choose to discuss narrow topics that seem more proximate and manageable. In any case, several elements of Campbell's effort have been controversial and may be somewhat off the mark, but his underlying message ought to be above controversy: More needs to be known about what reference providers do and how they do it, and more thought must be given to what they should be doing and why they should be doing it. This message is repeated and expanded in a later address (Campbell, 1993) that includes a mission statement for access engineers and fuller analyses of reference desk transactions and consumer needs.

Although Campbell and his critics articulate and in some sense are indicative of a crisis, the sense that reference service is entering or has entered a critical phase has been present for at least two decades. Vavrek (1974, 1978) seems first to have inquired whether there is a crisis in reference, though his angst derives from two trends we now accept as status quo—increasing use of paraprofessionals at the reference desk and reduced funding for reference. The belief that something is very wrong in the reference arena truly exploded onto the scene with a trio of articles published in 1984.

Miller's "What's wrong with reference" (1984) is the manifesto of the literature of crisis, touching the nerves of a generation of reference providers who previously had only a vague sense that something was amiss.

A malaise is abroad in reference departments everywhere. The annual reports make no mention of it, boasting instead of increasing numbers of searches performed, increasing numbers of reference books purchased, and increasing involvement of staff in committee work. The reports, however, do not mention the darker side of reference life. They do not mention that outdated works clog the reference shelves, and that new ones sit unknown and unused. They do not mention that many reference librarians are unfamiliar or uncomfortable with the new technological resources, many of which are going untapped. The reports do not mention that reference librarians are becoming so frazzled by the press of their various commitments that they are increasingly short-tempered with each other and impatient with those they serve. Nor do the reports mention that many reference librarians promise more service during instructional sessions than they have time to deliver in actual practice, and that many reference librarians do not often enough take the time that would be necessary to deal thoroughly with people's requests for information. . . . Essentially, we have succeeded in pushing ourselves beyond our levels of comfort and competence . . . we have reached beyond our grasp. (Miller, 1984, p. 303)

Miller (1984) describes vividly the tensions and frustrations of contemporary reference service, articulating "the consequences of our reference sprawl" (p. 303) and describing how the best and the brightest have been encouraged to overextend themselves into burnout. His proposed responses—creative reorganization of existing staff and planning—have proven to be less timeless.

Less noticed at the time but in the longer run nearly as significant as framers of the discussion are contributions by Bunge (1984) and Rettig (1984). Bunge, a library school professor who worked a variety of reference desks during a sabbatical leave, experienced first hand a "widespread unhappiness among reference librarians" (p. 128), owing to the conduct of public service "in a bureaucratic setting of limited resources" that induces a "psychological dissonance" (p. 129) between ideals and reality. More specifically, the explosion of sophisticated reference sources (both printed and electronic) and a wider range of users with more complex needs create tension, frustration, and feelings of inadequacy and loss of control. Rettig, taking the editorial route as associate editor of *Reference Services Review*, perceives a high attrition rate among reference librarians and attributes this phenomenon to the emotional wear and tear of constantly being "up" for emotionally draining desk service and endless rudimentary directional and instructional work. Rettig recommends in general terms that we redefine reference service, whereas Bunge promotes self-awareness, sharing feelings, developing client-centered service, and knowledge enhancements as needed responses.

Following W. Miller, Bunge, and Rettig, a cluster of articles in the mid-to-late-1980s helped to fashion an agenda of reference service issues. Chief among these are Hernon and McClure (1986, 1987b) and Miller and Rettig (1985). In the 1980s, Hernon and McClure conducted two unobtrusive tests of the accuracy of answers to government documents reference questions that culminated in the now well-known 55% rule (i.e., 55% of factual reference questions are answered correctly). This rule and the extensive body of literature that surrounds it are addressed later, but their 1986 article in *Library Journal* and 1987 symposium in *Journal of Academic Librarianship* jointly served as one of the last and perhaps most galling wake-up calls to the crisis in reference service: Not only are reference providers harried, burned out, overrun by technology, buried in printed material, and desensitized by a numbing and depersonalizing environment, but they also might be flat-out wrong nearly half the time! In the *JAL* symposium Hernon and McClure summarize their research and ask some pertinent questions (Is 55% acceptable? What do we need to increase the rate?). This is followed by five commentaries from librarians who discuss root causes, barriers to improved service, and the definition of accuracy, but none of whom mount a serious challenge to Hernon and McClure's findings.

Miller and Rettig are among the first participants in the crisis dialogue to provide a historical perspective on the issues and to propose significant structural changes to the status quo. Opening with a discussion of Green's (1876) classic article on reference service, Miller and Rettig observe that over the last century little has changed in our ideas regarding the nature and shape of reference service despite radical changes in our tools and environment. A major source of discontent among reference providers, then, is a decreasing sense of purpose due to continuation of an obsolete service model despite significant environmental change (in part resulting in what Bunge [1984] terms psychological dissonance). The solution, they argue, is a client-centered "personal shopper" approach that integrates reference, instruction, and online searching in the direct retrieval and delivery of information to users by reference providers, as distinct from the empowerment model of leaving users with what we have deemed to be appropriate tools. Rettig (1991, 1993d) later expands on his personal shopper model while assailing its antithesis, bibliographic instruction.

If the Miller and Rettig model sounds familiar, it is very much the argument of Campbell, despite the latter's desire to offload much existing reference traffic to self-service computers. If Campbell's notion of access engineering may rightly be viewed as a technological approach to a redefinition of the reference service model, one with the reference provider as leader and pathfinder, then Miller and Rettig here offer essentially the same alternative in a more humanistic form.

B. Funding and Budgeting

Few would suggest a lack of money is the root of the present crisis in reference service, but no one doubts that fiscal constraints factor heavily in the equation. Although much data are available on library expenditures in such broad categories as staff, materials, and operations, there are no composite data beyond individual institutions that afford a clear picture of the impact that declining fortunes for academic library funding has had on public services generally, much less reference services in particular. Since funding for reference services over time likely is a relatively stable proportion of library expenditure, however, upward and downward trends for libraries probably represent roughly equivalent trends within reference service units. A review of funding patterns for parent institutions is therefore a useful way of assessing in broad (albeit indirect) terms the recent fiscal toll on reference services.

Generally speaking, academic library budgets increased dramatically in the later 1960s, held more or less steady in the 1970s, and in the 1980s and 1990s have nearly returned to mid-1960s levels. A team lead by A. M. Cummings and funded by the Andrew W. Mellon Foundation (Cummings et al., 1992) found that expenditures for a selection of 17 university libraries as a percentage of university educational and general expenditures rose from 2.93% in 1966 to 3.76% in 1971; held more or less level through 1979 (3.82%); and has since declined to 3.08% in 1990 (pp. 30, 192). This pattern holds true for various categories of academic libraries and matches a recent assessment for all academic libraries from 1970 to the present (Goudy, 1993). In short, when viewed as a proportion of university expenditures, the remarkable funding expansion of the 1960s has almost entirely been lost in the last decade.

Still more discomfiting is the proportion of library expenditures within university instruction and departmental research expenditures and a comparison of staffing and operational expenditures within library budgets. In the case of library expenditures as a percentage of instruction and research expenditure, in 1990 the 17 universities studied by Cummings (1992) actually invested less in libraries (8.89%) than prior to the late 1960s expansion, which increased from 9.84% in 1966 to 11.49% in 1970. Within library budgets the myth that personnel costs have been gobbling up an increasing share of the budget clearly is not true since this portion of academic library budgets actually decreased from 62% in 1963 to 52% in 1991 while operational costs, including investment in new technologies, more than doubled. The trend of a decreasing portion of library budgets allocated to staffing costs is corroborated by Werking (1991), who further demonstrates that the phenomenon affected liberal arts colleges sooner and to a greater extent than large research libraries.

The literature abounds with anecdotal reports of massive serial subscription cuts, branch closings, staff reductions, and service cutbacks (e.g., Nicklin, 1992; Tomer, 1992) that place these disturbing but abstract statistics in a somewhat more immediate context. On the department level, the external pressures of fiscal restraint are coming to bear in several ways. The expectations of reference providers are decreasing even as those of users are increasing, and there is considerably more pressure to choose from among human, printed, and electronic resources without a clear sense in many situations of which represent the better long-term investments. The budget process is becoming more demanding, complex, and continual as pressure increases to economize and more sophisticated budgeting systems and tools are deployed (Fraley and Katz, 1987). Upward pressure to invest in new resources while maintaining the old and downward pressure to economize or even to reduce overall expenditures give added meaning to the term *middle management*—and considerably more so if one attempts to accomplish related decision making in a collegial fashion.

C. Impact of Technology

The revolutionary effects of technology in libraries are felt nowhere more than at reference service points. All library units and functions are experiencing both the positive and negative consequences of technology, but reference providers who perform as intermediaries, instructors, troubleshooters, consultants, and users for a great breadth of products and services offer a unique perspective on the technological revolution.

As of mid-1991, 97% of the Association of Research Libraries membership responding to a survey provide mediated searching services, 96% offer reference CD-ROMs, 45% support end-user online searching, and 37.5% access reference databases through their OPACs while another 48% are planning to do so soon (Tenopir and Neufang, 1992). The full range and implications of electronic resources at play in contemporary reference service, and likely to be at play in the near future, are assessed by Carande (1992), including OPACs, CD-ROMs, networks (and networks of networks), expert systems, and even virtual reality.

1. On the Reference Floor

The impact of technology on reference service has been extensive. In terms of retrieval capabilities, the new technologies provide greatly expanded subject access (especially keyword searching, which we now take for granted but in the larger scheme of things is truly revolutionary), direct user access, and "end user searching at a fixed and predictable cost" in contrast to the unpredictability of mediated searching (Miller and Gratch, 1989). A new array of retrieval tools induces reconsideration of services, how staff are trained and users instructed, and with whom strategic alliances are made (Simmons-Welburn, 1993; Tenopir, 1993). Significant changes in the reference work environment include increased business at the reference desk (or at least the perception thereof), more learning time needed for librarians, more time spent on such manual tasks as printer support and hardware troubleshooting, and both negative and positive impacts on the physical environment, depending on extent of space, networking, and decentralization of CD-ROMs (Gunning, 1992; Tenopir and Neufang, 1992).

Technology is changing the nature of reference service by broadening the provider's role as intermediary and imbuing the user with much greater latitude for independent action. There are clear winners and losers on both sides of the desk. For some, technology represents an invigorating opportunity to transcend old limitations; for others, the new technologies represent unwelcome impediments to accomplishing goals in familiar and time-tested ways.

For the latter, the impact of technology can often be described as computer anxiety or technostress. Even more potent when interacting with other forms of stress, technostress can be expressed as performance anxiety, information overload, or role conflicts that seriously undermine one's ability to work effectively (Bichteler, 1987; Kupersmith, 1992).

For CD-ROMs in particular, "problems of cost, instruction, standardization, space and security have never really been resolved, either for librarians or for end users" (Miller and Gratch, 1989, p. 387), a condition Zink (1990) attributes to insufficient planning and ad hoc deployment and funding from the outset. Giesbrecht and McCarthy (1991), drawing on surveys posted on PACS-L and Envoy 100, categorize objections to CD-ROM technology as psychological reasons, problem of multiple interfaces, increased teaching load, increased costs, increased stress, maintenance time, and hardware and software issues. The sheer rapidity and "riotous non-uniformity" (Kupersmith, 1992, p. 9) with which the technology has overtaken libraries have left many reference providers unable to adjust to new models for reference service or to incorporate a breathtaking proliferation of new systems. In short, most institutions and many individuals have experienced difficulty keeping up with the dramatic changes of recent years, and the extent to which this is true for institutions exacerbates the negative experiences for individuals. Indeed, organizational climate, including insufficient information and planning prior to deployment and insufficient investment at time of deployment, can appreciably increase staff resistance to technological change (Fine, 1986).

Given some fairly extreme reactions to technological change in the reference arena, it is surprising that "at the present time, automation doesn't appear to influence reference employee satisfaction" (Whitlatch, 1991). A study of library personnel in three major ARL libraries by Lynch and Verdin (1987) found reference personnel in 1986 significantly more satisfied than other groups in the library and slightly more satisfied than reference personnel in three university libraries in their 1971 to 1972 companion study (1983). More recently Estabrook, Bird, and Gilmore (1990) found that technology by itself did not influence the degree of job satisfaction of a group of library employees, including reference providers, in 1988.

It should be carefully noted that these studies occurred during the relatively early phases of the heavy infusion of technology into reference service and certainly do not take into account the most recent, arguably more complex wave of technology to reach the reference desk—the Internet, campuswide information systems, and readily accessible numeric (e.g., census) data. Still another consideration is the synergy of stressors, whereby the effect of a stressor can increase when combined with other sources of stress. If in fact there is widespread discontent among reference services personnel these days, and if much of the discontent expressed in print and public discussions seems focused on automation, the discontent could in fact derive from several sources that are not wholly revealed when reference personnel are asked about their attitudes toward automation.

2. On the Organization Chart

The rate of organizational change in response to extensive technological change has been slower than expected with about 80% of academic libraries in 1990 maintaining traditional divisions between public and technical services (Larsen, 1991), but there are signs major changes are under way or will occur soon in most major academic libraries. Among the changes expected are flatter organizational structures with specialists grouped across functional lines; more centralization and decentralization of operations and services, as appropriate to the technology; increased responsibility at all levels, especially clerical and support staff; and participatory decision making and goal setting (De Klerk and Euster, 1989; Johnson, 1991; Marchant and England, 1989). In recent years, a few libraries have reorganized into flatter organizations, but it is safe to say there has not been a stampede in this direction.

Hallman (1990) speaks of a cultural lag regarding change—a delay between material cultural change (technology) and accompanying changes in social structures. Following this principle, it should be expected that such large, conservative organizations as libraries would attempt many relatively cosmetic changes before undertaking major structural change. Under these circumstances, a substantial amount of real change is likely to occur at the lower levels before the parent institution addresses the need for overhaul.

This is precisely what has been happening in many reference departments in recent years. Although the broad mandate of the reference unit and its place in the library organization has not changed over the last 20 years, reference departments have been acccommodating the direct and indirect impact of technology by creating specialists and coordinators (sometimes even separate subunits) in such technology-intensive areas as database searching, instruction (Gunning, 1983), and CD-ROMs; establishing standing or ad hoc subgroups that focus on specific areas of responsibility aside from or in addition to any general assignments they might hold in common; and differentiating among information, reference, and consultation levels of service and the personnel appropriate to serve at these levels. Although at first glance these may appear to be relatively inconsequential changes, bear in mind they arise out of a reference ethos that historically has valued shared responsibilities, full-group decision making, minimal staff differentiation, and the ethic of serving all users at all times.

The purpose of these and similar innovations is to increase responsiveness to need through specialization or operational freedom to make decisions close to the point of need—in other words, to streamline the organizational modus operandi on a microlevel in the absence of meaningful restructuring at higher levels. These efforts are not well documented, but the author can offer the example of a department he managed through January 1994. With 23 staff members and programmatic responsibility for reference and information desks, instruction, CD-ROMs, government documents, and numeric data, the Research Services Department of the library at the University of California, San Diego, found it considerably more efficient, even essential, to maintain a system of coordinators, working groups with program responsibilities, and a general department steering team to manage the work of the department.

Yet these and similar efforts are decidedly limited in effectiveness for two reasons. First, reforms of this nature can go only so far in one unit in the absence of comparable change elsewhere in the organization. The economy of scale and responsiveness that come from bringing decision making closer to the point of need break down when individuals work beyond the department, as inevitably they must.

Second, reference departments typically remain caught between paper and digital technologies and so cannot yet effect a full shift to structures and work patterns most consonant with computer technology. A common model for implementation of technology entails movement from wholly manual processes, to development of parallel technical processes that emulate the manual, to elimination of manual processes, to true structural and operational innovation only after the manual elements are eliminated (De Klerk and Euster, 1989). In this scheme, reference services (which have not been as accustomed to the precision and detail of computer-based operations as, say, cataloging, and so have not been immersed in the technology to begin with) remain at an earlier stage of automation than most technical services operations. Reference necessarily continues to draw heavily on paper-based sources and routines, often combining paper and electronic resources (even paper and electronic versions of the same source) with little standardization of content, format, or operability (De Klerk and Euster, 1989).

Thus, the computer-based technologies run, and likely for several years will continue to run, parallel to paper-based technologies, mind-sets, service orientations, and organizational structures. Many if not most reference service units have stepped well into the future, but until parent organizations restructure to accelerate the process and the new technologies fully replace paper, these same units will be severely limited in the extent to which they can travel the path of organizational change to accommodate technological change.

Mediated searching came, was incorporated into reference routines and structures with some trepidation and anxiety, and now is receding as a service model that informs other areas of practice. OPAC and CD-ROM technology, and the hybrid of electronic journal indexes available through OPACs, arrived quickly and for some rudely, but reference providers have responded well and are incorporating these technologies into their routines, funding patterns, and organizational structures. Now reference personnel are bracing themselves for full-text retrieval, the Internet (and its successors), electronic journals, readily available numeric data, and sentence- and paragraph-level access to information through intelligent systems. Should they now return to the mediated "personal shopper" model for reference service, continue the direct-access approach to CD-ROMs and OPACs, or seek a new model that incorporates the best (and potentially the worst) of both models? This is one of the fundamental issues confronting reference providers today.

D. Burnout and Stress

Are academic reference librarians burning out? The answer, not surprisingly, depends on whom you ask and when they answered. One critical review of the literature (Fisher, 1990) concludes burnout probably is not a major problem for academic librarians, but there remains a basis for concern that burnout is more prevalent than some say and that a high degree of stress among academic reference providers is a trend that should be reckoned with before it becomes full-blown burnout. This may be especially true during the transition from materials- to user-centered services that place even greater emphasis on individual performance in potentially stressful situations.

Blazek and Parrish (1992) analyze the library science literature of burnout without limitation to type of library. They find that the preponderance of articles on the topic are concerned with reference rather than technical services librarians, probably due to the greater affinity of reference service with the classic helping professions of social work and teaching, the objects of a great deal of social scientific interest in the 1970s. It probably also is no coincidence that articles on burnout began appearing in library science journals in the early 1980s, in part as a concept migration from social science investigations in the 1970s but probably also in response to the rapid infusion of technology into libraries, especially in the reference arena.

In a literature review focusing on empirical tests for burnout among librarians, Fisher (1990) observes that the large majority of authors on librarian burnout hold the a priori assumption that the phenomenon exists to some significant extent despite limited empirical testing. Smith and Nelson (1983) based their study on a random sample of reference librarians in 75 universities in the United States, in part drawing on Forbes' Burnout Survey for their questionnaire. Their conclusion, that there is not a strong correlation between degree of burnout and the factors selected for study, is accepted by Fisher (1990) but rejected by Nauratil (1989), who challenges both the method of distributing questionnaires through department heads and the questionnaire itself. Haack, Jones, and Roose (1984) conclude that 14% of the respondents to a questionnaire administered at a conference indicate extensive burnout. Fisher strenuously challenges this conclusion, arguing that the sample was biased by limiting it to conferees, who are more likely to be overachievers than the larger population of reference providers, and that the respondents were unintentionally coached with a talk on burnout prior to administration of the questionnaire and solicitation of drawings.

Whether one, both, or neither of these studies is accepted, the conclusion remains that there is no reliable evidence of extensive burnout among academic reference providers. Still, this is not to say stress is not a problem or that the narrative articles on the subject are without merit. Libraries should in fact be prepared to deal with stress, and indeed burnout. Toward this end, Neville (1981) and Ferriero and Powers (1982) were among the first to make broad assessments of the topic, the former categorizing the issues into matters of concern to the individual, the organization, and the profession, and the latter a checklist of symptoms and contributing factors. Although not focused on academic librarians in particular, Bunge's (1987) general treatment of stress and Nauratil's (1989) broad social perspective are useful for all librarians.

Some stress is required to work effectively and efficiently, but too much stress can lead to burnout or ineffectiveness short of actual burnout (Caputo, 1991). This is the dilemma of stress—some is good, too much is bad. All library staff must perceive and manage stress and should use it as an opportunity for personal growth. There are no standard or generic stress management or burnout avoidance programs that work for all; much depends on individual makeup and unique manifestations of stress in each person. There is, however, a fairly standard list of coping mechanisms from which appropriate responses can be selected, ranging from techniques for the individual (Caputo, 1991; Ferriero and Powers, 1982; Neville, 1981), to environmental adjustments (Caputo, 1991; Ferriero and Powers, 1982; Neville, 1981), to far-reaching social reform (Nauratil, 1989).

E. Questions of Accuracy and Quality

The accuracy (and by extension, the quality) of reference service became a major concern of academic librarians in the mid-1980s, due in large measure to the study of government documents reference service by Hernon and McClure (1986, 1987a, 1987b). Their methodology is controversial and their findings are jarring.

> Unobtrusive testing of reference service is the process of asking reference questions (for which answers have been predetermined) of library staff members who are unaware that they are being evaluated. Collectively, these studies have shown that staff generally answer

50–60 percent of the questions correctly; make infrequent referral, either internal or external, to the library; fail to negotiate reference questions; and conduct ineffective search strategies. (Herman and McClure, 1986, p. 37)

Unobtrusive study methodology had been around for many years (McClure, 1984), as had unobtrusive studies of reference service with about the same results (Childers, 1991; Crowley, 1985; Hernon and McClure, 1987a), but Hernon and McClure brought this complex of issues into national focus—the stage was set with discussions of a general crisis in reference service and the dissemination of their results in two widely read publications reinforced these sentiments. Their findings have remained controversial among academic librarians, primarily on the points of the mix of libraries and reference desks tested and the nature and content of the questions employed.

Hernon and McClure coined what we now know as the 55 percent rule, which holds that between 50% and 60% of reference questions are answered correctly, or as they would say, produce a correct answer fill rate. An initial study focused exclusively on government documents questions at documents reference desks (McClure and Hernon, 1983) and their later, more widely discussed study (Hernon and McClure, 1987a) broadens this effort to include in-person documents questions at general and documents reference desks in a mix of public and academic libraries around the country. Most fully reported in book form, this latter study was summarized for *Library Journal* (Hernon and McClure, 1986) and discussed more broadly as a *Journal of Academic Librarianship* symposium (Hernon and McClure, 1987b).

The results and methodology of the later study (Hernon and McClure, 1987a) remain the point of departure for discussions of reference service accuracy. For this investigation Hernon and McClure designed (with the assistance of practicing librarians) 15 questions related to government documents and employed student proxies to administer the same 8 questions to 24 government documents reference desks and another 7 questions to 26 general reference desks. Overall, 61.8% of the questions were answered correctly, 64.6% at the documents desks and 59.1% at the general reference desks (Hernon and McClure, 1986). Reasons for incorrect answers include wrong data, 64.4%; "don't know" with no referral, 20.1%; and proxy incorrectly told appropriate source not available, 15.4% (Hernon and McClure, 1986).

As might be expected, the responses to unobtrusive studies of reference service have been many and varied, ranging from tongue-in-cheek humor to serious questions of method and analysis. On the light side, Plotnik (1985) wonders if half-right reference is such a bad thing, considering the track record of the media, government agencies, physicians, advice columns, and utilities. On the serious side, academic librarians have resisted accepting Hernon and McClure's findings, mostly on the basis of the narrow subject focus and factual nature of the questions that do not accurately reflect the range of questions and other demands on academic reference service, the mix of academic and public libraries used in the studies, and probably also a visceral distaste for a test methodology that for many runs counter to academic values and sensibilities.

The most serious challenge to Hernon and McClure is mounted by Whitlatch (1989), who questions both their methodology and their results in an obtrusive study of reference performance in five academic libraries. Whitlatch (1989) determines that 18.0% of reference inquiries comprise bibliographic citations, 11.3% are factual, and 70.7% are of an open-ended subject or resource-use nature. Thus, only 29.3% of these questions lend themselves to unobtrusive study—a considerably larger figure than the approximately 12% estimated by Childers (1987, 1991). Unobtrusive studies, therefore, tend to examine only a relatively small portion of what transpires at the reference desk.

From her sampling of reference questions Whitlatch (1989) also finds a success rate of 78.6% for factual questions, 70.5% for bibliographic citation inquiries, and 62.6% for subject-instruction encounters. And, if one wishes to factor for the appropriateness of these questions for the libraries in which they were asked, she determines that 60.7% of factual questions (17 of 28), 90.9% of bibliographic citation requests (40 of 44), and 93.3% of the subject-instruction exchanges (154 of 165) related to the course work and research missions of the institutions. Whitlatch's reference success rates, then, are considerably higher than Hernon and McClure's, and her results can be factored somewhat higher yet when regarding appropriateness of questions in relation to institutional missions.

Aside from success and correct answer fill rates and the issues of question content and mix of libraries surveyed, disturbing questions of overall quality and process remain for all types of libraries. Hernon and McClure relate what should be regarded as a high incidence of inappropriate termination of reference interviews even for a small portion of academic library reference performance; Elzy and others (1991) report only a 7.8 "librarian attitude factor" (p. 462) on a scale of 1 to 10; and in an unobtrusive study of academic and public libraries Durrance (1989) finds that more than one third of library users, judging on the basis of the librarian's interpersonal, listening, and interviewing skills, would not return to the same person.

Most of the tests discussed here were conducted prior to the broad implementation of online catalogs, CD-ROMs, and the addition of government documents records to online catalogs, but one wonders whether these resources would increase or decrease the success rates, considering also the many adverse side effects of this infusion of technology on both reference providers and users examined in the preceding discussion. What is an acceptable failure rate? What must be done to improve? Is "we're doing the best we can with what we have" good enough? Clearly more studies of academic reference performance are in order, but even more pressing is the need for academic libraries to measure the quality of their service in any of a number of ways, set benchmarks, and continually work for improvement.

III. Reshaping Reference Service

The various effects of technology and transformation of the scholarly communication system are compelling revision of some basic assumptions regarding reference service, many of which have gone unchallenged for over a century. Changing patterns in financial support and availability of staff; changes in the abilities, expectations, and even the composition of user groups; and increasing awareness of recent national trends and issues in reference service also are inducing broad and creative reconsideration of the current circumstance. These considerations in turn are leading to numerous changes that adapt to the present while preparing for the future.

As president of the American Library Association's Reference and Adult Services Division, Rettig (1992) captures this growing sentiment in his inaugural column in *RQ*.

> We find ourselves in an era of rethinking, reenvisioning, retooling, and reinventing. Technological developments have provided much of the impetus for revisiting abiding verities amidst new challenges . . . the telecommunications revolution offers opportunities to do entirely new things and to do old things in radically different ways. In other words, we must rethink, reenvision, retool, and reinvent reference service. (p. 463)

Rettig's follow-up column (1993a) details efforts to rethink the reference desk, merge service points, change staffing and service patterns, and cultivate librarian–user relationships independent of the desk or even the library; and his contribution to the proceedings of an institute (1993c) offers a more reflective review of these trends.

Other indications that fundamental changes within reference service units are well under way include: conference discussion group agendas and minutes, which report an increasing number of reductions in or overhauls of reference service; the results of a survey over LIBADMIN and LIBREF listservs for examples of structural reorganizations or redefinitions of functions or roles within reference departments (Lipow, 1992, 1993); and a set of two three-day Rethinking Reference institutes conducted in 1993 by Lipow. Lipow's institutes, whose proceedings and related material have been published (Lipow, 1993b), and which Oberg (1993a), Rettig (1993b), and Coder (1993) have reported, are particularly noteworthy for their inclusion of such national figures as Campbell and Massey-Burzio and a small working group approach to solving problems by participants.

A. To Desk or Not to Desk

Most would guess the notion of radically altering conventional reference desk service to be very recent, but it has been under discussion for over a decade. Hendrickson (1983) wonders aloud in an opinion piece if "there is any reason why, in a college or university library, patron–librarian interaction could not be expanded to replace the reference desk as the core of reference service?" (p. 81). The earliest true critic of the largely unchallenged tradition of the desk as the primary locus for reference service is Freides (1983), who in the same year observes that:

> Academic reference librarians have never defined their goals or the scope of their work beyond a general intention to assist readers with whatever they might need to facilitate their use of the library. Equally unarticulated and unexamined is the assumption that the hub of this assistance is the reference desk, where a reference librarian, or surrogate, is available to the reader at all times. The arrangement conveys an implicit promise never to let the reader go unserved, but it also pegs the service at a low level. The reference desk works best for directional questions and requests for specific factual information. It is not well designed for dealing with questions requiring interpretation or exploration. . . . By establishing the desk as the focal point of reader assistance, libraries not only expend professional time on trivial tasks, but also encourage the assumption that the low-level, undemanding type of question handled most easily and naturally at the desk is the service norm. (pp. 466–467)

Freides stops short of recommending abolishment of the reference desk, arguing instead for careful matching of types of questions with appropriate staff, an important principle in the alternative model of tiered information and reference service accomplished through multiple service points. Freides remains the single most powerful critic of the conventional reference service model and is cited by virtually every proponent of alternatives to this model, in part due to the power of her prose and in part because she articulates the structural shortcomings of reference desk service on a conceptual level well before the full impact of technology, especially CD-ROMs and OPACs, made these shortcomings more evident on a practical level.

Biggs (1985) reinforces Freides's arguments with the suggestion that we tend to value reference service by its quantity rather than quality, regarding as a "servile attitude" (p. 69) our compulsion to answer all questions from all people at all times. Biggs also raises the issue of professionalism and image derived from this attitude and arrangement, but she recommends curtailment of service hours and limitation of reference provision to librarians rather than eliminating or otherwise changing the nature of desk-oriented reference service.

Less constrained by the mental construct of the reference desk is Ford (1986, 1988), who presses the argument for eliminating the reference desk as commonly known. Beginning with the premise that " 'Renaissance' reference librarians serving all comers at a reference desk may no longer be a realistic solution for providing public services" (Ford, 1986, p. 492), she argues for a fresh look at our service models.

> So long as the reference desk model is uncritically accepted, librarians are not challenged to respond creatively to changes in materials, formats, and research opportunities for our users, and users are not challenged to use any of a variety of printed or computerized sources or aids. (Ford, 1986, pp. 493–494)

> Too much attention is being focused on trying to fix what exists rather than thinking about the future. The attention of practicing reference librarians is on the nitty-gritty day-to-day rather than long-range planning. . . . Reference departments and librarians have taken on new services but not given up or revamped old ones. What should the role of libraries and of librarians be and how should we relate to users? (Ford, 1988, p. 581)

Ford raises many more questions than she answers, but clearly her purpose is less to advance an alternate plan than to encourage thought about alternatives.

Two major efforts to restructure reference service have been documented in recent years. Shapiro (1987) reports an attempt at Michigan State University to establish a tiered information and reference service through the creation of an information-quick reference service point near the library entrance with more in-depth reference assistance available elsewhere. Shapiro reports this restructuring has significantly ameliorated the perceived problems of a volume of desk traffic that inhibited in-depth assistance, extensive use of professional time to perform clerical tasks, and lack of time to pursue adequately such activities as collection development, online searching, and instruction.

Efforts at Brandeis and Johns Hopkins universities reported by Massey-Burzio (1992, 1993) are bolder still. In response to a reference desk staffing situation that had been problematic for some time as instruction and online searching were added to department responsibilities and that worsened appreciably with the introduction of CD-ROMs, Massey-Burzio (1992) initiated at Brandeis the replacement of a conventional reference desk with an information desk and a research consultation service. The so-called Brandeis model consists of a highly visible information desk staffed by nonlibrarians, at which directional and brief information is obtained and from which referrals to librarians are made, and a less visible reference consultation service, which draws exclusively on librarians through a combination of office hours and service by appointments in a private, businesslike setting. Specific issues that motivated the Brandeis approach were concern for the quality of reference service, appropriate use of staff time, the image of professional librarians, and job satisfaction. In a later review of the Brandeis experience, enhanced by her re-creation of this model at Hopkins, Massey-Burzio (1993) observes that the reference consultation approach changes the relationship between user and librarian by "increas[ing] the value that patrons place on the reference librarian's work," whereas the prevailing "department store" model discourages in-depth assistance or long-term or follow-up consulting relationships (pp. 45–46).

If so many are disenchanted with the conventional reference desk and if the Michigan State, Brandeis, and Hopkins universities' efforts to restructure information and reference service have been so successful, why are libraries not hastening to emulate these institutions? First, the conservative nature of institutions should be recognized, especially large ones with collegial approaches to decision making, wherein major change requires a fair degree of consensus and therefore comes slowly. Second, on a more personal level major change can be threatening; in this instance, participants need to exchange the relative security of anonymity in a high-volume conventional reference environment for a consultation model in which one may be held more personally accountable. Finally, many institutions may be evolving incrementally along the lines outlined in this section and so are not reporting their experiences in the literature. This is true at the University of California, San Diego, which has established at the main entrance an information desk staffed by nonlibrarians who provide catalog instruction, directional and basic reference assistance, and referrals to individuals and other service points. The library also maintains a more or less conventional reference desk that relies heavily on referrals to specialists for in-depth consultations.

That the profession is evolving along these lines may also be indicated by reactions to two of the works discussed earlier. Both the Biggs (1985) and Massey-Burzio (1992) articles were the leads in *Journal of Academic Librarianship* symposiums and so were accompanied by several brief commentaries by others. Reactions to Biggs on the whole were negative and reactions to Massey-Burzio were largely positive. While the proposals from these authors were different in many respects, common issues addressed by the respondents (e.g., relationship between the desk environment and perceived professional status) and the nature and tenor of their comments do reveal a greater acceptance in 1992 than in 1985 for a major overhaul of the traditional reference desk service model.

B. Paraprofessionals at the Desk

The debate, as Oberg (1992b) says, is over. At one time a source of considerable controversy and anxiety, and on at least one occasion regarded as a portent of the demise of reference librarianship (Vavrek, 1978), paraprofessionals working extensively at the reference desk is a fait accompli. Much ink has been spilled discussing the pros, cons, and implications of this trend (Parmer, 1988), but the issue has quietly been settled offstage, largely by fiscal exigencies. The challenge now remaining is for libraries to maximize training and development opportunities for paraprofessionals so as to ensure high-quality service and to seek out the information-reference service model that most effectively balances the needs of users and staff to the benefit of the institution.

Increased employment of paraprofessionals at the reference desk is but one dimension of the restructuring that has occurred in academic libraries in recent decades. Goudy (1993) reports that from 1970/1971 to 1987/1988 the number of academic librarians increased 14.8%, while the number of support staff increased 50%. As of 1990, 88% of ARL libraries and 66% of smaller colleges and universities employed paraprofessionals at the reference desk (Oberg, 1992a). Lest one think the substantial presence of paraprofessionals at the reference desk is an isolated phenomenon, by 1990, 61% of the smaller colleges and universities were employing paraprofessionals for copy cataloging and 20% for original cataloging, including description, subject analysis, and classification (Oberg, 1992a). Indeed, many cataloging departments experienced and adapted to the fiscal constraints, migration of traditional librarian responsibilities to support staff, and major restructuring of individual responsibilities and department operations at least a decade before these trends were felt in force within reference departments.

In recent decades the movement for librarian faculty status, the explosion of technology, declining or static budgets, and an increasing emphasis on public services combined to create a tripartite structure in libraries consisting of librarians, paraprofessionals, and clericals (Oberg, 1992a). As librarians have become more engaged in activities commensurate with faculty or academic status, often outside the library, they have transferred to paraprofessionals many responsibilities that previously were reserved for professionals, creating a confusion of roles and in some quarters no small amount of discord (Hoffman, 1993; Oberg, 1993b). All library staff are working at higher levels due to the demands of automation and constrained budgets, but librarians have been slow to let go of some responsibilities while not clearly articulating what they are doing that remains distinctively different from that done by paraprofessionals. The result is uncertainty and disenchantment based in ambiguity.

Although librarians have increased their interest and involvement in teaching, collection development, research, and governance, paraprofessionals have of necessity increased their involvement in direct assistance of patrons in the reference arena, often alone or otherwise unsupervised. The benefits for librarians are obvious, but there is some evidence of reduced quality of service by paraprofessionals under certain circumstances, especially in the areas of referral, question analysis, and communication with users (Halldorsson and Murfin, 1977; Murfin and Bunge, 1988). More certain is consistently lower job satisfaction among paraprofessionals compared to that of librarians

(Kreitz and Ogden, 1990; Lynch and Verdin, 1983). Arizona State University West, which crafted from the inception of its library a reference service model based chiefly on reference desk paraprofessionals who make referrals to librarians as the paraprofessionals deem appropriate, reports some difficulties resulting from uncertainties surrounding the referral process and a high turnover rate due to the "lack of a good career ladder and good salaries" (Hammond, 1992).

Apparent shortcomings of paraprofessionals in the reference arena, though, are generally reported without a clear indication of the training and career development environment in which they are working. Certainly the same training and professional development opportunities afforded librarians when reference service was (at least presumed to be) an exclusively professional domain should be provided paraprofessionals. What professionals do that paraprofessionals do not undertake (e.g., teaching, faculty liaison, management, long-term planning) should be articulated clearly; paraprofessionals should be assisted in clarifying ambiguities at the other end of the spectrum, between paraprofessionals and clericals (Hoffman, 1993). And in the final analysis, all parties should acknowledge that innate abilities and interests, plus opportunities for training, career development, and collaboration, are more important ingredients for high quality reference service than professional status in and of itself.

C. Evaluation of Service and Personnel

The literature of reference service evaluation (or assessment) is as diffuse and disparate as reference service itself. To the extent there has been difficulty defining reference service, there has been difficulty agreeing on what and how best to evaluate it. Rettig (1991), for example, argues it is inherently difficult to undertake evaluations of reference service when there is no common understanding of what reference service is or what is its relationship to such other public services as bibliographic instruction. Until resolution of the fundamental issue of whether academic library public service is in the business primarily of delivering information or teaching users to acquire it themselves, he continues, we are not likely to agree on the standards and goals necessary for the meaningful evaluation of reference service. Still, the literature of evaluation is extensive if not cohesive, including several bibliographies and literature reviews (Baker and Lancaster, 1991; Bunge, 1977; Hults, 1992; Powell, 1984; Von Seggern, 1987) and an entire issue of *Reference Librarian* (Katz, 1984).

Reasons for undertaking reference service evaluation include the desire to make a better case for protecting or acquiring resources, acquire data for decision making, establish benchmarks for future measurement, compare performance with institutional peers (Baker and Lancaster, 1991), and demonstrate commitment to high-quality service (Von Seggern, 1987). Whatever the motivation, it is essential to articulate precisely what is to be evaluated in order to assure collection of meaningful data, for the goals of the evaluation process should dictate methodology (Hults, 1992). Von Seggern (1987) and Westbrook (1989) regard evaluation as part of a planning circle that begins with goals and objectives, continues with evaluation, proceeds through improvement of services based on evaluation findings, and begins anew with goals and objectives. In a similar fashion, Hernon (1987) urges the linkage of performance measures to evaluation and these results in turn to planning and decision making, a "utilitarian" approach that "deals with applications, impact, and usefulness of the data and presupposes that a primary purpose of data collection is to influence policies and decision making" (p. 450).

The world of evaluation is perceived and mapped differently by virtually every general commentator on the subject. Baker and Lancaster (1991) distinguish between macroevaluation (how *well* a system operates, e.g., proportion of questions not answered correctly) and microevaluation (*how* a system operates, e.g., why some questions were not answered correctly). Whitlatch (1992) makes the more usual distinction between quantitative and qualitative approaches with surveys, observation, and case studies chief among the latter; Von Seggern (1987) offers a taxonomy of answering success (including expert judgment, librarian or patron report, unobtrusive study), cost and task analysis, interview and communication, enumeration of questions, reference collections, staff availability, and use and nonuse of reference services; and C. Bunge (1977) describes cost-benefit analysis among other approaches. The single most useful guide to qualitative methods is Westbrook (1989), who provides descriptions, sample scenarios, administrative considerations, sources of potential bias, and companion methods for observation, interview, survey, content analysis, and other methodologies.

Beyond the controversial unobtrusive studies of reference service discussed earlier, some noteworthy approaches to evaluation have been reported from the field. Christensen and others (1989) discuss a five-part assessment of a reference service to gauge the impact of removing librarians from reference desk service. Using an unobtrusive test and surveys of patrons, student reference assistants, paraprofessional assistants, and librarian subject specialists, the authors ascertain an unacceptable level of quality for the desk service and call for establishment of performance standards among several other recommendations. That the authors used two methods and a total of five tests is noteworthy in that it points up an important principle of evaluation detailed by Westbrook. Whenever possible, she urges (1989), use a combination of methods—triangulation—to study a phenomenon so the result is more complete, accurate, and reliable.

Particularly nettlesome has been the problem of setting standards for and evaluating the performance of reference providers. Young (1985) characterizes reference work as a "creative and idiosyncratic process involving a personal, independent, and usually anonymous interaction with patrons" that resists objective assessment on the individual level, thereby allowing much poor reference work to go undetected (p. 70). Tyckoson (1992) also speaks of the complexity of the reference transaction in relation to evaluation methodologies, and both Tyckoson and Young eschew quantitative measures in favor of trait-based or behavioral assessments. Rubin (1991) offers one of the fuller descriptions of this approach, directly linking trait-anchored systems (that rate such performance traits as productivity, knowledge, judgment, etc.) and behavior-based systems (that measure such behaviors as "communicates well," "points vaguely," "treats users with courtesy," etc.) with goal-oriented standards. A collection of performance standards, evaluation forms, and survey results has been assembled by Gorman (1987).

More reference service evaluations are not undertaken because of the time involved, lack of material support, and lack of understanding of methods or possible applications of data. Other factors are a fear of scrutiny and an "uneasiness surrounding the evaluation of reference services [that] seem[s] to be attributable to the difficulty of reconciling management and professional perspectives," wherein managerial and reference provider worldviews are at odds both in the means and the ends of evaluation (Pierce, 1984, pp. 10, 19). Whatever the barriers, it is becoming increasingly clear they must be overcome as we are held more accountable by users and sources of funding to demonstrate the effectiveness of services and to justify investments made in them.

D. Changing Management and Managing Change

If there is one constant in reference service today, it is the persistence of change—in technology, the availability of resources, and patterns among our users. Some of the ways reference departments have for some time been using specialists, coordinators, dedicated subgroups, and task or working groups to bring resources and decision making closer to the point of need were examined earlier. These efforts have been accomplished largely in the absence of wholesale changes in either department or institutional structures, but all levels of the organization are thinking more earnestly about appropriate structural responses to current and anticipated pressures.

Among the more dramatic responses at the department level are consolidations of reference units, yet many of these efforts are not reported in the literature, such as the spate of reference and government documents merges in recent years. Kleiner (1987) chronicles and analyzes the centralization of separate humanities, social sciences, and sciences reference divisions accomplished at Louisiana State University in the late 1970s. Although the consolidation was not undertaken in direct response to many of the trends under discussion here, Kleiner's articulation of advantages and disadvantages of such a move remains relevant. Butcher and Kinch (1990) also address the issue of consolidating and reorganizing a reference department, but primarily as a reminder of the political dimensions of such change outside the library.

Libraries are becoming more complex, both in the degree of sophistication required to use them effectively and within the organizations themselves. One clear manifestation of this increasing complexity is the deterioration of traditional boundaries between technical and public services. DeDonato (1991) speaks of the convergence of reference and technical services within access services, driven in part by the rise of a global thinking that transcends traditionally parochial thought in both reference and technical services. Among the consequences of this convergence are changes in job descriptions whereby reference librarians become more engaged in the development of library systems and technical services librarians become more directly user-focused.

As traditional demarcations break down, the increasing complexity of reference departments and their parent organizations places a greater premium on effective working alliances and communication. In recent years the matrix model of management has emerged in the library literature and on the conference circuit, in part to satisfy the need for an organizational complexity that outstrips conventional hierarchical structures and in part simply to describe much informal coping activity that has transpired within such units as reference departments. Johnson (1990) provides a thorough review of the nature and origins of matrix management, and Euster and Haikalis (1984) assess the value of this approach in the context of a case study. The chief characteristics of a matrix organization are dual reporting relationships and reliance on "consultation, compromise, cooperation and negotiation" to accomplish tasks; potential problems are "anarchy and self-absorption," "power struggles," and excessive overhead (Euster and Haikalis, 1984, pp. 358, 360).

The lesson of matrix management beyond the ability to accomplish some tasks more effectively in some situations might be that in many instances the process is nearly as important as the result, especially when a particular effort may have reverberations beyond the task or project. New structures and alternative means of organizing may be attempted, and many of these are appropriate and necessary, but caution should be exercised not to lose sight of the need for effective communication among individuals and groups in complex organizations with unclear missions and blurred roles. This is the clear message of the Harvard College Library (Lee, 1993), Yale University technical services (Lowell, 1993), CSU–Long Beach (Johnson, 1993), and University of Arizona (Rawan, 1993; Williams, 1993) reorganizations, and it is a major leitmotiv in a monograph directed toward progressive managers in traditional organizations (Cargill and Webb, 1988).

IV. The Future of Reference

The future of reference service is to a great extent being shaped by forces well beyond the control of reference providers. Networking, restructuring, pluralism, and automation on the global level; and distributed computing, the centrality of networks, information access in lieu of ownership, and the convergence of media into a digital system on the campus level (Heterick and Sanders, 1993) are some of the leading broad-based forces now affecting academic libraries. More directly related to conventional library services are commercial information services, rapid document delivery, the proliferation of highly specialized databases and networks, and electronic imaging (Malin-conico, 1992).

As the electronic university emerges, it becomes increasingly clear that the scholarly communication system is undergoing a transformation that holds major implications for libraries and library public services. Lewis (1988) observes that "the issue is no longer library automation: it is remaking the structure of scholarly communication" (p. 291), and Lyman (1991) advocates re-creation of a scholarly communication system brought to a state of crisis by "radical changes in the economics of the traditional print library, in addition to fundamental changes in the nature of scholarly communication brought about by technology" (p. 34). Battin (1984) urges focus on the library as concept and function, rather than on narrow and (even then) obsolete definitions of librarian and library. With this perspective, she advocates more clearly associating the library's destiny with an evolving process of scholarly communication, a common thread for the library in all the economic and technological change underway.

Most observers agree that a major paradigm shift now underway in academic research libraries is dramatically changing the concept of the library, its role in the scholarly communication system, and the type of services it provides, including (indeed, especially including) reference. Some describe this shift as moving from a materials-oriented to a services-oriented paradigm, others as a movement from either bibliographic to information access or from document description to document delivery. Miksa (1989), in one of the more succinct and thorough portrayals of this transformation, speaks of movement away from a collections-centered library where all activities, structures, and even mental patterns (including those of reference providers and users) derive from and are defined by the on-site collection. In its place is emerging the user-centered paradigm, which in the new technological environment addresses the information needs of users independent of location and time, providing a new organizing principle that emphasizes access engineering over warehousing and arranging, full-text over bibliographic access, and delivery over processing.

Several other glimpses into a future that will affect reference services have appeared in recent years. Gorman (1991) offers up a tour de force of academic libraries a decade hence, addressing in turn the issues of funding, buildings and space, materials and access, staffing, and users. Govan (1991) discusses in realistic terms the impact of technology and other forces on research libraries, especially those with large staffs and print collections, while focusing on some of the practical dimensions of getting from here to there. Personnel issues are addressed by Creth (1991), whose principal concerns lie with redefining the roles of librarians, organizational structures that accommodate new communication and information systems, and qualifications required for all library personnel; and Veaner (1985b), who explores the attributes, attitudes, knowledge, and skills of the future library employee. Other worthwhile explorations of the future and what it might take to get there have been written by Woodsworth and others (1989), Veaner (1985a, 1990), and White (1990a, 1990b).

A. The New Reference Service

What will be the general character of reference service in coming years? Predictions in this area are no more reliable than those for the library as a whole, but a collation of the larger trends noted in previous sections and the insights of some thoughtful public services librarians suggest some distinct possibilities. Cargill (1992) in particular outlines several areas that warrant attention. Reference philosophy and services, she projects, likely will emphasize proactive user services, accommodate an increasing range of user understanding and abilities, depend much more on linked information management systems, regenerate the reference teaching role in electronic ways that support self-instruction, and more closely survey user needs. In addition, access to reference services will become more oriented to remote electronic and telephone paths, be arranged more by appointment and be of a consultative nature, and entail more user fees.

Major portions of Cargill's vision are affirmed by Rettig (1993a, 1993c), who notes four areas of experimentation occurring within reference service: tiered service, floating (or roving) reference providers, increased liaison work, and more user studies. The common denominator in these efforts is "a renewed and refreshing emphasis on the needs of individual users" (1993c, p.

81), an awareness that needs to deepen further. Toward this end, Martell (1983) offers an organizational model for a user-centered library.

The need for technical skills and understanding of complex computer-based systems, a major dimension of Cargill's vision, permeates a symposium on the future reference librarian in *Reference Services Review*. For example, Rockman (1991) speaks of a new technical orientation, Massey-Burzio (1991) notes the need for continuing education and the involvement of reference librarians in the development of systems, Ritch (1991) notes how the paper-based information explosion alone has outstripped traditional reliance on memory and experience at the core of traditional reference desk service and prescribes a reference team approach that blends technical and subject knowledge, Zink (1991) underscores the need for training and continuing education, and Hale (1991) views the increasing presence of technology as the chief tool in customizing reference services. These views on the need for more technical expertise and involvement in information systems are shared by Veaner (1985b) and Creth (1991).

Although greater involvement in technology is universally acknowledged as essential for the future of reference service, librarians should be careful not to be consumed by it. Swan (1993) encourages readers to "resist the unexamined, widely repeated claims that all the answers are electronic" (p. 44), fearing that without considerable political action along with the technical work there may result systems for which access is allocated to those who can pay the most. In a general essay on the future reference librarian, Surprenant and Perry-Holmes (1985) see commitment to humanistic values as the basis for individual, or what we are now calling user-centered, service. And Bunge (1993) urges retention of certain values and visions while proceeding into an unknown future, among them the notion of reference as a value-added service fashioned for individual needs, the value of personal dignity and individual rights, and the requisite professional autonomy and authority to meet user needs.

Reference providers have always advocated user-centered values, service tempered by humaneness and professionalism, and involvement in the technology of the day; however, the emphasis now is on degree of involvement and degree of user-centeredness. Emphasizing matters of degree, however, is inherently ambiguous and significant uncertainty naturally emerges when new and difficult choices have to be made. Martin (1990) describes the new paradox of public service created by the proliferation of electronic resources, an ongoing explosion of paper sources, increasingly complex libraries and information systems, and continuation of traditional service models.

To provide the same level of service to everyone may mean that we provide the highest level of service to no one. Is equality worth the price of inadequate service? If we say yes to everyone, does it mean that the service we provide our "primary clientele" is diminished? (p. 21)

Choices must be made for users and service providers, and choices must be made that will promote realization of a vision that is not yet clear to all those making the choices. Therein lies the crux of contemporary reference service, and therein can be found the dilemma of contemporary reference service models.

B. Paradigms Lost, Paradigms Regained

Historical perspectives often enable the present to be seen more clearly or the future more accurately, so it may be of benefit to look at reference service models and principles of the past before reviewing emerging options for the future. One germane facet of the history of reference service is the extent to which the quantity and nature of service have varied among institutions. The provision of reference service prior to the present generation is often thought to be stable, uniform, and even monolithic, but Rothstein (1955) shows that this is clearly not the case. Drawing on the early reference theorist Wyer (1930), Rothstein denotes three general philosophies of reference that form a service model continuum ranging from highly personalized service with limited instruction to a highly instructional model with limited personal assistance in retrieving information. Between these extremes lies a model, a sort of golden mean, that attempts to balance the elements of instruction and direct assistance.

Rothstein and others argue that the early reference theorists largely eschewed the information delivery model, but Wagers (1978) demonstrates that these same theorists in fact advocated providing information directly. Practitioners, of course, marched to different drums altogether by engaging in any number of variants between the theoretical extremes (McElderry, 1976; Rothstein, 1989; Schiller, 1965). Constants in the history of reference service, then, are a tension between the information and instruction models of reference service and considerable variation in the ways and extents to which these models have been applied and even understood in retrospect.

In recent decades and for a variety of reasons, instruction has become a full-fledged movement to the extent in many cases of forming administrative units and operational goals both within and outside conventional reference departments. Whether a cause or a symptom, the tension between the so-called instruction and information models of reference service has increased appreciably during this same period. Dusenbury (1984), speaking of instruction within the reference service context, presents one of the more forceful defenses of the instruction model.

If one accepts that education is, fundamentally, the progressive mastery of public knowledge, and that the purpose of information is to transmit why things are as they are, not
merely enumerate what they are, it would be ironic (and more than a little depressing) to
structure learning in such a way that the learner would not have, as a basic component
of education, the ability to independently explore an area of concern or interest. Students
at every level should be able to find information independently and should have been
taught how to find the best information available. This is not an elitist idea designed to
increase the status of librarians. (p. 102)

Leading opponents of the instruction model are Schiller (1965), Wilson
(1979), and, most recently and perhaps most vocally, Rettig (1993d; Miller
and Rettig, 1985).

Actually, Rettig opposes both the instruction model, particularly its
embodiment in the bibliographic instruction movement, and the conventional
information model. The current extended version of the instruction model
doesn't work because it is taking a correct-answer approach in an era when
users can and should be free to explore and to make judgments on their own
(1993d), and the "access to information model" is no longer effective because
so much technology has rendered libraries unworkable and the reference desk
"a service that isn't meant to be taken seriously" (p. 141). Rettig thus decries
both models and pleads for the construction of information systems that can
be used intuitively and without assistance.

Rettig generalizes the approach of bibliographic instruction without acknowledging recent efforts to adjust instruction to the demands of technology
by emphasizing information literacy and independent navigation of electronic
systems, and he understates the inseparable dimension of instruction present
in virtually all reference service, but even so he most certainly is on the useful
path of seeking to reformulate a reference service model that accommodates
the practical realities of contemporary reference service. In similar fashion
Nielsen (1982), whose observation that conflict over roles divides us at a time
we can least afford divisiveness remains an appropriate reminder, argues that
both the information and instruction models are doomed to obsolescence.
While Nielsen does not offer a clear alternative or synthesis, he concludes
with the hope that movements emphasizing sharing, humanism, and holistic
approaches in other service professions might provide the basis for new
reference service models.

Others have attempted recombination of reference service principles and
roles. Martell (1984), noting fragmented roles, unexamined assumptions, and
the lack of a reference service agenda, calls for "an integrated role model that
pulls together reference services rather than fragments them" (p. 85). Gunning
(1984) follows with an outline of such a model, bringing reference, collection
development, online searching, and instruction together in subject specialists
configured in either relatively large or relatively small administrative units.

As discussed earlier, some libraries are opting for this model in smaller units as they flatten the organizational structure and emphasize subject orientation. Others have taken this concept a step further by making all librarians integrated subject specialists, leaving all other operations and management to nonlibrarians (Johnson, 1993).

Swanson (1984) expresses reservations about the integrated model, especially in larger research libraries that "are too complex, the tasks too complicated and the patron needs too varied and unpredictable for integrated role model librarians to meet all of them effectively or any individual librarian to have the skills and abilities to provide all services needed" (p. 90). Her particular reformulation, which she calls an extended traditional model, combines some aspects of the integrated service model in traditional departmental divisions with matrix management and other techniques to transcend customary administrative boundaries. Still another approach is the dual-function assignment that combines technical (usually cataloging) and public (usually reference) services (Paster, 1991); the notion, implications, and facets of mediated reference service are explored in an issue of *Reference Librarian* (Ewing and Hauptman, 1992).

Two decades ago some public services librarians began responding to the present crisis by emphasizing one portion of the collective reference personality, the impulse to teach. Now another segment, small but growing, questions this focus and urges greater emphasis on direct provision of information. Meanwhile experiments with electronic tools and resources are undertaken, some have eliminated the reference desk, alternative staffing patterns are examined, and a variety of service models are considered, but we consistently return to a fundamental tension between teaching and delivering.

Contrary to popular belief, especially in a period of great change and uncertainty when a simpler past is sought, there has never been a dominant theory of reference or less than a smorgasbord of service models determined largely by local exigencies. There has always been tension between information and instruction, between providing and showing how to find information. The varieties of these models are legion. In recent decades, first the massive expansion of higher education, the information explosion, and the increasing complexity of libraries, then severe fiscal constraints coterminous with a technological revolution, have all converged to inflict great stress on all aspects of and among all participants in academic library reference service. The consequence of these strains has been to particularize rather than unify our responses as we seek many solutions to what appear to be many problems.

A review article is not the place to attempt resolution of this issue, if indeed it is resolvable. Identifying, experimenting with, reporting and discussing, and choosing from among many service models and elements may be the key, with the mix wholly dependent on such local circumstances as institutional mission and character, professional cultures, capabilities of staff, budget realities, and aspirations and priorities. Each day, choices are made by reference providers working with users, and larger and more difficult planning choices are made in response to the challenges of dwindling resources and burgeoning technology. It is all the more important, then, that reference providers stand back from their local service models; question, analyze, and compare them with alternatives; and consciously choose that which serves their local interests best rather than permit the future to choose for them.

V. Conclusion

This will be the last review article to focus on reference service as a discrete operational unit subject to independent analysis. Public services are converging in ways that are rendering insignificant such conventional distinctions as reference, instruction, liaison, document delivery, and database searching. The traditional dichotomy of technical and public services is eroding as academic libraries move from materials- to user-centered organizational models. Higher education, driven by technological developments that also are transforming the scholarly communication system, is forcing an unprecedented degree of library integration into the electronic fabric of the new university. Not only will isolated examination of reference service soon be conceptually invalid, but it will also simply be impossible.

No longer can academic librarians afford to view themselves in a self-referencing fashion, and no longer can the literature of academic librarianship afford to focus on the library as a closed or nearly closed system. Libraries are being transformed by technology, but it is the manifestation of technology in a changing scholarly communication system and a complex set of user communities that bring into focus the true implications of technological change. The library service perspective will no longer simply be incorporation of technology into its normative behaviors; the impulse will instead be to understand the revolution underway in scholarly communication and to understand users from their perspective rather than that of the library. Instead of approaching these phenomena from the library looking outward, academic librarians will seek to understand them in and of themselves, to find the place of the library and its services within the interactions of faculty and students among their colleagues. The next review article relevant to what is now known as reference service will address the scholarly communication system, university communites, and library services from a perspective outside the library.

Acknowledgment

The author wishes to express appreciation for the thoughtful editing and commentary of Richard Hume Weking on an early draft of this article.

References

Baker, S. L., and Lancaster, F. W. (1991). *The Measurement and Evaluation of Library Services*, 2d ed. Information Resources Press, Arlington, Virginia.

Battin, P. (1984). The library: Center of the restructured university. *College & Research Libraries* **45**, 170–176.

Bichteler, J. (1987). Technostress in libraries: Causes, effects, and solutions. *Electronic Library* **5**, 282–287.

Biggs, M. (1985). Replacing the fast fact drop-in with gourmet information service: A symposium. *Journal of Academic Librarianship* **11**, 68–78.

Blazek, R., and Parrish, D. A. (1992). Burnout and public services: The periodical literature of librarianship in the eighties. *RQ* **31**, 48–59.

Bunge, C. (1977). Approaches to the evaluation of library reference services. In *Evaluation and Scientific Management of Libraries and Information Centres: Proceedings of the NATO Advanced Study Institute* (F. W. Lancaster and C. W. Cleverdon, eds.), pp. 41–71. Noordhoff, Leyden.

Bunge, C. (1984). Potential and reality at the reference desk: Reflections on a 'return to the field.' *Journal of Academic Librarianship* **10**, 128–133.

Bunge, C. (1987). Stress in the library. *Library Journal* **112**, 47–51.

Bunge, C. (1993). Vision and values: Touchstones in times of change. In *Rethinking Reference in Academic Libraries: The Proceedings and Process of Library Solutions Institute No. 2* (A. Lipow, ed.), pp. 33–35. Library Solutions Press, Berkeley.

Butcher, K. S., and Kinch, M. P. (1990). Who calls the shots? The politics of reference reorganization. *Journal of Academic Librarianship* **16**, 280–284.

Campbell, J. D. (1992). Shaking the conceptual foundations of reference: A perspective. *Reference Services Review* **20**, 29–35.

Campbell, J. D. (1993). In search of new foundations for reference. In *Rethinking Reference in Academic Libraries: The Proceedings and Process of Library Solutions Institute No. 2* (A. Lipow, ed.), pp. 3–14. Library Solutions Press, Berkeley.

Caputo, J. S. (1991). *Stress and Burnout in Library Service*. Oryx Press, Phoenix.

Carande, R. (1992). *Automation in Library Reference Services: A Handbook*. Greenwood Press, Westport, Connecticut.

Cargill, J. (1992). The electronic reference desk: Reference service in an electronic world. *Library Administration & Management* **6**, 82–85.

Cargill, J., and Webb, G. (1988). *Managing Libraries in Transition*. Oryx Press, Phoenix.

Childers, T. (1987). The quality of reference: Still moot after 20 years. *Journal of Academic Librarianship* **13**, 73–74.

Childers, T. (1991). Scouting the perimeters of unobtrusive study of reference. In *Evaluation of Public Services and Public Services Personnel* (B. Allen, ed.), pp. 27–42. University of Illinois, Graduate School of Library and Information Science, Champaign.

Christensen, J. O., Benson, L. D., Butler, H. J., Hall, B. H., and Howard, D. H. (1989). An evaluation of reference desk service. *College & Research Libraries* **50**, 468–483.

Coder, A. (1993). Rethinking reference: New models and how to get there. *Hawaii Library Association Journal* **44**, 14–16.

Creth, S. D. (1991). Personnel realities in the university library of the future. In *The Future of the Academic Library. Proceedings of the Conference Held at the University of Wisconsin in September 1989* (E. P. Trani, ed.), pp. 45–62. Graduate School of Library and Information Science, University of Illinois, Champaign.

Crowley, T. (1985). Half-right reference: Is it true? *RQ* 25, 59–68.

Cummings, A. M., Witte, M. L., Bowen, W. G., Lazarus, L. O., and Ekman, R. H. (1992). *University Libraries and Scholarly Communication: A Study Prepared for the Andrew W. Mellon Foundation*. Association of Research Libraries, Washington, DC.

De Klerk, A., and Euster, J. R. (1989). Technology and organizational metamorphoses. *Library Trends* 37, 457–468.

DeDonato, R. (1991). How did we get here: Thoughts on the convergence of reference and technical services. *Reference Librarian* 34, 27–35.

Durrance, J. (1989). Reference success: Does the 55 percent rule tell the whole story? *Library Journal* 114, 31–36.

Dusenbury, C. (1984). Reference service: Software in the hardware age. In *Academic Libraries: Myths and Realities. Proceedings of the Third National Conference of the Association of College and Research Libraries* (S. C. Dodson and G. L. Menges, eds.), pp. 94–109. Association of College and Research Libraries, Chicago.

Elzy, C., Naurie, A., Lancaster, F. W., and Joseph, K. M. (1991). Evaluating reference service in a large academic library. *College & Research Libraries* 52, 454–465.

Estabrook, L., Bird, C., and Gilmore, F. L. (1990). Job satisfaction: Does automation make a difference? *Journal of Library Administration* 13, 175–194.

Euster, J. R., and Haikalis, P. D. (1984). A matrix model of organization for a university library public services division. In *Academic Libraries: Myths and Realities. Proceedings of the Third National Conference of the Association of College and Research Libraries* (S. C. Dodson and G. L. Menges, eds.), pp. 357–363. Association of College and Research Libraries, Chicago.

Ewing, M. K., and Hauptman, R., eds. (1992). *The Reference Librarian and Implications of Mediation.* (Reference Librarian, 37). Haworth Press, New York.

Ferriero, D. S., and Powers, K. A. (1982). Burnout at the reference desk. *RQ* 21, 274–279.

Fine, S. (1986). Technological innovation, diffusion and resistance: An historical perspective. *Journal of Library Administration* 7, 83–108.

Fisher, D. P. (1990). Are librarians burning out? *Journal of Librarianship* 22, 216–235.

Ford, B. J. (1986). Reference beyond (and without) the reference desk. In *Energies for Transition: Proceedings of the Fourth National Conference of the Association of College and Research Libraries* (D. Nitecki, ed.), pp. 179–181. Association of College and Research Libraries, Chicago.

Ford, B. J. (1988). Reference service: Past, present, and future. *College & Research Libraries News* 49, 578–582.

Fraley, R. A., and Katz, B., eds. (1988). *Finance, Budget, and Management for Reference Services.* (Reference Librarian, 19). Haworth Press, New York.

Freides, T. (1983). Current trends in academic libraries. *Library Trends* 31, 457–474.

Giesbrecht, W., and McCarthy, R. (1991). Staff resistance to library CD-ROM services. *CD-ROM Professional* 4, 34–38.

Goodyear, M. L. (1985). Are we losing control at the reference desk? A reexamination. *RQ* 25, 85–88.

Gorman, K. (1987). *Performance Evaluation in Reference Services.* (SPEC Kit, 139). Association of Research Libraries, Office of Management Studies, Washington, D.C.

Gorman, M. (1991). The academic library in the year 2001: Dream or nightmare or something in between? *Journal of Academic Librarianship* 17, 4–9.

Goudy, F. W. (1993). Academic libraries and the six percent solution: A twenty year financial overview. *Journal of Academic Librarianship* 19, 212–215.

Govan, J. F. (1991). Ascent or decline? Some thoughts on the future of academic libraries. In *The Future of the Academic Library. Proceedings of the Conference Held at the University of Wisconsin, September 1989* (E. P. Trani, ed.), pp. 24–44. Graduate School of Library and Information Science, University of Illinois, Champaign.

Green, S. (1876). Personal relations between librarians and readers. *Library Journal* **1**, 74–81.

Gunning, K. (1983). The impact of user education and computer searching programs on reference services. In *Reference Service: A Perspective* (S. H. Lee, ed.), pp. 79–88. Pierian Press, Ann Arbor, Michigan.

Gunning, K. (1984). An integrated model of library information service. In *Academic Libraries: Myths and Realities. Proceedings of the Third National Conference of the Association of College and Research Libraries*, pp. 93–96. Association of College and Research Libraries, Chicago.

Gunning, K. (1992). The intelligent reference information system: The effect on public services of implementing a CD-ROM LAN and expert system. *Library Administration & Management* **6**, 146–153.

Haack, M., Jones, J. W, and Roose, T. (1984). Occupational burnout among librarians. *Drexel Library Quarterly* **20**, 46–72.

Hale, M. L. (1991). Getting ready for tomorrow—or today. *Reference Services Review* **19**, 77–80.

Halldorsson, E. A., and Murfin, M. E. (1977). The performance of professionals and nonprofessionals in the reference interview. *College & Research Libraries* **38**, 385–395.

Hallman, C. N. (1990). Technology: Trigger for change in reference librarianship. *Journal of Academic Librarianship* **16**, 204–208.

Hammond, C. (1992). Information and research support services: The reference librarian and the information paraprofessional. *Reference Librarian* **37**, 91–104.

Hendrickson, L. (1983). Deskless reference services. *Catholic Library World* **55**, 81–84.

Hernon, P. (1987). Utility measures, not performance measures, for library reference service? *RQ* **27**, 449–459.

Hernon, P., and McClure, C. R. (1986). Unobtrusive reference testing: The 55 percent rule. *Library Journal* **111**, 37–41.

Hernon, P., and McClure, C. R. (1987a). *Unobtrusive Testing and Library Reference Service*. Ablex Publishing, Norwood, New Jersey.

Hernon, P., and McClure, C. R. (1987b). Library reference service: An unrecognized crisis: A symposium. *Journal of Academic Librarianship* **13**, 69–80.

Heterick, R. C., and Sanders, W. H. (1993). From plutocracy to pluralism: Managing the emerging technostructure. *EDUCOM Review* **28**, 22–26.

Hoffman, S. L. (1993). Who is a librarian? *Library Mosaics* **4**, 8–11.

Hults, P. (1992). Reference evaluation: An overview. *Reference Librarian* **38**, 141–150.

Johnson, G. (1993). *Managers, Matrix and Multiple Choice in an Organizational Structure*. Paper presented at California Academic Library Managers program, Transforming the Organization: Academic Libraries in the 1990s, Claremont, California, December 9.

Johnson, P. (1990). Matrix management: An organizational alternative for libraries. *Journal of Academic Librarianship* **16**, 222–229.

Johnson, P. (1991). *Automation and Organizational Change in Libraries*. G. K. Hall, Boston.

Katz, B., ed. (1984). *Evaluation of Reference Services*. (Reference Librarian, 11). Haworth Press, New York.

Kleiner, J. P. (1987). The configuration of reference in an electronic environment. *College & Research Libraries* **48**, 302–313.

Kreitz, P. A., and Ogden, A. (1990). Job responsibilities and job satisfaction at the University of California libraries. *College & Research Libraries* **51**, 297–312.

Kupersmith, J. (1992). Technostress and the reference librarian. *Reference Services Review* **20**, 7–14, 50.

Larsen, P. M. (1991). The climate of change: Library organizational structures, 1985–1990. *Reference Librarian* **34**, 79–93.

Lee, S. (1993). Organizational change in the Harvard College Library: A continued struggle for redefinition and renewal. *Journal of Academic Librarianship* **19**, 225–230.

Lewis, D. H. (1988). Inventing the electronic university. *College & Research Libraries* **49**, 291–304.

Lipow, A. G. (1992). Reorganization in reference departments: Summary of responses. LIBREF and LIBADMIN listservs. January 6. 212 lines.

Lipow, A. G. (1993a). Reorganization in reference departments: A summary of survey responses. In *Rethinking Reference in Academic Libraries: The Proceedings and Process of Library Solutions Institute No. 2* (A. Lipow, ed.), pp. 207–212. Library Solutions Press, Berkeley.

Lipow, A. G., ed. (1993b). *Rethinking Reference in Academic Libraries: The Proceedings and Process of Library Solutions Institute No. 2*. Library Solutions Press, Berkeley.

Lowell, G. (1993). *Lessons Learned in Yale's Technical Services Reorganization*. Paper presented at California Academic Library Managers program, Transforming the Organization: Academic Libraries in the 1990s, Claremont, California, December 9.

Lyman, P. (1991). The library of the (not-so-distant) future. *Change* **23**, 34–41.

Lynch, B. P., and Verdin, J. A. (1983). Job satisfaction in libraries: Relationships of the work itself, age, sex, occupational group, tenure, supervisory level, career, commitment, and library department. *Library Quarterly* **53**, 434–447.

Lynch, B. P., and Verdin, J. A. (1987). Job satisfaction in libraries: A replication. *Library Quarterly* **57**, 190–202.

Malinconico, M. (1992). Information's brave new world. *Library Journal* **117**, 36–40.

Marchant, M. P., and England, M. M. (1989). Changing management techniques as libraries automate. *Library Trends* **37**, 469–483.

Martell, C. R. (1983). *The Client-Centered Academic Library: An Organizational Model*. Greenwood Press, Westport, Connecticut.

Martell, C. R. (1984). A house divided: Public service realities in the 1980s. In *Academic Libraries: Myths and Realities. Proceedings of the Third National Conference of the Association of College and Research Libraries*, pp. 85–101. Association of College and Research Libraries, Chicago.

Martin, R. R. (1990). The paradox of public service: Where do we draw the line? *College & Research Libraries* **51**, 20–26.

Massey-Burzio, V. (1991). Education and experience: Or, the MLS is not enough. *Reference Services Review* **19**, 72–74.

Massey-Burzio, V. (1992). Reference encounters of a different kind: A symposium. *Journal of Academic Librarianship* **18**, 276–286.

Massey-Burzio, V. (1993). Rethinking the reference desk. In *Rethinking Reference in Academic Libraries: The Proceedings and Process of Library Solutions Institute No. 2* (A. Lipow, ed.), pp. 43–48. Library Solutions Press, Berkeley.

McClure, C. R. (1984). Output measures, unobtrusive testing, and assessing the quality of reference services. *Reference Librarian* **11**, 215–233.

McClure, C. R., and Hernon, P. (1983). *Improving the Quality of Reference Service for Government Publications*. American Library Association, Chicago.

McElderry, S. (1976). Readers and resources: Public services in academic and research libraries, 1876–1976. *College & Research Libraries* **37**, 408–420.

Miksa, F. (1989). The future of reference II: A paradigm of academic library organization. *College & Research Libraries News* **50**, 780–799.

Miller, C., and Rettig, J. (1985). Reference obsolescence. *RQ* **25**, 52–58.

Miller, W. (1984). What's wrong with reference: Coping with success and failure at the reference desk. *American Libraries*, **15**, 303–306, 321–322.

Miller, W., and Gratch, B. (1989). Making connections: Computerized reference services and people. *Library Trends* **37**, 387–401.

Murfin, M. E., and Bunge, C. (1988). Paraprofessionals at the reference desk. *Journal of Academic Librarianship* **14**, 10–14.

Nauratil, M. J. (1989). *The Alienated Librarian*. Greenwood Press, Westport, Connecticut.

Neville, S. H. (1981). Job stress and burnout: Occupational hazards for service staff. *College & Research Libraries* **42**, 242–247.

Nicklin, J. L. (1992). Rising costs and dwindling budgets force libraries to make damaging cuts in collections and service. *Chronicle of Higher Education* **38**, A1, A28–A30.

Nielsen, B. (1982). Teacher or intermediary: Alternative professional models in the information age. *College & Research Libraries* **43**, 183–191.

Oberg, L. R. (1992a). The emergence of the paraprofessional in academic libraries: Perceptions and realities. *College & Research Libraries* **53**, 99–112.

Oberg, L. R. (1992b). Response to Hammond: Paraprofessionals at the reference desk: The end of the debate. *Reference Librarian* **37**, 105–107.

Oberg, L. R. (1993a). Rethinking reference: Smashing icons at Berkeley. *College & Research Libraries News* **54**, 265–266.

Oberg, L. R. (1993b). Reference services in an on-line environment: Some implications for staffing. In *Rethinking Reference in Academic Libraries: The Proceedings and Process of Library Solutions Institute No. 2* (A. Lipow, ed.), pp. 71–76. Library Solutions Press, Berkeley.

Parmer, C. (1988). Paraprofessionals in the literature: A selective bibliography. *Journal of Education for Library and Information Science* **28**, 249–251.

Paster, A. L. (1991). Dual function librarianship: What makes it work? *Reference Librarian* **34**, 3–13.

Pierce, S. (1984). In pursuit of the possible: Evaluating reference services. *Reference Librarian* **11**, 9–21.

Plotnik, A. (1985). Half-right reference. *American Libraries* **16**, 277.

Powell, R. R. (1984). Reference effectiveness: A review of research. *Library and Information Science Research* **6**, 3–19.

Rawan, A. (1993). *Restructuring the Library to Meet a Changing Environment*. Paper presented at California Academic Library Managers program, Transforming the Organization: Academic Libraries in the 1990s, Claremont, California, December 9.

Rettig, J. (1984). The crisis in academic reference work. *Reference Services Review* **12**, 13–14.

Rettig, J. (1991). Can we get there from here? In *Evaluation of Public Services and Public Services Personnel* (B. Allen, ed.), pp. 3–26. University of Illinois, Graduate School of Library and Information Science, Champaign.

Rettig, J. (1992). Rethinking reference and adult services. *RQ* **31**, 463–466.

Rettig, J. (1993a). Rethinking reference and adult services: A preliminary report. *RQ* **32**, 310–314.

Rettig, J. (1993b). Academic reference service astride a fault line. *Wilson Library Bulletin* **68**, 53–56.

Rettig, J. (1993c). Islands in a sea of change. In *Rethinking Reference in Academic Libraries: The Proceedings and Process of Library Solutions Institute No. 2* (A. Lipow, ed.), pp. 77–84. Library Solutions Press, Berkeley.

Rettig, J. (1993d). To BI or not to BI? That is the question. In *Rethinking Reference in Academic Libraries: The Proceedings and Process of Library Solutions Institute No. 2* (A. Lipow, ed.), pp. 139–151. Library Solutions Press, Berkeley.

Ritch, A. (1991). Back to the future: From "Desk Set" to desklessness? *Reference Services Review* **19**, 74–76.

Rockman, I. (1991). Reference librarian of the future: Introduction. *Reference Services Review* **19**, 71–72.

Rothstein, S. (1955). *The Development of Reference Services through Academic Traditions, Public Library Practice and Special Librarianship.* Association of College Libraries, Chicago.

Rothstein, S. (1989). An unfinished history: A developmental analysis of reference services in American academic libraries. *Reference Librarian* **25/26**, 365–409.

Rubin, R. (1991). Evaluation of reference personnel. In *Evaluation of Public Services and Public Services Personnel* (B. Allen, ed.), pp. 147–165. University of Illinois, Graduate School of Library and Information Science, Champaign.

Schiller, A. R. (1965). Reference service: Instruction or information. *Library Quarterly* **35**, 52–60.

Shapiro, B. J. (1987). Trying to fix "What's wrong with reference." *Journal of Academic Librarianship* **13**, 286–291.

Simmons-Welburn, J. (1993). New technologies and reference services. *RQ* **33**, 16–19.

Smith, N. M., and Nelson, V. C. (1983). Burnout: A survey of academic reference librarians. *College & Research Libraries* **44**, 245–250.

Surprenant, T. T., and Perry-Holmes, C. (1985). The reference librarian of the future: A scenario. *RQ* **25**, 234–238.

Swan, J. (1993). The electronic straitjacket. *Library Journal* **118**, 41–44.

Swanson, P. (1984). Traditional models: Myths and realities. In *Academic Libraries: Myths and Realities. Proceedings of the Third National Conference of the Association of College and Research Libraries*, pp. 85–101. Association of College and Research Libraries, Chicago.

Tenopir, C. (1993). Choices for electronic reference. *Library Journal* **118**, 52–54.

Tenopir, C., and Neufang, R. (1992). The impact of electronic reference on reference librarians. *Online* **16**, 54–60.

Tomer, C. (1992). The effects of the recession on academic and public libraries. *Bowker Annual* (C. Barr, ed.), pp. 74–84. R. R. Bowker, New Providence, New Jersey.

Tyckoson, D. A. (1992). Wrong questions, wrong answers: Behavioral vs. factual evaluation of reference service. *Reference Librarian* **38**, 151–173.

Vavrek, B. (1974). Is there a current crisis in reference librarianship? *Pennsylvania Library Association Bulletin* **29**, 119–121.

Vavrek, B. (1978). When reference librarianship died: It began in Detroit. *RQ* **17**, 301–305.

Veaner, A. B. (1985a). 1985 to 1995: The next decade in academic librarianship, part I. *College & Research Libraries* **46**, 209–229.

Veaner, A. B. (1985b). 1985 to 1995: The next decade in academic librarianship, part II. *College & Research Libraries* **46**, 295–308.

Veaner, A. B. (1990) *Academic Librarianship in a Transformational Age: Program, Politics, and Personnel.* G. K. Hall, Boston.

Von Seggern, M. (1987). Assessment of reference services. *RQ* **26**, 487–496.

Wagers, R. (1978). American reference theory and the information dogma. *Journal of Library History* **13**, 265–281.

Werking, R. (1991). Collection growth and expenditures in academic libraries: A preliminary inquiry. *College & Research Libraries* **52**, 5–23.

Westbrook, L. (1989). *Qualitative Evaluation Methods for Reference Services: An Introductory Manual.* Office of Management Services, Association of Research Libraries, Washington, DC.

White, H. S. (1990a). Pseudo-libraries and semi-teachers, part I. *American Libraries* **21**, 103–106.

White, H. S. (1990b). Pseudo-libraries and semi-teachers, part II. *American Libraries* **21**, 262–266.

Whitlatch, J. B. (1989). Unobtrusive studies and the quality of academic library reference services. *College & Research Libraries* **50**, 181–194.

Whitlatch, J. B. (1991). Automation and job satisfaction among reference librarians. *Computers in Libraries* **11**, 32–34.

Whitlatch, J. B. (1992). Reference services: Research methodologies for assessment and account-ability. *Reference Librarian* **38,** 9–19.

Williams, K. (1993). Total change at the University of Arizona. In *Rethinking Reference in Academic Libraries: The Proceedings and Process of Library Solutions Institute No. 2* (A. Lipow, ed.), pp. 67–69. Library Solutions Press, Berkeley.

Wilson, P. (1979). Librarians as teachers: The study of an organization fiction. *Library Quarterly* **49,** 146–162.

Woodsworth, A., et al. (1989). The model research library: Planning for the future. *Journal of Academic Librarianship* **15,** 132–138.

Wyer, J. I. (1930). *Reference Work: A Textbook for Students of Library Work and Librarians.* American Library Association, Chicago.

Young, W. F. (1985). Methods for evaluating reference desk performance. *RQ* **25,** 69–75.

Zink, S. D. (1990). Planning for the perils of CD-ROM. *Library Journal* **115,** 51–55.

Zink, S. D. (1991). Will librarians have a place in the information society? *Reference Services Review* **19,** 76–77.

The Information Needs of Children

Virginia A. Walter
Graduate School of Library and Information Science
University of California
Los Angeles, California 90024

I. Introduction

There is some evidence that the current paradigm for public library service is increasingly customer driven. The Public Library Association's planning and role-setting process, for example, is based on determining a particular service population's needs and designing a specific service plan to meet those needs (McClure et al., 1987). It rejects the notion of one model for library service that would apply in all situations and specifically cautions library administrators to avoid trying to be all things to all people. *Output Measures for Public Library Service to Children* (Walter, 1992) revisits the concepts of selecting library roles based on the needs of a community's *children* and shows how each of the 8 roles could be implemented for children.

This new emphasis on customer-driven, market-oriented library service assumes that librarians know how to analyze their communities and assess the needs of their users. There is a significant body of research to assist the adult services specialist.[1] Very little is known, however, about either the information needs of children in general or the techniques that could be used to determine the information needs of children in a particular community. This article briefly reviews the existing relevant literature and reports the findings of a research study designed to identify and categorize the informa-

[1]There have been too many good studies of adult information needs to list them all, but the pioneering work of Brenda Dervin, Ching-Chih Chen, and Peter Hernon should be mentioned. There have also been studies of the information needs of specific client groups, such as battered women (Roma M. Harris, "The Information Needs of Battered Women," *RQ*, Fall 1988, pp. 62–70) and adults who are learning word processing (Pierrette Bergeron and Michael S. Nilan, "Users' Information Needs in the Process of Learning Word-Processing: A User-based Approach Looking at Source Use," *The Canadian Journal of Information Science*, **16**, July 1991, pp. 13–27). More recently Cheryl Metoyer-Duran has identified information needs of adults in ethnolinguistic communities by studying the role of information gatekeepers (Cheryl Metoyer-Duran, *Gatekeepers in Ethnolinguistic Communities*, Norwood, New Jersey, Ablex, 1993).

tion needs of 10-year-old children in southern California. Implications of this
study for practice and research are discussed.

II. What Is Known about the Information Needs of Children?

A. Definitions

There is no knowledge base at present that is specifically devoted to the
information needs of children. Some of the research on general or adult
information needs is helpful, however, in establishing definitions. Dervin
and Nilan (1986) surveyed the existing research on information needs and
concluded that it could be divided into two paradigms, traditional and alternative. In the traditional paradigm, information is seen as an objective commodity and users as processors of information. The focus tends to be on observable
behaviors and the use of information systems. In the alternative paradigm,
information is seen as socially constructed. In this view, people need information to make sense of specific situations and to solve specific problems. Its
focus is on the user, not the information system. Thus, Ching-Chih Chen
and Peter Hernon (1982) emphasize that an information need is more than
a question asked of an information provider. They begin by defining information broadly as "all knowledge, ideas, facts, data, and imaginative works of
mind which are communicated formally and/or informally in any format"
(p. 5). They then assert that an information need occurs whenever people find
themselves in situations that require some form of knowledge for resolution.

Dervin conceptualizes an information need as an impediment preventing
an individual from moving forward in cognitive time and space. The person
is faced with a gap that must be bridged by "asking questions, creating ideas,
and/or obtaining resources" (Dervin, 1989, p. 77). Such gaps do not occur
in the abstract but arise out of particular critical events and situations.

Andrew Green (1990) contributes to the discussion by distinguishing
among information needs, wants, and demands. His subjects are college
students, but his conclusions are applicable to children as well. He finds that
needs share certain defining elements. They are instrumental and purposeful
and, unlike wants, they are contestable. You cannot argue with a child who
says he *wants* a book about superheroes, but you can debate whether he *needs*
it. Needs are, not illogically, related to necessity. If the teacher says that a
child must bring in a book about black widow spiders in order to get an A
in class, then the child indeed *needs* a book about black widow spiders. Without
it, she cannot get an A. Green finds that the element, however, that most
clearly distinguishes a need from a want or a demand is that there is no
necessary self-awareness of a need. People frequently need things without

being aware of the need (Green, 1990, pp. 65–67). This is a particularly important aspect of children's information needs. With their more limited experience of the world, children lack the frame of reference to articulate many of their most pressing information needs. Adults must articulate those needs for them.

B. Methods for Determining Information Needs

The Librarian's Thesaurus defines information need as "that need which library services or materials are intended to satisfy" (Soper, 1990, p. 2). The author further explains that community analysis is the method used by librarians to identify characteristics of a target population and infer what library services and information would be most appropriate for them. She specifies techniques that are used in community analysis, such as observing environmental characteristics, studying demographics, observing patterns of library use, and interviewing key informants (Soper, 1990, 29).

Roger Greer and Martha Hale (1982) have been strong advocates for community analysis as the basis for determining a library's role. Their methodology involves data collection and analysis from four perspectives: demographics, community organizations, service- and product-providing agencies, and life-styles. Each of these perspectives can be tailored to look specifically at children in a community. Census and school data give demographic information about children. Children belong to community organizations such as 4H, Camp Fire, and Boy Scouts. It is relatively easy to identify agencies that provide services to children and families, such as child care and recreation centers. One can also determine agencies and institutions that provide products of interest to children, such as skateboards and baseball cards. Life-styles can be deduced by observation, interviews, or focus groups that tease out the answer to questions such as What is life like for children here? Are the streets safe? How do children get around? What do children do after school? What are the reading scores? What do people think of the local schools?

It is not always clear from the literature on community analysis how to make the leap from knowledge about the community to knowledge about people's information needs. Assume that one has learned from community analysis that 38% of the residents of a particular community are under the age of 14, that the children are overwhelmingly African-American and poor, that reading scores are going up, that crime and personal safety are major issues, that social services are abundant but poorly coordinated, and that organized recreational opportunities are lacking. What can one deduce about the information needs of children and their caregivers in this community? Some experts claim that only a needs assessment focused on individuals can answer that question.

Brenda Dervin's sense-making methodology is one of the most widely adopted techniques for conducting such needs assessments. Through timeline interviews, the researcher probes the individual's efforts to acquire information needed to bridge a cognitive gap in a particular critical incident (Dervin, 1983, 1989). Variants of the sense-making technique have been used extensively by Dervin and others to assess information needs in a variety of settings.

Robert Grover (1993) has presented a conceptual model for diagnosing information needs in the context of a school library media program. He proposes a two-stage process: systematic analysis of both the school and the community followed by one-on-one interaction with a user at the point when he or she has decided to seek information, normally the reference interview. He asserts that the reference interview can become a vehicle for diagnosing information need by applying knowledge of information psychology, how individuals seek, acquire, organize, process, utilize, and store information. He suggests that practitioners draw from many disciplines to create their usable information psychology theory base—role theory, cognitive theory, communication theory, and so on. Grover's model is useful for detailing the complexity of the information environment in which young users are placed and for suggesting the interdisciplinary tools available to information practitioners for understanding that environment, but it falls short of providing specific needs assessment techniques.

C. Research on Children's Information-Seeking Behavior

There has been some research on children's information-seeking behavior that sheds light on the needs that presumably stimulate the behavior. Carol Kuhlthau's work is perhaps the most developed in this area. She has conceptualized the relationship of information-seeking behavior to stages of cognitive and affective development. Although her research has focused on adolescents, it shows how constructivist theory, in particular, can illuminate our understanding of information seekers' behavior. Of particular interest to understanding needs is her explication of the uncertainty principle as a major aspect of what she calls the information search process (Kuhlthau 1993). She has demonstrated how uncertainty about defining or articulating an information need can cloud the initiation of the search process. Children are likely to experience particular difficulty in formulating their information needs and are more likely to experience unmet needs.

A small study from New Zealand highlighted the difficulty children have formulating search strategies even when the object of the search was predetermined. The researchers used intensive qualitative techniques to analyze sixth graders' efforts to find specific information about birds in their school library to satisfy a class assignment. The researchers found that the children did not have an adequate knowledge base to allow them to narrow and broaden their search strategy appropriately. In addition, the children had difficulty both finding and interpreting information about books in the catalog and locating specific books on the shelves (Moore and St. George, 1991). Given the difficulties that these children had when the information object was given them, imagine the obstacles that exist when children must also articulate the original information need.

The Science Library Catalog Project is a long-term research study being conducted at UCLA to investigate a variety of issues related to children and information retrieval in electronic environments (Borgman et al., 1990; Walter and Borgman, 1991). Among the findings from this research relevant to information needs is that just as recognition memory develops before recall memory, children are more likely to be able to *recognize* a search term that is relevant to their inquiry than to be able to generate an appropriate search term independently. This suggests that children would also have difficulty articulating an information need but might recognize one if it were suggested to them.

III. Research on Children's Information Needs in Southern California

A. The Conceptual Framework

The study reported here was conceptualized as falling into the alternative paradigm described by Dervin and Nilan (1986) and owes much to Green's clarification of information needs (1990). It assumes that children have information needs that, if met, would enable them to solve problems and resolve particular situations. It assumes that children are frequently unaware of these needs.

A further assumption of the study is that while children are frequently unaware of their information needs, significant adults in the lives of children minister to the information needs that *they* perceive to be important. Children are seen in this society as developing human beings in need of socialization and education. Frederick Elkin and Gerald Handel (1978) define childhood socialization as "the process by which we learn the ways of a given society or social group so that we can function within it" (p. 4). They go on to explain that many adults contribute to this process, both informally and formally. Much of this education takes the form of providing information.

Examples of adult information providers in children's lives include parents, teachers, nurses and other health professionals, coaches, ministers, child care workers, social workers, and police officers, as well as librarians. These adults are, with differing degrees of overt intentionality, inferring information needs in children and trying to meet them. Thus, a teacher will perceive that children need to have more information about world geography and will develop lesson plans to meet that need. Police officers will see a need to provide children with information about the dangers of addictive drugs or the alternatives to gangs. Nurses see that children need to have information about risky behavior that could cause AIDS. Ministers may find that children need to have information about ethics or morals. Parents may identify a need in their children for practical information about earthquake preparedness or bicycle safety. A soccer coach may see the need to impart both concrete information about the rules of the game and more abstract information and values relating to fairness and competition.

What distinguishes these information needs from the conventional wisdom about adult information needs is that all are imposed on children by others. Children surely have self-identified information needs and wants, but much of the information that is provided to them is information they never asked for. Children also receive information from sources other than well-meaning adults. Television and peers are the two most salient. When television programmers aim to inform rather than entertain children, they do not ask children what they want to know but rather decide independently, sometimes based on expert consultations, what it is appropriate for them to know. Other children are probably the most frequently sought source of information by children, but they do not ordinarily cast themselves in the role of information providers.

This study seeks to create a cohesive model of children's information needs as identified by adults who have the responsibility for educating, socializing, and caring for children in various capacities, by adults who also function as information providers to children.

Recognizing that children's information needs will change as they develop, this study looks at children at a particular stage in their development, at the time when they are 10 years old. At 10, children are in the exciting developmental stage that Piaget termed concrete operational (Siegler, 1991). Their thought processes are well developed, and they are particularly receptive to information that will give them mastery over an uncertain world. They are capable of learning critical thinking skills that will help them evaluate information.

The study also draws from the ecological perspective of such researchers as James Garbarino and his colleagues (1989) who integrate variables about the child's place in the social world with Piagetian stage theories. These theories help us to understand the differences, for example, in the information needs of a 10-year-old Chicano boy in east Los Angeles and a 10-year-old Jewish girl from a wealthy Connecticut bedroom community.

Finally, the study is informed by social construction theory in its various manifestations. The researcher assumes, like Peter Berger and Thomas Luckmann (1966), that all social reality, not just information, is socially constructed. It assumes that childhood is a fluid social construction and that much of the purposeful activity of childhood is directed at making sense of that social world. As Jerome Bruner and Helen Haste (1987) explain, "through such social life, the child acquires a framework for interpreting experience, and learns how to negotiate meaning in a manner congruent with the requirements of culture. 'Making sense' is a social process; it is an activity that is always situated within a cultural and historical context (p. 1)."

B. The Target Population

In order to account for cultural and social variables, the research was conducted in two different southern California counties, Los Angeles and Santa Barbara. There are 2,326,110 young people under the age of 18 in Los Angeles County.[2] They are ethnically diverse; 27% are Anglo, 50% are Latino, 11% are African-American, and 11% are Asian-American and other. A study by the advocacy organization Children Now (1993) shows that children in Los Angeles County rank worse than the California average on 9 out of 12 benchmarks of children's well-being: eighth-grade achievement scores, high school dropouts, infant mortality, health checkups for needy children, violent crime, births to teens, preventable teen deaths due to homicide, child support payments, and children living in poverty.

Santa Barbara County is less densly populated; there are only 85,887 people under the age of 18 living there. Although it is also ethnically diverse, it is less so than Los Angeles County; 52% of the children are Anglo; 40% Latino; 3% African-American; and 5% Asian-American and other. In contrast to Los Angeles children, Children Now finds that Santa Barbara children are doing better than the California average in all but two of the benchmarks: late or no prenatal care and child abuse reports.

C. The Methodology

Because of the underlying assumption that children's information needs are largely determined and supplied by adults, the decision was made to collect data from adults rather than children. The goal was to obtain rich, qualitative data that would lend itself to deep analysis. This data was collected, therefore, through lengthy interviews with key informants in the two counties. Adults who work with children in a variety of capacities were identified in both locations. Efforts were made to contact people who reflected the ethnic diversity of the child populations. Parents were excluded but will be targeted in a follow-up study. A total of 25 key informants were finally interviewed, 15 in Los Angeles County and 10 in Santa Barbara County. The researchers

[2]All demographic data is from *The Children Now County Data Book 1993: Facts for Community Action* (Oakland, California, Children Now).

tried to find parallel informants in both settings (i.e., a school nurse from both communities). This was largely, but not completely, successful. Although the informants in Santa Barbara County were all from the city of Santa Barbara and may have been disproportionately involved in providing services to less affluent children, the informants from Los Angeles County reflected economic and geographic diversity, as well as cultural diversity. They were drawn from many different parts of Los Angeles County—the affluent Westside, Santa Monica, the South-Central ghettos and barrios, Chinatown, and Echo Park. Table I summarizes the key informants in both counties.

Each informant was interviewed by the principal investigator; in most cases, a research assistant was also present for the interview. A standard

Table I Summary of Key Informants

Title or profession	Gender	Ethnicity	County
Child care provider	Female	Asian	L.A.
Child care administrator	Female	African-American	L.A.
Child care administrator	Female	Latino	S.B.
Children's librarian	Female	Latino	L.A.
Children's librarian	Female	Anglo	S.B.
Classroom teacher	Female	Anglo	L.A.
Community organizer	Male	Latino	S.B.
4H administrator	Male	Anglo	S.B.
Girl Scout leader	Female	Anglo	L.A.
Minister	Male	Anglo	L.A.
Police officer	Male	Anglo	S.B.
Police officer	Male	African-American	L.A.
Probation worker	Male	African-American	L.A.
Probation worker	Male	African-American	L.A.
Probation worker	Female	Anglo	L.A.
Probation worker	Female	African-American	L.A.
Recreation center director	Male	African-American	S.B.
Recreation center director	Male	Latino	L.A.
Soccer coach	Male	Anglo	L.A.
School administrator	Male	Latino	S.B.
School nurse	Female	Asian	L.A.
School nurse	Female	Anglo	S.B.
Social worker	Female	Latino	L.A.
Social worker	Female	Latino	S.B.
Social worker	Male	African-American	S.B.

open-ended interview protocol was used in each session. The following questions were asked.

1. In your area of expertise, what do you see as the primary information needs of children. In other words, what do you think children need to know or have information about in the area of health, the law, recreation, and so on?
2. Where and how do children find this information currently? How well are those information needs met? Who (if anyone) provides them with the information?
3. In your area of expertise, what are the major information gaps in children's lives? What information do they need that they are not getting?
4. Why does this gap occur? How could it best be filled? Who could best get this information to children?
5. Do you have any ideas about other information needs of children, outside of your particular area of specialty?
6. What could be done to improve the quality and quantity of information that California children receive? What are the barriers to kids getting the information that they need? How could these obstacles best be overcome?

The interviews were conducted over a period of 6 months, from June to December 1992. The interviews ranged from half an hour to 3 hours. The principal investigator and two research assistants took extensive notes and coded the notes for recurring themes. They shared their understanding of what they had heard and validated their interpretations of what they had heard by independent analyses, which were brought together and synthesized by the principal investigator. Information needs that were identified by two or more informants were separated and grouped with like information needs and relative weights were assigned based on frequency and intensity of references to it by the informants. The result was a hierarchical model of children's information needs.

D. The Findings

1. There Is a Hierarchy of Children's Information Needs

As the data were analyzed, it became clear that some needs were mentioned and given more importance than others. A hierarchy of children's information needs began to emerge that resembled in remarkable ways Abraham Maslow's familiar model of human needs.

Self-actualization
Esteem

Love and belonging
Safety
Physiological needs[3]

The model of children's information needs can be summarized as follows. Note that some broad categories of information need are placed at more than one level of the hierarchy; this reflects different dimensions or functions of the need in question.

Self-actualization: Formal education or curriculum needs, leisure activities, ethics and values
Esteem: Multicultural awareness, emotional awareness, social system knowledge (legal, economic, etc.), sex education, ethics and values
Love and belonging: Multicultural awareness, emotional awareness, leisure activities, interpersonal skills, ethics and values, sex education
Safety: Crime avoidance, traffic rules, emergency procedures, basic literacy, sex education
Physiological: Personal hygiene; nutrition; general health issues; AIDS prevention; drug, tobacco, and alcohol abuse; child abuse; sex education

What is significant for understanding the model is that the adult informants gave the greatest stress to the items at the lower rungs of the hierarchy. The following summary indicates the number of times that broad subject areas at different levels of the hierarchy were mentioned and gives a quote or two to impart a flavor of the concern and a sense of the context in which it was raised. Sex education, ethics and values, and multicultural awareness, which are listed at different levels of the hierarchy, are discussed as separate topics.

Physiological and safety needs were the two categories of needs mentioned most often and given the most stress in terms of their importance for children. AIDS, for example, was mentioned as a critical information need by 12 of the 25 informants. A school nurse from Santa Barbara pointed out, "They need to know about the consequences of risky behavior before their hormones take over; then it's too late; they won't hear it anymore." The 4H administrator said, "They don't ask about AIDS, but they're curious. They heard about Magic Johnson, and it freaked them out." A day care administrator said, "They need straight facts in terms they can understand."
Ten adults talked about the need for realistic information about gangs, drugs, alcohol, and tobacco. All the probation and police officers pinpointed needs in this area, of course. One probation officer said, "The older kids are using the little ones to commit crimes because they know they can escape

---

[3]Maslow's hierarchy of needs has been reprinted in hundreds of psychology and management texts, but its original explication can be found in Abraham H. Maslow, *Motivation and Personality*, 2d ed. (New York, Harper & Row, 1970).

the justice system. We have to help the young ones resist this, to see the negative consequences of what they're doing. There is so much hype from the media about the commercial goodies that the kids can't afford. We have to help them see alternatives." Another pointed out, "Ten-year-olds don't have any idea how the justice system works, what happens when you're arrested, come to trial and go to jail. They need that information." A police officer said, "Kids want truthful, frank answers about drugs. They've been lied to."

Eight adults talked about the need for children to know basic health and nutrition facts. A school nurse from the Chinatown area in Los Angeles talked about the immigrant children she serves whose parents are often unfamiliar with Western medicine or with the health care services that are available. "The children have to educate their parents," she said. "We have to teach the kids about everything from head lice to TB if we want the families to get the information." The Santa Barbara nurse said, "I've got kids who do the family meal planning, grocery shopping, and cooking. They've got to have some information about nutrition."

Information about household emergency procedures was mentioned by 10 adults. A child care administrator said, "We have 200 to 300 kids on our waiting list for afterschool care. They are all self-care kids right now. They need to know what to do when they're home alone, how to call 911, how to contact their parents at work."

At the third level of the hierarchy, love and belonging, information about effective interpersonal skills, was mentioned by 5 informants. The minister said, "It's one thing to try to teach the value of fair play; you've got to give them information about how to operationalize that." A probation officer said, "They need to know effective ways to resolve conflict, to say no and stay out of trouble." Three respondents talked about children's lack of understanding of their own emotions. A social worker who does a great deal of counseling observed, "They don't know how to recognize or label what they're feeling. They can't distinguish between anger, fear, and anxiety, so they just lash out."

Although many of the informants talked about children's need for self-esteem, few related this to specific information needs other than cultural awareness. One who did, however, was a child care administrator in Los Angeles, who said, "Children have questions that are raised by the media, like, 'How could I live like that?' Or, 'How do people get to be famous?' We need to give them realistic information about how the system works and how they can change the system."

One of the few specific information needs that could be placed at the self-actualization level was mentioned by a child care provider who works with poor Latino and Asian children in Los Angeles. "My kids need to experience beauty," she said. "They need to go to museums and concerts, learn how to play the piano, take ballet lessons. They are missing some of the essence of being human." One librarian also talked in terms that can be related to self-actualization. "Most just ask for homework materials. I know they're missing great literature that would enrich their lives, but they just won't read it."

The need for information about sex was mentioned in so many different contexts that it seemed to fall in all but the top rung of the hierarchy. At the level of physiological needs, the informants felt that children need to know enough about sex to prevent unwanted pregnancies, sexual abuse, and sexually transmitted diseases, including AIDS. Although it is uncommon for a 10-year-old to be sexually active, many will be exposed to risky behavior within the next few years, and there was much agreement that they need the information early, before sexual activity begins. The onset of puberty is beginning in some 10-year-olds, and many of the informants specified the need to know about such basic developmental occurrences as menstruation. One school nurse said that 10-year-olds often asked her questions that demonstrated tremendous ignorance about sex: Can boys have babies? Why don't boys have periods? Don't babies come out of belly buttons? Concerns about child abuse in particular led to placing sex education in the safety category of the hierarchy. There were many concerns raised about gender relations, and this aspect of sex education is included under love and belonging. Finally, 3 of the informants talked about the need for greater self-esteem, particularly in girls, as one aspect in preventing early pregnancies, and this accounts for placing sex education in the esteem level as well.

The interviews were conducted in the months immediately following the 1992 civic unrest in Los Angeles. It is not surprising that needs for multicultural awareness, sensitivity, and understanding were raised in multiple contexts. One community worker said, "Darker-skinned kids need cultural reinforcement. It's like they're invisible to mainstream society." There was widespread agreement that more cultural awareness and sensitivity was needed for children to get along in their increasingly diverse societies. The classroom teacher said, "There is unbelievable prejudice and ignorance. Some of my Chinese kids think black skin will rub off if you wash it, and I still hear black children on the playground chanting rhymes like, 'Chink chink Chinaman sitting on a fence.' You just keep plugging away at it and hoping that familiarity won't breed contempt."

The need for information about ethics and values was a thread that ran through many interviews. It is difficult to know where to categorize it. In many cases, it was an overarching theme or framework for the informant's remarks. It is not surprising that the minister was concerned with issues of ethics and values. He said, "Kids ask me religious questions. It was tough during the Gulf War. They wanted to know, How can people hate? How can people hurt people? Where is God? Why doesn't he stop it?" But many of the informants raised questions of values. The soccer coach, for example, was talking about children's needs for survival skills, knowing how to get along on the streets. Then he added, "Children don't have anyone at home on a regular basis to tell them what behaviors are inappropriate. They aren't learning right from wrong." One child care administrator said, "Who's talking to these kids, telling them what's right and wrong?" A probation officer said, "Children need to know the consequences of their behavior. They don't have a moral framework." A child care administrator said, "Children need information that will help them develop effective and morally appropriate coping skills."

2. There Are Multiple Providers of Information and Misinformation to Children

The informants identified many appropriate sources of information for children: parents, extended family members, teachers, helping professionals of all kinds. Many of these information providers do not have accurate information or the ability to communicate it effectively to children, however. New immigrant parents were mentioned repeatedly as lacking critical information that they would ordinarily be passing on to their children in a culture where they were more proficient with the language and institutions. Several informants pointed out that even information-literate parents often lack the time to communicate all the information that children need. In addition, some of the most critical information needs are sensitive and difficult for many parents to talk about with their children—sex being the most obvious. Schools seem to be stretched far beyond their capabilities to provide information, as more functions are assigned to them.

As a result, children receive a disproportionate amount of information from the media and peers. The informants agreed that much of the information from these sources was, in fact, misinformation. The child care administrator observed, "Television raises so many false hopes without giving children the tools to attain them." A police officer said, "They pick up most of what they know (about drugs) on the streets, and most of it's just plain wrong."

3. There Are Significant Unmet Information Needs of Children

Along with misinformation, the informants agreed that many information needs of children simply go unmet. The minister admitted, "Many questions probably go unanswered. Many kids don't even articulate the questions they have." A child care administrator said, "So many never get the information at all; that's part of the frustration." Both librarians agreed that they don't get asked the most basic questions in children's lives. "Maybe they're embarrassed to ask," said one. "Or they think we won't have the answers."

The most commonly mentioned unmet information needs were those clustered in the two lower rungs of the hierarchy: basic survival skills, emergency procedures, and basic health and sex information (including AIDS prevention).

4. There Are Identifiable Barriers to Meeting Children's Information Needs

The informants had many ideas about why children were not getting the information they need to lead healthy lives and develop according to their fullest potential. At one level, several argued that children's lack of information simply reflected the low status of children in society. A social worker said, "We haven't invested serious public money in children for years now." Cultural and language barriers were also mentioned frequently. Several spoke eloquently about the increasing complexity of society. One social worker said, "There is so much more that children need to know now than there was when we were kids. Their parents are overwhelmed; the social institutions are overwhelmed. It's no wonder the children are floundering." The 4H leader lamented the fragmentation of the service delivery system for children. "I try to keep informed about what's available for children," he said, "but agencies keep changing and going under and there's no coordination at all." The school administrator blamed the limited time that children spend with caring adults. "They're always with other kids or watching TV," he said.

Other obstacles to meeting children's information needs seem to be related more to the ineffectiveness of the information providers. A police officer said that adult communication styles were ineffective in getting important messages across: "It takes a while to establish rapport with kids. We tend to be too authoritarian, and that turns them off." One of the social workers agreed: "We should be identifying leaders among the kids and getting the information to *them*. Give them more responsibility. Make information-getting more hands-on; that's how kids really learn." A school nurse echoed this: "We've got to make information exciting, experiential. Media has numbed kids, made them stop asking questions. We've got to stimulate children to start asking questions again." Others suggested that we use media and information technology to stimulate children's interest. A police officer urged that information videos be produced, "the glitzier the better." The school administrator suggested using computer games to get important information across.

E. Discussion

It was interesting to discover how few of the respondents were accustomed to thinking about children in terms of information. As the interview progressed, many of them seemed to find this worldview helpful. One social worker mused, "I never thought before how much of the time what I am doing is giving kids information or how much time I spend looking for information in my job." It is also interesting how few of these professionals thought of the library as a source of information for themselves or the children they serve. Only the classroom teacher and the 4H leader mentioned the library as a potential resource for children. Two respondents specifically discounted the library. A probation worker said, "Don't expect kids to get this stuff from books and libraries. Books are way too passive." The minister said, "Forget the library. This isn't really about information; it's about relationships."

The pervasiveness of perceived unmet information needs at the most basic level of the hierarchy is particularly worrisome. Many of the information needs cited as being largely unfilled—health and sex education, basic survival skills, emergency procedures—are areas that conventional wisdom has assigned to parents to pass on to their children. School personnel confirmed that they felt pressure to try to teach these but they felt overwhelmed by the challenge. The classroom teacher said, "I have fifth graders who can't even read yet, much less find Peru or Saudi Arabia on a map. What's my job? Should I be focusing on basic academic skills and knowledge or trying to teach these children how to survive?"

It is possible that children have slipped into some adult roles without our noticing it or adequately preparing them for these roles. More children seem to be acting in consumer roles, for example. Several respondents talked about children doing the family grocery shopping for their families because their parents worked or felt uncomfortable with the language. Middle-class children often have significant amounts of money of their own to spend. A recent *Los Angeles Times* article reported that children between the ages of 4 and 12 spent $8.6 billion in 1991 and, unlike other customers in this recessionary era, their spending continues to increase (Stabiner, 1993).

Other respondents talked about the influence of television advertising on children and the need for children to know how to evaluate critically product claims. A police officer said, "So they all want Air Jordans just because they're on TV, and the older dudes are wearing them, and they look cool. So they put pressure on their mothers to buy these $60 shoes or they steal them or they run some drugs to get the money, and man, they're just tennis shoes? No tennis shoes are worth that much."

There was surprisingly little difference in the responses of professionals working with children in Los Angeles and in Santa Barbara. *All* children seem to be information poor. For children who are already at risk of not reaching their full potential and well-being because of poverty or other social factors, access to basic information could be a critical variable in their development. There are serious implications for policy and practice to be addressed.

IV. Implications

A. For Practice

Joan Durrance (1989) challenged the information profession to translate information needs into actual, meaningful library services. The model of children's information needs presented here has a number of implications for library practice. One is that children's librarians should focus more attention on providing information to parents and other caregivers, in the language and format that is most appropriate for them. Existing programs such as the partnership between the Association for Library Service to Children and Head Start are good exemplars.

Second, children's librarians should aggressively collect and disseminate information to children about basic survival skills. Relatively little of this information is found in traditional trade books. It is more likely to exist in pamphlets, magazines, and nonprint formats. Some of the most accurate and accessible information about AIDS for children, for example, is found not in books but in children's magazines and pamphlets, neither of which are systematically acquired, stored, indexed, or marketed as an information resource in the library. Some information might be delivered most effectively in hands-on programs where children could participate and practice putting the information to use.

Third, the traditional children's library emphases on storytelling and fiction reading should be recast consciously as vehicles for communicating information about cultural diversity and ethics and values. The cultural dimensions of sharing folklore are obvious, but we need to do even more to market the best novels for children, which so frequently treat moral and ethical issues with sensitivity and art. Perhaps children's librarians have been too exclusive. They need to recruit other professionals, parents, concerned citizens, and volunteers of all ages as partners in the promotion of storytelling and quality reading as an important source of critical cultural and ethical information for children.

Fourth, librarians need to broaden their approach to service delivery. It is apparent that many children can no longer come to public libraries during their off-school hours. Many participate in afterschool child care programs. Many are self-care children who are instructed to go straight home after school. The streets in even middle-class neighborhoods are frequently considered unsafe for unaccompanied children, particularly after the recent spate of highly publicized child molestation and murder cases, such as the Polly Klaas incident in northern California. Librarians must design delivery systems that get the information to the children rather than waiting for the children to come to the information.

Fifth, the methodology used to construct this model of children's information needs could be implemented as a community-based needs assessment by any librarian. By replicating the research described here, a librarian will acquire a useful network of child advocates as well as deep information about the condition of children in a particular community.

B. For Research

The model presented here needs further amplification and validation. The principal investigator is currently doing follow-up research with parents and with the subject domain of AIDS information. It would also be useful to replicate the study focusing on children at other ages: 2, 4, and 6 would be interesting points in children's development to target.

In addition, although this research specifically targeted adults as the most appropriate sources of data about children's information needs, it would be useful now to go on and apply Dervin's sense-making techniques with children, defining critical situations related to the areas of information need identified here. If nothing else, such research would give a sense of children's information "wants," which are also legitimate targets for library services.

V. Conclusion

This article has presented a model of the information needs of 10-year-old children in southern California that was developed through qualitative empirical research, the analysis of data from in-depth interviews with 25 professionals who work with children in a variety of capacities. The model is a hierarchical model, based on Maslow's hierarchy of needs. The research showed that the greatest degree of unmet need lay in the bottom two rungs of the five-tier hierarchy, at the physiological and safety levels.

Although the findings from this study have significant implications for the practice of children's librarianship, they also have disturbing implications for the conditions of children in our society. It is distressing to learn that the people who are responsible for providing critical services to children see that young people are so lacking in the information that they need to thrive. At the dawning of the great information age, policy specialists enthuse about the great electronic information highway. With the proliferation of computers in more classrooms and homes, many children will be ready to cruise the new electronic highways and byways with ease and delight. Hopefully, they will find information there that will enrich their lives. I worry, however, about the children whose most basic information needs are still unmet—their needs for information that will keep them safe and healthy. Will Internet provide a 9-year-old girl with the information she needs to escape from an abusive stepfather? Who is developing client servers for children who cannot read? Are there electronic hostels for children who need to stop over for awhile and steep themselves in information about other small and powerless people who have nevertheless slain dragons, climbed mountains, found true love, survived unspeakable horrors—and prevailed?

Acknowledgments

The research for this study was funded by a grant from the UCLA Academic Senate. The author wishes to acknowledge the contributions of her research assistants on the project, Olivia Flisher and Kyle Broenkow, both of whom were students at the Graduate School of Library and Information Science at the time.

References

Berger, P. L., and Luckmann, T. (1966). *The Social Construction of Reality: A Treatise on the Sociology of Knowledge.* Doubleday, New York.

Borgman, C. L. et al. (1990). Children's use of an interactive catalog of science materials. *Proceedings of the 53rd American Society for Information Science Annual Meeting,* **27,** 55–68.

Bruner, J., and Haste, H., eds. (1987). *Making Sense: The Child's Construction of the World.* Methuen, London.

Chen, C., and Hernon, P. (1982). *Information Seeking: Assessing and Anticipating User Needs.* Neal-Schuman, New York.

Dervin, B. (1983). *An Overview of Sense-Making Research: Concepts, Methods, and Results to Date.* Unpublished paper presented at the annual meeting of the International Communication Association, Dallas, TX.

Dervin, B. (1989). Audience as listener and learner, teacher and confidante: The sense-making approach. In *Public Communication Campaigns* (R. E. Rice and C. Whitney, eds.), pp. 67–85. Sage, Newbury Park, California.

Dervin, B., and Nilan, M. (1986). Information needs and uses. *Annual Review of Information Science and Technology* **21,** 3–33.

Durrance, J. C. (1989). Information needs: Old song, new tune. In *Rethinking the Library in the Information Age* (A. Mathews, ed.), pp. 159–177. U.S. Department of Education, Washington, DC.

Elkin, F., and Handel, G. (1978). *The Child and Society: The Process of Socialization.* 3d ed. Random House, New York.

Garbarino, J. et al. (1989). *What Children Can Tell Us: Eliciting, Interpreting, and Evaluating Information from Children.* Jossey-Bass, San Francisco.

Green, A. (1990). What do we mean by user needs? *British Journal of Academic Librarianship* **5**, 65–78.

Greer, R. C., and Hale, M. L. (1982). The community analysis process. In *Public Librarianship: A Reader* (J. Robbins-Carter, ed.), pp. 358–366. Libraries Unlimited, Littleton, Colorado.

Grover, R. (1993). A proposed model for diagnosing information needs. *School Library Media Quarterly*, **21**, 95–100.

Kuhlthau, C. (1993). *Seeking Meaning: A Process Approach to Library and Information Services.* Ablex, Norwood, New Jersey.

McClure, C. R., et al. (1987). *Planning and Role Setting for Public Libraries.* American Library Association, Chicago.

Moore, P. A., and St. George, A. (1991). Children as information seekers: The cognitive demands of books and library systems. *School Library Media Quarterly*, **19**, 161–168.

Siegler, R. S. (1991). *Children's Thinking*, 2d ed. Prentice Hall, Englewood Cliffs, New Jersey.

Soper, M. E. (1990). *The Librarian's Thesaurus: A Concise Guide to Library and Information Terms.* American Library Association, Chicago.

Stabiner, K. (1993, August 15). Get 'em while they're young. *Los Angeles Times Magazine*, 12–16, 38.

The Children Now County Data Book 1993: Facts for Community Action. (1993). Children Now, Oakland, California.

Walter, V. A. (1992). *Output Measures for Public Library Service to Children: A Manual of Standardized Procedures.* American Library Association, Chicago.

Walter, V. A., and Borgman, C. L. (1991). The science library catalog: A prototype information retrieval system for children. *Journal of Youth Services in Libraries*, **4**, 159–166.

Information Management Systems Planning: A Process for Health Science Libraries and Institutions

Elizabeth K. Eaton
Health Sciences Library
Tufts University
Boston, Massachusetts 02111

I. Introduction and Background

Today the concept of an information highway is headline news. The Vice President is its biggest promoter. Through the news media the readers are made increasingly aware of the ups and downs of the public and private sectors' struggle to both control and utilize this valuable resource. Standards, policies, and strategic planning for the information highway's use could direct the activity surrounding it and minimize the ongoing confusion. Strategic planning to manage information technology results in integration and inclusiveness, eliminating duplication of resources and fragmentation of effort.

This article discusses the academic health institutions' approach to information management and the derived benefits. Medical libraries have played a critical role in this information management process. Today's academic and public libraries face similar challenges and, hopefully, can apply methods and lessons here to their own changing environments.

The National Library of Medicine (NLM) in 1979 contracted with the Association of American Medical Colleges (AAMC) to study trends in biomedical information transfer and to assess related implications for health sciences libraries (Cooper, 1983). This contract culminated in Matheson and Cooper's paper, "Academic Information in the Academic Health Sciences Center: Roles for the Library in Information Management" (Matheson and Cooper, 1982), which examined the implications of changing information technology for faculty, students, and practitioners. Acknowledging the fiscal constraints, the authors urged academic health science centers to move more aggressively to exploit the potentials of this change. Specific strategies for strengthening the existing information systems were made. One suggestion described how a technologically sophisticated library system could play a new role in maintaining the preeminence of American medicine. They recommended that a strategically placed national agency, such as the NLM, act as a catalyst by connecting acdemic health science centers into a networked system. Referred to as the Matheson report, it became a blueprint for intramural and extramural NLM programs and principles of the report were incorporated into NLM planning and budget documents for fiscal year 1984/1985. In March 1983, NLM announced and received Request for Proposals (RFPs) to conduct institutionwide strategic planning for information resources management. Thus, the NLM formally began the Integrated Academic Information Management Systems (IAIMS) program, which "set out to catalyze a new, computer-supported information management environment in medical teaching and research institutions" (National Library of Medicine, 1989).

A Report to the NLM Board of Regents, January 1989, summarized the purposes of the IAIMS concept: "The goals of the IAIMS program are to foster the use of information technology to enhance the efficiency and effectiveness of the biomedical community, and to prepare medical libraries to discharge crucial and evolving functions in this new information-intensive environment" (National Library of Medicine, 1989).

The initial NLM contract posed questions and problems relating to organizational and individual responses to rapid advances in technology. During the 1970s, the first desktop personal computers and the decentralization of computer services provided evidence of the advances in high-speed computing. Independent of each other, computing and communications were improving at the annual rate of 25% during the 1970s and 1980s (Dertouzos, 1991). In the 1970s, computer services were shared among many users; in the 1980s, desktop productivity tools resulted in their decentralization. In the 1990s, computing power is mobile, and the world of information is electronically available. What at first was considered a luxury or novelty quickly became de rigueur (Tesler, 1991). In the 1970s, libraries began to automate their library information systems, including online public access catalogs (OPACs). A few OPACs available in the late 1970s were typically found on stand-alone computers or limited mainframe/dumb terminal link. Today most academic libraries are automated and now OPACs are accessible electronically. "Catalogs are coming online daily" (Rega, 1993), according to the *1993 OPAC Directory*, which listed 280 dial-in and Internet-accessible catalogs in the United States. Meanwhile, the scientific literature explosion continued. An estimated 25,000 biomedical journals today may reach 50,000 in 50 years (Lock, 1992). The number of full-text online sources has grown by 600% in the last 7 years; in 1985 online texts totaled 535 and numbered 3077 in 1992 (Orenstein, 1993; Tenopir and Berglund, 1992).

Recognizable technological changes in 1979 prompted leaders to urge planning. "Without a vision of the goal, and a concrete demonstration of feasibility, . . . fruitful change is difficult to initiate. . . . The environment must be receptive for a successful transplantation" (Matheson and Cooper, 1992, p. 22). "The library is the logical and necessary place to begin a process of planned change" (Matheson and Cooper, 1992, p. 45).

The Matheson report and the NLM's IAIMS program threw down the gauntlet to health science libraries. Those libraries that did not receive a formal challenge, either from granting agents or their own administrators, nevertheless saw the changes coming and felt the pressure.

Questions posed a decade ago regarding future scenarios and possible solutions are still being asked today. What impact does information technology have on institutions? What do academic institutions need to do? What role can libraries play? Once these scenarios are defined, how might they be accomplished?

This article addresses these and related questions through an examination of specific institutional IAIMS programs, which include strategic planning, prototype and model development, and implementation. The issues faced and the successes achieved may be applied to many institutions. The cultural, behavioral, and leadership requirements for a successful IAIMS may be inferred for successful problem solving in other areas (National Library of Medicine, 1989).

II. Information Technology in the Health Sciences—Historical Perspectives

IAIMS's and the AAMC's activities in the early 1980s did not happen coincidentally. The goal of integrating information management systems of health sciences libraries with those of medical schools and their teaching hospitals evolved from a shared environment and culture. These institutions had arrived at similar crossroads in this era of advancing technology. Often instigated by the library, changes occurred simultaneously in both the academic institutions and the teaching hospitals with whom the schools were physically and programmatically linked. Library automation, clinical and hospital automation, and computing in medicine were developing as fast as technology would allow.

A. Computer Applications in Libraries

A health science library survey of automated records management in the United States and Canada conducted in 1980 identified 8 online catalogs; 15 either batch or online automated circulation systems; and 20 systems that used their machine records to produce book or computer-output-microfiche (COM) catalogs. The survey was sent to all 139 libraries on the Houston Academy of Medicine–Texas Medical Center mailing list for the *Annual Statistics for Medical School Libraries in the United States and Canada, 1978–79* (Lyders, 1980). Of the 139 questionnaires sent, 93 usable responses were obtained from an overall return rate of 69% (Grefsheim et al., 1982).

In 1980, however, most library catalogs were still manual. This same survey showed that only 57 had any machine-readable records (50 in MARC or MARC-compatible format, 7 in other formats), and only 32 were actively engaged in converting some or all their records to machine-readable format (Ruxin and Hill, 1983).

Several conclusions about the automation process were drawn from the survey. First, the reported online automation developments were mostly the results of universitywide system developments, involving both the academic libraries and the health sciences libraries. Second, these automated medical libraries were successful only with the cooperation of the campus or medical center computer facility and its personnel to maintain and operate the system (Grefshein et al., 1982).

Early library automation brought together institutional departments that had operated separately with no history of cooperation. As found in the survey, the computing and communications departments, cozily centralized and in charge of all aspects, were being invited or requested to become partners in library automation. At Tufts University, for example, librarians were solely responsible for direct input of bibliographic records, which only they could input, delete, or edit. Computer Services was in charge of machine maintenance and operation and daily network delivery. Communicating with both the computing department and the library staff, a library systems director managed the workload, system updates, backups, and training. Without the cooperation of these two formerly disparate and separate departments and without computer-services support, universitywide library automation would not have progressed. These early library automation projects served in many instances as models for cooperative developments in their institutions.

Although only half the health sciences libraries had MARC records by 1980, all were engaged in online searching of databases. NLM had produced its first computerized *Index Medicus* in August 1964. A prototype online system called AIM-TWIX, based on the *Abridged Index Medicus*, covering the 100 most-referenced *Index Medicus* journals, was made available in 1970. Due to high demand, fully implemented MEDLINE (MEDLARS on-line) became available in October 1971. By using MEDLINE, health professionals, via computer terminals, gained access to citations to all the articles in biomedical journals indexed for *Index Medicus*. Including such fields as nursing and dentistry, the database covered approximately 3,000 biomedical journals (Mehnert and Leiter, 1988).

B. Computer Applications in Medicine

Medical problems have played a seminal role in developing computer logic. Medical informatics, a relatively new multidisciplinary academic field, attempts to provide the theoretic and scientific basis for the use of automated information systems in biomedicine. The field includes health practitioners, computer scientists, engineers, librarians and information scientists, and management personnel. In the 1980s, the initial practical demonstration of the power of the methods of informatics (to store and retrieve information, to compute quantities, and to control events) was already having a profound effect on health care affairs because of its focus on the fundamental processes of medical treatment and information (Lindberg and Schoolman, 1986). The National Library exerted strong leadership in developing computer applications for information transfer in medicine in response to the AAMC's Matheson report.

Clinical Information Systems and Hospital Information Systems

"The development of the microprocessor in the mid-1970s created a revolution in computing power that caused a dramatic increase in the ability to manage information with an overall reduction in cost. This advancement has allowed mankind to control information in the same way that the industrial revolution allowed it to harness machines" (McNeely, 1991, p. 533).

The rapid evolution of the microprocessor influenced the clinical laboratory. A clinical information system typically analyzes and displays the laboratory results. Clinical information systems (CIS) are defined as computer-supported applications with a relatively large and long-term database containing clinical data, which are used to assist in the management of patient care. The CIS is an application of information system technology (Blum, 1986).

Sometimes used to describe the larger CIS, the term *hospital information system* (HIS) is interchangeable with patient care systems, so-called because patient-care personnel input records. Basically, the CIS produces laboratory data and is one component of an HIS. The HIS definition is situational, as each institution defines its HIS in terms of results. At first, computer vendors concentrated on capturing data that could be used for Medicare cost reinbursement. As development progressed, HIS systems were designed to analyze total institutional patient care needs. Early on, this approach became hospital automation, networking or interfacing automated systems into a larger system and building interfaces between systems. Work continues today to build a better, more integrated HIS, pulling disparate systems together for synthesis and sharing of clinical laboratory and MEDICARE reports, for instance. Networking allows each functional division of a hospital to both choose and own the optimal information processing system, which is possible with the 1990s technology and data communication standards for operability (Korpman, 1991).

The typical clinical information system from 1950 to 1960 consisted of one or two log books supplied by manually transcribing worksheets. In the late 1950s, several new developments affected the evolution of clinical laboratories (Krieg, 1991).

1. The increase in third-party reimbursement reduced the need for physicians and patients to address the trade-offs of costs-versus-quality, which changed the view of the primary goals of a new generation of medical residents and students toward optimal patient care. More tests were ordered, thus increasing the laboratory workloads.

2. Automated analyzers were introduced, allowing a technician to produce 10 to 20 times more reportable results per hour than with the manual method. For example, Mount Sinai Hospital in New York did 260,000 tests in 1965; once an autoanalyzer (Sequential Multiple Analysis-Plus Computer) was installed, the chemistry department was doing 8,000 to 10,000 tests per day (Bronzino, 1982).

3. These events increased job opportunities in clinical pathology, clinical chemistry, clinical microbiology, transfusion medicine, laboratory medicine, and medical technology.

In the 1960s and 1970s, rapidly developing computer technology applications for science and technology automated previous routine clerical tasks. There existed a spirited debate regarding whether to computerize around dedicated laboratory minicomputers or to share the hospital's mainframe computers. Influenced by the 1971 Johnson report commissioned by the College of American Pathologists, which recommended dedicated laboratory computers, minicomputers became the choice method of laboratory computerization.

In the 1970s and 1980s, interest in laboratory computerization was high. Workshops sought comparisons across systems. In 1971, one of the first modern laboratory information systems by Laboratory Computing, Inc., (LCI) was based on the DEC PDP-12 minicomputer, which was soon superseded by the PDP-11 family. Use of these computers influenced the software; systems developers no longer were limited to assembly language. The high-level language FORTRAN was replaced by Massachusetts General Hospital Utility Multi-Programming System (MUMPS), a programming language permitting online modification without interruption of function. Programmers within a department were able to implement changes and additions. Another important development in the 1970s was the successful interfacing of the minicomputers' laboratory information system with HIS (Krieg, 1991).

Evolution of the laboratory systems continued into the 1990s. These systems became more complex, more cost effective, and more user friendly. Improvements in software made possible further networking and integration with HIS.

Although similar to those of the 1980s, the clinical information systems of today have applications that serve every area of the laboratory in an integrated way. They are beginning to employ relational database technology. Trends will be toward: (1) increased use of database technology for laboratory management and quality assurance; (2) further employment of microcomputers as workstations, LANs, or even as entire systems; (3) increasing use of decision-support systems (i.e., medical informatics); (4) adaptation of mass storage of data and images; (5) further implementation of such technology as bar codes, voice input, image analysis, and data manipulations; and (6) greater connectivity to the hospital information systems and physicians' office systems.

There are two basic models for clinical information systems. The first is for hospitals that have a limited number of patients, who are treated for longer periods of time and whose admissions require a great deal of information. The facility is typically large, with other functions included, such as a hotel, business office, and personnel. The second model is for the ambulatory care setting, such as an office practice or health maintenance organization. Here, there are more patients, seen for shorter periods, but needing long-term follow up and other nonmedical functions. Information processing costs are greater compared with other costs of the facility, just the opposite of the hospital model. Thus, the two types of clinical information systems differ in character (Blum, 1986).

The early HISs were targeted to reduce labor costs, which were shown to be one fourth of total hospital costs. It was speculated and later proved that automated processing could reduce labor costs (Blum, 1986). The ambulatory care centers emphasized an automated patient medical record system to keep the physician informed and to assist in the patient follow-up actions and reports. Several of the early HIS played an important role in the prototype evaluation period in the 1970s. The NLM's IAIMS programs supported these developments, emphasizing their contribution to medical informatics.

The HISs' scope varied. As more information systems were strung together, more services were added—not only CIS information but also radiology images. By 1988, 25% of daily production images were digital, replacing film; these digitized images could be accessed over networks using standardized output signals (Lodwick and Taaffe, 1988). About this time an HIS was thought of as an integrated system that included all information pertaining to clinical care. By this time most library systems and the major bibliographic database, MEDLINE, had been networked and were accessible online. Thus,

library services and access to such databases as MEDLINE were added to
the menus of information available on HIS or health campus networks.

We have to thank the microprocessor, the AAMC's seminal report, Nina
Matheson, who recognized how it all fits together, and NLM, which supported this concept philosophically and financially through its IAIMS programs and its research and development of MEDLINE. Medical informatics
now plays a key role in clinical decision making. To be fully effective, the
various systems must be integrated; NLM's IAIMS programs provide an
incentive to achieve the desired integration.

III. The National Library of Medicine's IAIMS Program

NLM's IAIMS program required an institution to follow three sequential
phases: (1) a planning phase of about 2 funded years, (2) a prototype phase
to explore and introduce technologies of about 3 years, and (3) a 5-year
implementation phase to introduce a networked and coordinated information
and communications program (National Library of Medicine, 1989). Because
there are well-documented programs, today we have a carefully recorded
history of the change process. The phases and the awards are shown in
Table I.

The IAIMS projects prompted institutions to address these questions.

What are the institutional policies regarding information technology? Who
is responsible, computer services, libraries, or other departments?

What distinguishes a leader in information technology? Are the leaders CEOs,
CIOs, library directors, or directors of computing?

Is there a common vision for both the schools and the hospitals? Is this vision
accepted and shared by administration and faculty or are they left to the
visionaries?

What fruitful changes are necessary?

Table I IAIMS Phases and Awards

Phase	Description	Award
2 years	Planning award	$250,000
3 years[a]	Model development	$1,200,000
5 years[a]	Full implementation	$750,000/annum

[a] Changed in 1993 to a two-tiered system. Phase II and III merged.

Is the environment receptive for a successful transplantation?
What has happened to technology diffusion or information diffusion in academic institutions?

The stated requirements for the NLM Phase I Planning Grants identify steps to create fruitful changes on an institutional basis. They are:

1. Preparation of an environmental forecast for the institution's next decade
2. Development of an institutional information policy
3. Identification or selection of leadership for planning of academic information management
4. Involvement of all sectors of the academic medical center including faculties, staff, and students
5. Specification of desired strategic outcomes
6. Establishment of the planning process, including goals and timetables (National Library of Medicine, 1986).

During the NLM Phase II Model Grant period, NLM made monies available for testing IAIMS-related concepts on a small-scale basis in the environment involving information related to the research, education, and/or patient-care mission of the institution. These were only granted if there existed a written institutionwide IAIMS strategic plan.

As stated in the *1986 NLM Fact Sheet*, only those health sciences institutions that had completed an IAIMS plan and could demonstrate examples of successful modeling of critical elements of their plan could request NLM assistance to proceed with full-scale implementation of Phase III (National Library of Medicine, 1986).

NLM expanded the initial IAIMS prototype programs by announcing a four-tiered grant application structure: (1) planning phase, (2) model development phase, (3) implementation phase, and (4) IAIMS-related research (National Library of Medicine, 1983). NLM announced and received RFPs from institutions to conduct institutionwide strategic planning for information resources management. These first awards went to Columbia University, Georgetown University, University of Maryland, and the University of Utah.

The AAMC followed up with complementary events: completion of the "Physicians for the Twenty-First Century, a Report by the Panel on General Professional Education of the Physician and College Preparation for Medicine (GPEP)"; a plan for a 4-day seminar, Information Management in the Academic Medical Center, scheduled for January 1985 (this 4-day seminar on information technology in academic medical centers has continued to draw new audiences annually); and plans for a symposium in March 1985, Medical Information Sciences and Medical Education (Cooper, 1984).

The 1984 GPEP report acknowledged the role of information science in preparing physicians for the twenty-first century. This report called for the development of the skills necessary "in the collection of information from and about patients, . . . in the identification and critical appraisal of relevant literature and clinical evidence, and in the continuation of effective learning." Recommendation 6 of its third conclusion encouraged the use of computers to help physicians retrieve information from the literature and analyze and correlate data about patients (Association of American Medical Colleges, 1984).

Currently medical education has been undergoing one of the most intense reassessments it has experienced in at least 25 years. Factors driving this reassessment include the 1984 GPEP report; the 1993 report, *Assessing Change in Medical Education: The Road to Implementation;* the growing body of knowledge required to practice medicine; and the health care reform movement.

A. IAIMS Awards

Through the end of 1991, NLM reviewed for funding 70 applications from 40 institutions. From these, 31 awards were made to 17 institutions and organizations: 16 planning grants, 10 model development grants (2 partially funded and 5 at a full-implementation funding level) (Lindberg, West, and Corn, 1992).

B. Changes to a Two-Tiered Program

In 1992, NLM adjusted the IAIMS Program to reflect experiences learned, to take advantage of accomplishment made, and to permit continued progress. This reflected the learning about designing and operating integrated information systems and the changed technologies. The factor that changed the most was the institutional information network, because by this time networks were part of institutional infrastructure and no longer required the support they had earlier. NLM, also, no longer saw the need for separate introduction and demonstration periods. Their findings were that institutions applying recently were more advanced at both the Phase I and Phase II levels. Given this, the program was redesigned into a two-phase support program (National Library of Medicine, 1993).

1. The first phase continued to support planning and initial systems operations in order to show institutional readiness for full IAIMS.
2. The second phase would be similar to previous support for full institutionwide implementation (Lindberg, West, and Corn, 1992).

Because of this change, only those institutions funded in the three-phase sequential IAIMS programs are considered as examples.

IV. First Four IAIMS Sites

As Wayne Peay, Director of the Health Sciences Library, the University of
Utah, states, "IAIMS encompasses an enormous range—from the minutiae
of data communications protocols to the staggering problems of intitutional
information policy" (Peay, Butter, and Dougherty, 1986).

A brief review of the initial four IAIMS Planning Grants recipients
and their accomplishment illustrates similarities and differences. Common
elements begin to appear (National Library of Medicine, 1987).

A. Columbia Presbyterian Medical Center (CPMC)

This institution received one of the initial Phase I Planning Grants. It went
on subsequently to receive Phase II and Phase III awards. A major factor in
the need for planning was a new facilities program. Their teaching hospital,
Presbyterian Hospital, began building a tertiary care hospital on the CPMC
campus and a new community hospital 2.5 miles north. At the same time
Columbia University was building a research park. Both projects increased
the demand for online remote access to hospital records, etc., and sharpened
the need to plan information systems that effectively satisfied this requirement. Similar to all academic medical centers, CPMC was seeking more
efficient ways of managing the ever-increasing volume of biomedical knowledge, trying to avoid unplanned growth of incompatible ad hoc systems and
to construct a curriculum that would enable health professions students to
learn to work with computers in an era in which automated data systems
were expected to increase exponentially.

The planning took 18 months and involved representatives of the community, both clinical and research faculty, librarians, administrators, and hospital personnel. This planning resulted in a strategic planning document. On
the strength of this document and coordinated campus efforts CPMC was
awarded both a model and implementation grant (Henrickson, Goldstein,
and Levy, 1986).

B. Georgetown University

Chosen in September 1983 Georgetown was one of the first sites to conduct
a strategic planning study leading to the design of an institutionwide IAIMS.
They, too, subsequently were awarded both Phase II and Phase III grants. In
the 2-year planning phase, Georgetown University Medical Center engaged in
three major activities: (1) a strategic planning process for IAIMS; (2) an
institution self-study, including an environmental forecast; and (3) a 10-year
implementation plan. Their overall goal was an IAIMS plan that would

improve information flow by linking the medical center in an electronic network of distributed systems. Outcome was a timely strategic plan with two major goals: (1) to improve academic information management and the transfer of biomedical information and (2) to create a center of excellence and prototype IAIMS to serve as a national resource and example for other academic health science centers. NLM awarded them a further 3-year model IAIMS grant in September 1985, which provided seed funds for the pilot phase, with Georgetown contributing resources. Georgetown's IAIMS chose five projects that concentrated on supporting changes in health professional education and clinical care. These were to build a communication network system; launch a neurosciences model experiment to automate the department of neurology using a cluster approach for internal and external transfer of information; enhance clinical problem solving at all levels; enhance communication among executives of the medical center units; and provide training and education resources through an academic information management center to be based in the medical library. A focal point in the Georgetown IAIMS, the library emerged as an essential component of IAIMS. All the projects received continuing support from Georgetown. Having achieved success in the second phase, Georgetown received a third-phase full 5-year implementation grant (Broering, 1986).

C. University of Maryland at Baltimore (UMAB)

Distinguished by its breadth, this IAIMS prototype proposal involved all the schools and their affiliations with the University of Maryland Medical Center. Its objective was to integrate all the major functional areas on campus, including research, clinical care, education, and administration. UMAB used the IAIMS initiative as the catalyst for. a campuswide strategic planning process. Although the proposal was initially intended to produce consensus when reviewed by representatives of all the campus schools and medical institutions, it was approved as a policy document for the campus as a whole. The implementation of the strategic plan involved the enhancement of the core facilities to support a distributed system. In the first phase they created a campus network, providing an information utility environment, including decision support systems (DSS) and applications software that enabled users to respond interactively to nonrepetitive problems. The network also provided campuswide access to the Health Sciences Library DSS.

The Hypertension Pilot or "vertical slice" served as the Phase II prototype. The Hypertension Center, an interdisciplinary center without walls designed to coordinate numerous hypertension-related activities, involved resources across the spectrum of departments and schools and cut across administration, education, clinical services, and research. Building a database of greater than 100,000 subjects would demonstrate the need for rapid electronic information transfer, challenges of large-scale databases, and the coupling of many different computers; it would allow rapid communication between clinicians, researchers, students, and administration in diverse locations and provide rapid, continued access to the health sciences library resources. It would serve as a working model for campuswide database needs (Wilson et al., 1986).

D. The University of Utah (Phases I and II)

This university saw the potentials of the Matheson report and realized that IAIMS offered an institutional rather than a library framework for assertive long-range planning and management of information resources. The library proposed to the administration the value of an integrated library system (ILS). The deans endorsed the project and appointed an ILS Planning Committee, which included representatives from the School of Medicine, College of Nursing, College of Pharmacy, College of Health, and University Hospital. In response to the March NLM RFP, the ILS Planning Committee became the IAIMS Task Force (Peay et al., 1986). The fortuitous appointment of Dr. Homer R. Warner, Chair of the Department of Medical Informatics, as the special assistant and principal investigator for the proposed IAIMS project satisfied another important attribute of a Phase II IAIMS program, which was that medical information sciences be organized as an academic department of the school of medicine (Matheson and Cooper, 1982).

Dr. Warner designed the Health Evaluation through Logical Processing (HELP) system, a comprehensive, hospital-based computer system for acquiring medical information and implementing medical logic. It was the keystone of the IAIMS at Utah, serving as a real example of the importance of the IAIMS efforts, particularly as an administrative model for information management. Utah's strengths were the HELP system and a supportive vice president for health sciences. During the IAIMS planning process a series of self-studies, which included future scenarios written by task forces, which were initially thought of as intellectual exercises, became incorporated into the institutional plan. Utah was funded for the IAIMS Program Phase II (Peay et al., 1986).

V. 1986 IAIMS Awards and Common Elements

These four were the first. In 1986, NLM funded the next four IAIMS sites. They were Baylor College of Medicine, Harvard University, University of Cincinnati, and the Johns Hopkins University.

Johns Hopkins and Harvard received Phase I funding. The University of Cincinnati went through Phases I and II. Baylor extended IAIMS development into the third phase. At Baylor, Dr. G. Anthony Gory viewed the exploitation of advanced information technology as a key to increased organizational effectiveness. To succeed, he said, the institution must muster an impressive array of technologic and intellectual resources, and probably make significant organizational changes (Gory, 1990).

Among other institutions receiving both Phase I and Phase II funding were the American College of Obstetricians and Gynecologists, Washington, DC; the University of Pittsburgh; and the University of Michigan (the latter two were partially funded).

Duke University received a Phase II and III award. Faculty and staff at Duke University Medical Center (DUMC) had participated since 1969 in a series of plans for effective information management. "By the mid-1980s this combination of centralized and entrepreneurial efforts had resulted in the development of a set of independent systems which collectively provided a rich array of end user functions but without the advantages of integration" (Stead et al., 1993, p. 225). DUMC carried out a series of institutional planning efforts from 1983 to 1985 and concluded that the time was right to establish an IAIMS at DUMC. They developed a strategic plan for achieving IAIMS and obtained grant funds to test a model. Based on their model they revised their strategic plan in 1989. With that as the foundation they applied and received IAIMS funding for an implementation project in 1990 (Stead et al., 1993).

1. The impetus was a new building or program.
2. Institutions used the IAIMS initiative as a catalyst for campuswide strategic planning; the plan became institutional policy.
3. Almost always a medical information science was organized as an academic department, and its chair or chief became an active IAIMS participant.
4. The model phase was interdisciplinary, coordinating resources for administration, education, clinical care, and research.
5. Campuswide access to both library information services and clinical information systems existed. The library played a major role.
6. Today all sites have campuswide communication networks with Internet access.
7. Medical libraries played a key role in the integration process.

Looking more closely at the IAIMS process can illustrate how an institution begins to think organizationally, what is involved, and how to move from thinking to action. The following examination of Tufts University's IAIMS activity illustrates these points.

VI. Tufts University IAIMS Planning Grant

Tufts University School of Medicine (TUSM) received a planning grant in 1990. The events leading to this grant can best be understood by knowing some brief background information about Tufts.

Tufts University Health Sciences Campus is a confederation of separately administered institutions, which have cooperative arrangements to fulfill the shared missions of patient care, education, and research. It includes the following major units: Tufts University's four health sciences schools (medicine, dentistry, veterinary medicine, and the Sackler School of Biomedical Sciences) and the U.S. Department of Agriculture Human Nutrition Research Center on Aging. The Health Sciences institutions constitute the Boston campus of Tufts University, which has a main campus for the arts and sciences and engineering in Medford, Massachusetts, and a third campus for the veterinary school's clinical teaching facilities.

Affiliated with TUSM, the New England Medical Center includes the New England Medical Center Hospital, a Boston-based 500-bed, specialized diagnostic and referral center, providing inpatient and outpatient care, research institutes, and other health service organizations. New construction, with a 1994 completion date, will add another 200 inpatient beds. Affiliated with these institutions but geographically remote are an outstanding and diverse group of thirty-plus clinical care organizations. Together TUSM and NEMC are called the Tufts Health Science Campus (THSC).

The mission of the THSC IAIMS program is to provide the members of this confederation comprehensive and integrated access to local and national biomedical information, which will enhance each constituents' ability to fulfill its respective mission vis à vis patient care, teaching, and research. Further, as high-quality research is the driving force behind improvements to patient care and education, the IAIMS mission is to manage biomedical information in a manner that supports, enhances, and facilitates research (Tufts University, 1993).

The planning impetus began with construction for the Tufts Health Sciences Education Building, a new teaching facility. The Planning Committee set up program concepts and project criteria. In addition, another committee, the Clinical Library Sites Committee, looked at new concepts of publishing. Representation on the Planning Committee was broad, reaching from the Dean of Medicine to faculty and students, headed by the Associate Provost for Sponsored Research and the University Librarian. The New England Medical Center; the Schools of Medicine, Veterinary Medicine, and Dental Medicine; the Sackler School of Biomedical Graduate Sciences; and their library were to share the facility. The Educational Media Center, a joint NEMC and Tufts service, was to occupy a space near the first-floor auditoriums.

In 1983, the Health Sciences Library, after having an acting director for a year, hired a new director. Shortly thereafter, in fall 1983, the groundbreaking ceremony was held for the new education building. The plans for the physical structure and the intellectual arrangement were finalized. For the next 3 years, the library staff designed and organized the move from a 12,000 square foot facility, with 50% of the collection in off-campus storage, to a new 44,000 square-foot space, which would house the entire collection on four floors. In 1985 the faculty, students, and staff began to occupy the recently named Arthur M. Sackler Center for Health Communication. Its opening ceremony featured a United States-China live teleconference.

In 1987, a year after the building was fully occupied, the University Provost named an Associate Provost for Information Technology (APT) to oversee the information technology development. A consummate consultant, the APT asked relevant questions, made connections previously unnoted between individuals sharing similar interests, and in general was a marvelous person to whom one could both listen and talk. He understood the need to focus on the accomplishment of the missions of education, research, and clinical care. It was under his guidance that the Tufts Health Sciences Education Building Committee and the Clinical Library Sites Committee were reorganized into the Communication and Computing Committee (CCC) for the Health Sciences Campus. The purpose of the committee was to recommend to the Council of Health Sciences Deans plans and policies for the development and operation of institutional computing and communication resources and to provide ongoing oversight of these resources. At this time, network plans were designed to connect the affiliated hospitals including NEMC, Tufts' closest and largest teaching hospital. Under the APT's tenure the library leadership was also reorganized. Instead of a University Librarian, the directors of the four major Tufts libraries: Veterinary, Arts and Sciences, Health Sciences, and the Ginn Library at the Fletcher School of Law and Diplomacy, formed the University Library Council (ULC), the chair of which rotates among the directors. The University Systems Librarian was also included as a member. The ULC's responsibilities are strategic planning for library resources, including electronic databases; arranging and maintaining all librarywide contractual arrangements; overseeing the promotion process of Tufts librarians; and participating in consortium arrangements, including serving on the Boston Library Consortium's Board of Directors.

In 1988/1989, well aware of the IAIMS planning initiative and with the help of the CCC, the APT applied for the Phase I Planning Grant. It was approved with a high rating but not funded. A year later, however, NLM notified Tufts that funding was available. The APT's untimely death had left the grant without a principle investigator (PI). Because of her early participation in planning and developing technology support, the Health

Sciences Library Director was selected to head the IAIMS Planning Committee and to become the PI.

A. The Targeted Outcome: A Strategic Plan for the Health Sciences Campus

The process of developing a strategic plan began in earnest when Tufts received funding for the IAIMS Planning Grant. The new CCC formed a core group from its membership and designated them as the IAIMS Program Team, whose chair was the PI. Their specific responsibility was the day-to-day work necessary to formulate an Information Management Strategic Plan. This integrated planning team was principally responsible for the university and the hospital's decision to jointly plan and implement the campuswide network. The committee gained the cooperation of all those engaged at departmental and school levels in information technology projects and served a vital coordination function.

The IAIMS Planning Committee with the CCC produced two products during the first year, the first being a Health Sciences Campus Computing Resource Guide for faculty and students—a nuts-and-bolts outline of available computing services, courses, databases—and a description of how to utilize or receive training. Second, the CCC sponsored a day-long campus information fair, which demonstrated educational software and advanced computer technology. Many sites published an IAIMS newsletter. In lieu of its own publications, due to partial and thus limited funds, the committee published articles in campus newspapers and other campus releases.

Chosen to represent the widest institutional interests, the IAIMS Program Committee (IPC) members included the Associate Provost for Research, who had been chair of the early building planning committees; the chair of the Library and Information Resources Committee, who also shared a long history of involvement with information resources on the health sciences campus; the chair of the Department of Anatomy and Cellular Biology, formerly chair of CCC and developer of a model interactive video program for neuroscience; the vice president and chief information officer of NEMC; the director of Communication and Technical Services; an internationally known informatics researcher, who was professor of medicine and chief of the Department of Clinical Decision Making and Medical Information Sciences; the telecommunications director from Tufts Computing and Communications Services (TCCS); and the current chair of the Computer and Communication Resources Committee.

At their bimonthly meetings the committee set criteria and goals, conducted a self-study program to access the current state-of-the-art at the health sciences campus and set about defining their institutions.

B. Focus Group Method of Self-Study

To determine campus interest and expertise, the IPC members chose the Focus Group Method of self-study. This method consisted of selecting groups of participants who represented the four areas the NLM had identified as major areas of responsibilities for a health science campus: administration, research, clinical care, and education. The IPC Committee met 24 times with 16 different focus groups from April to October of the planning grant's first year. The list of groups included Clinical Pathology; Purchasing; Basic Science department managers; deans of schools of medicine, veterinary and dental science; clinical/research; educational media; the USDA's HNRC; and others. Focus group discussions were not restricted to the area represented by that group. For example, a research group was free to comment on administrative needs. Conversations at meetings were stimulated by a series of questions sent out prior to the meeting so that people could consider the issues and formulate their thinking in advance.

Data collected portrayed a vivid and consistent picture of the information management needs of the campus. Needs and problems recurred from group to group, which indicated a strong consensus. Emerging patterns of issues were then organized around major areas of need.

The following trends were observed in the focus groups, which came to be called by the rubrics of their reports:

Focus groups displayed a wide range of ability and expertise in computer usage.

Those whose primary role was administration raised issues regarding tracking and sharing of information between departments, as well as having to "move" this information.

Thus Functions of the Network referred to both online transmission of information and common network services.

Clinicians and researchers tended to be familiar with computers and networking. Already familiar with how a network could function, they were most concerned with how the network would perform, how it would be supported, its increased availability, and policies about its use.

These Network Descriptions included performance, availability, network management, and policies.

Researchers, deans, and other educators provided information for the sections called Curriculum Aides and Research Aides. The hospital clinicians described how a Clinical Information System should perform.

C. Results of the Focus Groups: Network Groups

From the focus groups and a literature review designed to identify other institutional members who had perhaps been missed, the IPC created network groups, a collection of individuals who shared common interests. More often than not these individuals, who had engaged in similar research on the same campus, had neither met each other nor, surprisingly, did they know of each others' research. For example, the NEMC Radiation Oncology Computer Bioengineer, a national expert on archiving clinical radiation images, first met the chairman of the Anatomy and Cellular Biology Department, whose research project included capturing and archiving clinical images for research and teaching, at a focus group meeting. These two people formed the core of the imaging network group and were designated project leaders of the image library project, which aimed to create a dynamic database comprised of a variety of clinical diagnostic and other digitized images, including two- and three-dimensional images.

The network groups had as their charge to define more closely the needs identified by the focus groups and to identify the Health Sciences Campus's strengths and deficits with respect to these needs. Although the network groups formed in the early stages of the writing of the strategic plan, it became obvious that the subjects they addressed could be considered the core of the strategic plan, provide fertile ideas for model developments, and be expanded to the implementation plan. These subjects or needs fell into categories that one could classify as definitions of the problems perceived and experienced by the users or customers.

Among the network groups named were Imaging, Administration, Clinical Care and Research, Curriculum, Curriculum Support, Affiliated Institutions, Library, Electronic Classroom, Network, and Standards. While the committee was performing the self-study, TCCS and ULC were simultaneously formulating their strategic plans. The ULC plan covered electronic resources and their availability, while the TCCS plan included campuswide resources, the campus network, budgets, and implementation timetables. Incorporating these plans into an overall strategic plan strengthened the Health Sciences Campus' plan.

The outcome of defining needs was a set of strategic objectives.

1. Establish a permanent department to plan and organize information technology and to provide vision, expertise, leadership, coordination, and implementation of the IAIMS strategic planning process on the Health Sciences campus.

2. Provide for a campuswide, universal-access, high-performance, digital communication network capable of handling advanced information technologies into the next century.

3. Implement an integrated and seamless virtual institutional database by incorporating existing and new databases into a campuswide IAIMS. Over time and wherever practical, existing databases should be made accessible on the network. The greatest challenge, both technical and organizational, is to integrate the patient-care databases into the campus information system.

4. Extend campus-network access to faculty, clinicians, students, and staff at the teaching and clinical affiliates; encourage these institutions to develop integrated information systems of their own, to which Tufts could connect and interact.

5. Build information technology resources to support strategies for curriculum development on the Health Sciences Campus; create an academic resource center to serve as an environment for developing innovative pedagogical techniques and courseware.

6. Strengthen the existing Medical Information Sciences Division (medical informatics) to enable it to provide a leadership role on campus in developing state-of-the-art biomedical application of information technology.

To reach these objectives, the IPC inventoried what had been done, which clarified what was left to be done. Up to this point the committee had

1. Prepared a needs statement
2. Stated the strategic objectives
3. Formulated an outline of the implementation plan
4. Involved the CCC and the potential customers in network groups
5. Facilitated joint planning between the campus departments and the campus networks

D. Changes to IAIMS

During the planning period NLM changed the structure of the IAIMS proposal from a three- to a two-tiered system. NLM also changed the second word in IAIMS from Academic to Advanced—Integrated Advanced Information Management Systems—which indicated an increase in scope to include not only the academic campus but also the hospitals and other affiliated organizations. Tufts planners regrouped and decided to try for a full-implementation grant; previously their target had been the Phase II model stage.

E. Outstanding Issues at Tufts

Tufts' planning had come to a critical point. To move ahead with the implementation plan and the application for the third-phase IAIMS, all involved persons, departments, and organizations, including Tufts-affiliated hospitals, had to approve and support the plan. The model Phase II might have facilitated this but, because of the change, Tufts had folded its model phase into its full-implementation phase.

Tufts also needed to discover and address issues previously unsolved or, worse, not yet encountered; those issues to be addressed were

Who needed to be contacted from top down or bottom up?

What and who had been forgotten?

What were the unresolved issues the IPC faced or identified but had not dealt with?

How could they keep the network groups together once they had accomplished both objectives of defining the needs and completing an implementation proposal?

What would be the success criteria? How would Tufts know if it had reached its goal?

The list of important people to contact was fairly straightforward. Top down meant the president, the deans of all the Health Sciences Campus schools, and chief and administrator at NEMC and other affiliated institutions. Because both clinical and basic-science faculty were involved in the network groups, it was important for them to discuss the plan personally with both their division and department chiefs. Appointments for these personal visits were made. This top down group needed to both approve and support the plan financially or with staff time contributions, which could be counted as institutional support.

The bottom up group would include departmental support staff, department managers, computer-support personnel, and administrative and curriculum-support personnel. This group would be involved in the daily operation of the plan; their enthusiasm, suggestions for improvement, and final approval would be needed. Staff time contributions would again count as institutional support.

The committee reviewed the list to determine who had been forgotten. TUSM had appointed a new dean of the School of Medicine in June 1992, a new university president in September 1992, and several new department chairs. To gain their support, it was important to bring them on board immediately and keep them informed.

New initiatives and programs were being introduced during the planning process. Again, the problem arose of how to keep abreast of developments and whom to contact. Tufts, for example, had been awarded a Robert Wood Johnson Foundation planning grant for training primary-care physicians. As the national health-care-reform program was then developing, this initiative would become a major focus within the curriculum. Contact and continuing dialogue with this group, for one, would be very important.

F. What Were the Unresolved Issues That the IPC Faced?

The proposed creation of an information management office for the Health Sciences Campus implied reassignment of responsibilities that were seen as sources of power by TCCS, which up until then had total authority over computing and communications. Although the IPC members had discussed and agreed on this issue, the director of TCCS needed to be consulted in the presence of the top health science campus administrators, specifically the dean and the executive dean of TUSM.

The current laboratories and classrooms did not support the image-storage or resolution requirements of state-of-the-art technology. An electronic-classroom for the dissemination of electronic text, image data for neuro-science and other teaching, would answer these needs. The administration and support questions, however, needed resolution. This would involve the TCCS for sharing power with the director of information technology on the Health Science Campus, the library for management, and the administration for support.

Clinical information systems focused on dedicated departmental operations, laboratory, radiology, and so on, and did not provide practicing physicians a unified patient view. Nor did the clinical information systems store or archive data for longitudinal research purposes. The NEMC Management Information Systems staff had been working with clinical groups but without direct input from the basic scientists at Tufts. Because Tufts and NEMC have different governing bodies, joint planning became imperative.

While individuals and new initiatives were being brought into the information loop, the IPC committee needed to keep the established network groups engaged in planning. Taking advantage of expertise and interests of existing faculty is critical for any institution; at Tufts, with limited resources, it was imperative. Thus, in order not to lose their forward momentum, the network group needed a new focus. Their new assignment was to write their relevant sections of the implementation plan.

VII. Defining Success

Having carefully worked through this planning process and brought together many, if not all, of the people working in information technology at Tufts, the IPC still needed to determine if the process was successful.

This brings the discussion back to the definition of success. First, success had been defined as having a written document with input from all customers at all levels. Each success criterion achieved, however, resounded like Pandora's box. It was not enough; more action ensued; more issues surfaced. The planning process became an ever-evolving, truly iterative process.

The planning phase's success criterion, in fact, was the final written document, the Strategic Plan. Then as a follow-up to the written plan, a second tier of the success criteria was a grant application for the implementation phase (III), which was submitted to NLM. These two documents helped the institution to

1. Prioritize needs.
2. Develop a budget and timetable for each project and program, which was useful for all future planning.
3. Identify key faculty and staff as program leaders. (Recognizing faculty in this manner builds loyalty; the process created a loyal and dedicated IAIMS faculty and staff.)

During the site visit, each key person involved in IAIMS projects, including affiliated hospital faculty, staff, and top administrators, spoke to the defined project needs. At that point, the IAIMS Program Committee was confident that they had a critical mass for implementation.

Is the Tufts Health Sciences Campus different today than it was before IAIMS? The answer is yes, in the following ways:

1. A written plan exists with widely supported priorities; both a strategic information-technology plan and a campuswide network plan were produced.
2. Staff and faculty became more knowledgeable, and they expect more and participate more in information technology changes.
3. A joint telecommunications network with NEMC exists. Joint project participation set up a means for future discussion of policy issues, such as who should have access to clinical information.
4. Tufts has moved toward cooperative rather than duplicative efforts among its core facilities, libraries, computer centers, and educators. According to an article by Dr. Edward Brandt, this commonly results from the IAIMS programs and can only enhance continuing medical education and lifelong learning (Brandt, 1990).
5. A central player in this endeavor, the library served as a model. Its model is the integrated library system, which provides access to library catalogs and other information systems worldwide via the Tufts campus network and the Internet.
6. Electronic communication has become a high priority for NEMC and other affiliated hospitals. Models based on this connectivity are developing for research, clinical care, and education.

During a recent visit an attendee asked the PI what one thing stood out as vital to success. The answer was a focused IAIMS staff. Particularly if the library director maintains two roles, both as director and PI, staying focused becomes imperative. Tufts' modest staff were dedicated and focused on the defined outcome. An IAIMS PI must be someone who has his or her heart and mind focused on an outcome. The advice a physician gave to a patient who had hurt her ribs skiing could be adopted for those undergoing institutional change: "You won't hurt yourself; if you can, just ski through the pain." Working to create change can be personally painful, but success awaits those who can stay focused and "just ski through the pain"; that is, persevere!

A. Meetings

Benefits derived from meetings were valuable as both background information and in developing action plans. Several particularly useful meetings, which sharpened the intellectual understanding of the IAIMS process, are listed as follows.

1. The IAIMS Consortium Meetings were initiated in 1989. The IAIMS consortium now has a dozen members, who explore ways to improve intellectual and technical exchanges between the member sites. The consortium promises to accelerate greatly the developmental efforts at each cooperating IAIMS site and may provide a mechanism for increasing the transfer of IAIMS experiences to nonparticipating health science institutions (Lindberg et al., 1992).

2. The Symposium on Computer Applications in Medical Care (SCAMC) is held annually. Paper topics range from the descriptions of IAIMS site projects and the many clinical information systems being developed or used to innovative curriculum developments.

3. The AAMC continues to offer its management education program, Information Technology in Academic Medical Center, in Snowmass, Colorado. The faculty offer a review of IAIMS concepts; speakers from IAIMS institutions provide updated information. Others from the attending institutions (often a mix of financial officers, planners, librarians, deans, and computer technologists) act together to discuss the IAIMS issues. The Snowmass environment is conducive to continuing these discussions over dinner.

4. In 1991, in conjunction with the American Medical Informatics Association (AMIA), the Medical Library Association (MLA) sponsored a post-MLA conference on Unified Medical Language for IAIMS. These symposiums take place every few years after the MLA's annual meeting.

5. NLM, which has presented good technology programs, has a plethora of information. Their electronic conference center is open for all to visit at NLM in Bethesda, Maryland.

B. Other Benefits

Another benefit from working through an IAIMS initiative was that the momentum inspired others. Several examples are listed as follows.

The ULC's strategic planning focused on IAIMS issues of sharing and cooperative planning with TCCS, as well as on broadening the access to information to the campus at large, which included dial-in and Internet access potentials.

The TCCS's five-year plan had a more user or customer orientation and incorporated the IAIMS planning issues.

The NEMC/Tufts backbone and communications planning was an open process and included the entire Health Sciences Campus.

A budget was created to define and provide dollar values to present and future resource needs.

A further benefit was that campus liaisons and collaborations have continued with refreshing regularity. A new esprit de corps developed, which will benefit all future projects requiring interaction among colleagues. Examples are:

NEMC's Radiology Department and the Tufts' Neurosciences basic-science faculty continued their research interests in image transfer and storage.

The Robert Wood Johnson Foundation Planning Committee extended its liaison work to the library and computer services.

Other grants and contracts were submitted to support IAIMS concepts and models.

The third- and fourth-year medical school curriculum included more outreach and computer technology in both its teaching and administrative functions.

C. Results of Planning

These events may have occurred sooner or later since information technology and communication networks have progressed faster than one could keep up with. Being organized, however, and having a strategic plan with which to channel energies helps provide the necessary direction and incentives. There is every reason to believe that the IAIMS initiative has guided this process at Tufts.

VIII. Conclusion

Tufts is just one example of an institution involved in an IAIMS initiative. When it began, Tufts tried to compare itself with other IAIMS sites to see how to structure its plan. It became obvious that Tufts had strengths and weaknesses that were unique in all areas, from administration to clinical care. Recognizing this point, Tufts designed a plan that spoke specifically to Tufts.

It created ongoing momentum. Each institution has such strengths as administrative support and a library. Each institution needs to take advantage of
these strengths to create institutional change and to harness the potential of
information technology.

References

Association of American Medical Colleges (AAMC). (1984). Physicians for the twenty-first
    century: Report of the project on the general professional education of the physician and
    college preparation for medicine. *Journal of Medical Education* **59**(11, part 2), 13, 149–160.
Blum, B. I. (1986). Clinical information systems—A review, in medical informatics (special
    issue). *The Western Journal of Medicine* **145**, 791–797.
Brandt, E. N. (1990). Continuing education/beyond higher education. *Bulletin of the Medical
    Library Association* **78**(2), 157–160.
Broering, N. C. (1986). Beyond the library: IAIMS at Georgetown. *Bulletin of the Medical Library
    Association* **74**(3), 249–256.
Bronzino, J. D. (1982). *Computer Application for Patient Care*. Addison-Wesley, Menlo Park,
    California.
Cooper, J. A. D. (1984). Perspectives on the planning of integrated management systems. In
    Planning for IAIMS: Proceeding of a Symposium Sponsored by the National Library of Medicine,
    October 17, 1984, pp. 8–10.
Cooper, W. G. (1983). Program implications for the National Library of Medicine. *Bulletin of
    the Medical Library Association* **71**(4), 433–434.
Dertouzos, M. L. (1991). Communications, computers and networks. *Scientific American* **265**(3),
    62–71.
Gory, G. A. (1990). *Phase III IAIMS at Baylor College of Medicine*. The body of the Phase III
    IAIMS proposal submitted to the NLM, March 1, 1990.
Grefsheim, S. F., Larson, R. H., Bader, S. A., and Matheson, N. W. (1982). Automation of
    internal library operations in academic health sciences libraries: A state of the art report.
    Bulletin of the Medical Library Association **70**(2), 191–200.
Hendrickson, G. L. F., Goldstein, R. K., and Levy, R. I. (1986). IAIMS at Columbia: A
    strategic plan and model project. *Bulletin of the Medical Library Association* **74**(3), 243–248.
Korpman, R. A. (1991). Health care information systems; patient-centered integration is the
    key. *Clinics in Laboratory Medicine* (March), 203–221.
Krieg, A. F. (1991). Laboratory information systems from a perspective of continuing evolution.
    Clinics in Laboratory Medicine (March), 73–82.
Lindberg, D. A. B., and Schoolman, H. M. (1986). The National Library of Medicine and
    Medical Informatics, In Medical Informatics (special issue). *The Western Journal of Medicine*
    145, 786–790.
Lindberg, D. A. B., West, R. T., and Corn, M. (1992). IAIMS: An overview from the National
    Library of Medicine. *Bulletin of the Medical Library Association* **80**(3), 244–246.
Lock, S. P. (1992). Perspective from the editor of the British Medical Journal. *Bulletin of the
    Medical Library Association* **80**(2), 107–109.
Lodwick, G. S., and Taaffe, J. L. (1988). Radiology systems of the nineties: Meeting the
    challenge of change. *Journal of Digital Imaging* **1**(1), 4–12.
Lyders, D. ed. (1980). *Annual Statistics of Medical School Libraries in the United States and Canada,
    1979–1980*, (2d ed.). Association of Academic Health Sciences Library Directors, Houston
    Academy of Medicine–Texas Medical Center (AAHSLD, HAM–TMC).

Matheson, N. W., and Cooper, J. A. D. (1982). Academic information in the academic health sciences center. *Journal of Medical Education* **57**(2), 1–93.

McNeely, M. D. D. (1991). Advances in medical informatics during the 1980s. *American Journal of Clinical Pathology* **96**(Suppl. 1), S33–S39.

Mehnert, R. B., and Leiter, J. (1988). The National Library of Medicine. In *Handbook of Medical Library Practice*, Vol. III (4th ed.). (L. Darling, D. Bishop, and L. A. Colaianni, eds.), pp. 157–158. Medical Library Association, Inc., Chicago, Illinois.

National Library of Medicine (NLM). (1983). *NLM News*, 38(3), 1–2.

National Library of Medicine (NLM). (1986). *Extramural Programs Fact Sheet, Integrated Academic Information Management Systems (IAIMS) Planning and Development Grants*. IAIMS Programs, Bethesda, Maryland.

National Library of Medicine (NLM). (1987). *IAIMS and Health Sciences Education: Support of Health Sciences Education by Integrated Academic Information Management Systems. Proceeding of a Symposium sponsored by the National Library of Medicine*, March 12, 1986. IAIMS Program Office, Bethesda, Maryland.

National Library of Medicine (NLM). (1989). *The Integrated Academic Information Management System (IAIMS) Program: A Report to the NLM Board of Regents*. January 1989.

National Library of Medicine (NLM). (1993). *Extramural Programs Fact Sheet, IAIMS: Integrated Advanced Information Management Systems*. Office of Grants Inquiries, Bethesda, Maryland.

Orenstein, R. M., ed. (1993). *FullText Sources Online*. BiblioData, Needham, Massachusetts.

Peay, W. J., Butter, K. A., and Dougherty, N. A. (1986). IAIMS and the Library at the University of Utah. *Bulletin of the Medical Library Association* **74**(3), 238–242.

Rega, R., ed. (1993). *OPAC Directory 1993: An Annual Guide to Online Public Access Catalogs and Databases*, Meckler Publishing, Westport, Connecticut.

Ruxin, O. K., and Hill, S. E. (1983). Cataloging and Classification: Automation and Computer-Based Networks, Cataloging of Special Materials. In *Handbook of Medical Library Practice*, Vol. II (4th ed.). (L. Darling and D. Bishop, eds.), p. 292. Medical Library Association, Inc., Chicago, Illinois.

Stead, W. W., Bird, W. P., Califf, R. M., Elchlepp, J. G., Hammond, W. E., and Kinney, T. R. (1993). The IAIMS at Duke University Medical Center: Transition from model testing to implementation. *M. D. Computing* **10**(4), 225–230.

Tenopir, C., and Berglund, S. (1992). Fulltext searching on major supermarket systems. *Databases* October, pp. 15–16.

Tesler, L. G. (1991). Networked computing in the 1990s. *Scientific American* **265**(3), 86–93.

Tufts University (TU). (1993). *Tufts Health Sciences Campus Strategic and Implementation Plan for Integrated Advanced Information Management Systems: IAIMS*. IAIMS Planning Committee, Tufts University School of Medicine, Boston, Massachusetts.

Wilson, W. P., Ball, M. J., Zimmerman, J. L., and Douglas, J. V. (1986). The IAIMS initiative at the University of Maryland at Baltimore. *Bulletin of the Medical Library Association* **74**(3), 257–261.

Public Library Funding: Issues, Trends, and Resources

Brian A. Reynolds
San Luis Obispo City-County Library
San Luis Obispo, California 93403-8107

Public librarians in the United States play a vital role in modern life. With little fanfare, they help people navigate in an increasingly complex and interconnected world. These librarians understand better than anyone else why people must be literate, aware, and involved in public life. Public libraries are vital to the survival of our democratic culture and the preservation of the United States as a leader in the world community.

Today's public librarians know that the existence of their institutions may no longer be taken for granted. They cannot afford to be reactive; they must become proactive. Rather than providing a static mix of services, public libraries are adapting to changing community needs and are engaging social issues not only within library buildings but also in the streets of our communities and over electronic highways.

The social, economic, and political landscape of the United States is evolving at a dizzying pace. Facts, assumptions, and values are altered continuously. In an earlier era, information was scarce and poorly distributed; public libraries gathered, sorted, and made it available to customers on site. Today, most people are bombarded with too much information. Information overload is common. The new role for public libraries is to extract from an overabundance of data, customized informational packages for their clients. These packages are then distributed in a timely manner to wherever the customer might be: in the library, at home or office, or around the globe.

The fact that we live in the information age is so well-known as to be a cliché. The acquisition and intelligent use of information are necessary to the individual; they are also commodities vital to our economy and society. The rapid changes of modern life alter the information environment constantly. No matter how well people were educated or what they knew yesterday, new data must be acquired and processed today in order to be prepared for tomorrow. A democratic society that wishes to remain economically and politically viable depends on an informed, active citizenry. Today's public library is a crucible in which information becomes knowledge. These libraries are the only social agency which is equipped to sustain lifelong learning needs for everyone.

In recent years, technology (specifically, computerization of library processes, plus internal and external databases) has been a major creator of change. The effects of technology on society and public library service since the 1970s are probably as significant as those engendered by the invention of movable type in Europe during the 1400s. Technology has the promise to improve the breadth and depth of public library service dramatically while simultaneously reducing traditional barriers of convenience and timeliness. Nonetheless, the technology is not free; it requires rigorous and complicated management.

Public library use statistics are at an all time high. Public library leaders are inspired by new visions of service and accountability to customer needs. Quantum improvements in services through technology and telecommunications demonstrate enormous potential. The irony is that far too many public libraries are in financial trouble. Nationwide—and especially in California—public library budgets are being slashed: open hours reduced, book budgets cut, and library staff laid off. This phenomenon has serious implications not just for the institutions themselves but also for our entire society.

An analysis of public library funding issues is important for many reasons. Public libraries are a mirror for the society they serve; the programs they offer and appropriate funding patterns depend on societal conditions. Today, the social, political, and technological environment in which public libraries operate is changing at a phenomenal rate. The funding climate for public libraries has become unstable.

The current public library funding crisis is widespread and dramatic. The level of danger tends to inhibit creative thinking and promote crisis or reactive management. Constantly changing conditions seem to reduce the time needed to look for solutions. The good news is that the current mess is forcing us to analyze, streamline, and chart better directions for the future. Changes in public library programs and funding sources will not be cosmetic or superficial. Fine-tuning of traditional habits will be inadequate. Stabilizing and sustaining public library funding needs over time will require qualitative changes in how services offered to the public are marketed, developed, and priced.

This essay will cover three topics: a history of public library funding issues; current public library funding formats; and the trends or resources that will help promote strong public libraries today and tomorrow. Essay content is drawn from library literature as well as my 20 years of professional library experience. For the last 11 years I have been a public library director in California—a state where libraries are under siege (Vogel, 1993).

I. History

The Age of Reason conveyed the idea that people could improve their lives and the world around them through intellectual effort. This philosophy was pivotal to the development of democratic forms of government and the emergence of the free public library. In order for people to govern themselves, they must be literate and informed on the issues of the day. Our Founding Fathers understood this.

In the summer of 1731, Benjamin Franklin was one of the first 50 cosigners to the charter for America's first subscription library, the Philadelphia Library Company. Members paid 40 shillings each to join and agreed to pay 10 shillings annually. This subscription library soon was joined by many similar libraries in cities such as New York and Boston (Dickson, 1986).

The first tax-supported public libraries were created in New England. The public library in Peterboro, New Hampshire, founded in 1833, is the oldest free public library in the world to be supported by taxation (Dickson, 1986). The Commonwealth of Massachusetts passed its famous Act of Authorization to Establish a Public Library in the City of Boston in 1848 (Curley, 1990). By 1850 there were nearly 700 public, private, academic, and subscription lending libraries in the United States. Over the next century, many of these libraries would form a foundation for today's network of tax-supported public libraries (Curley, 1990).

Forty-five years before the birth of the United States, the seeds of today's public libraries were planted. By the early 1900s, tax-supported public libraries had become the dominant information provider nationwide. These public libraries were free in two key aspects: (1) they were free to the user in that no service was denied because of lack of ability to pay and (2) they were also free because an attempt was made to provide materials of all kinds, on all sides of an issue, and one did not have to pass a political or religious test to access these materials. This democratic institution called a public library was unique in the world and probably unique in human history. In 1991, there were more than 9000 separate public library agencies nationwide with more than 15,000 outlets ($4.9 bil. for public libraries . . . , 1993).

The first major event of the current public library funding crisis began in the summer of 1978, with the passage of California's Proposition 13. This measure cut property tax support of local government by 57%, required most new local tax measures to be approved by voters with a two-thirds majority, and shifted responsibility for most fiscal decisions away from cities and counties to the state of California. Other states passed similar measures in subsequent years (e.g., Massachusetts, Oregon, Colorado).

Outside California, most public libraries continued to flourish. Herbert Goldhor reported a nationwide jump in the public library *Index of Expenditures* between 1984 and 1985 of 9.7% (Goldhor, 1986). One year later, Goldhor reported public library spending making the biggest jump in a decade, rising 10.7% in 1986 over the level of 1985 (Goldhor, 1987).

In a 1986 *Library Journal* editorial, John Berry praised public libraries for their value and efficiency. The nationwide per capita spending level of public libraries stood at $11.14. Yet, while this represented a 51% per capita spending increase since 1980, cost per circulation had only increased 15% (Berry, 1986).

By 1988, the nationwide public library per capita spending index had risen to $14.24, for an average annual increase over 1985 of about 9%. Regionally, per capita spending varied widely. The Northeast and West spent $17.14 and $17.15, respectively; the South languished at $10.55 per capita. Alaska led the pack in per capita spending at $35.19, with Mississippi earning dubious honors at $4.44 per capita (Selsky, 1990).

By the early 1990s, the California public library "flu" had spread: A *Library Journal* article entitled "Library Budgets Survey '91: Hard Times Continue" described a nationwide crisis (Quinn and Rogers, 1992). Public library use continued its upward trend, but funding fell in the opposite direction. This 1992 "Hard Times" article featured a photograph of Multnomah County (Oregon) Librarian Ginnie Cooper hanging up a sign showing all 14 branches would be closed an additional day per week.

For Californians, this was nothing new. The Shasta County Public Library gained national notoriety when it closed briefly in 1988. In Butte County, California, the public library's future was "uncertain as county faces bankruptcy" (Marquand, 1990). Elsewhere in the nation, service levels at even major urban libraries were worse than during the Depression. Boston Public Library operated with fewer staff, and the New York Public Library was open fewer hours (Gurwitt, 1992). The latest California county in danger of closing is Merced. Serving over 200,000 citizens with a $1.4 million annual budget and 83 staff, the Merced County Library was scheduled to close January 1, 1994 (La Ganga, 1993).

Public library budget troubles began to receive broad media coverage. *California Journal*, a nonpartisan review of California politics, featured the crisis in early 1993: "Libraries are the underpinning of our democracy. . . . Yet libraries are taken for granted and viewed as non-essential when it comes to cutting the budget," said California State Librarian Gary Strong. As societal pressures dump more social problems on libraries, Santa Cruz City-County Librarian Anne Turner noted that: "In many cases, libraries are left to be the only symbol of government presence in a neighborhood" (Schilling, 1993).

The American Library Association, under the guidance of 1992 President Patricia Glass Schuman, developed a nationwide campaign publicizing library funding problems. Writers Octavia Butler and Kevin Starr have championed public libraries in *Omni* magazine and the *Los Angeles Times* (Butler, 1993; Starr, 1993). The plight of public libraries was featured by ABC's *World News Tonight*, on a recent "American Agenda" segment (Plight of public libraries . . . , 1993).

One major contributor to the public library funding crisis has been a persistent, nationwide economic recession. The most populous state, California, is mired in the deepest economic downturn since the Great Depression. Relative to other government agencies, libraries of all types seem to be taking cuts much deeper than average. Around the United States many public libraries are suffering the worst budget cuts in history. But economic conditions are not the only reason. In his candidate's statement for the ALA Presidency, Arthur Curley wrote that the current crisis in library funding is a direct result of economic recession, "but even more the product of eroded commitment to educational and cultural priorities than of societal poverty" (Curley, 1993).

Public opinion surveys consistently show that citizens place public libraries near or at the top of the priority list of all local governmental services. Satisfaction with service levels rarely scores below the 90% range. Recent surveys also show majority support for national per capita spending levels at *double* current levels (Public wants increased support, 1993). Yet, in many communities around the United States, public libraries are dying. Public library funding elections are being defeated. This apparent paradox lies at the heart of any discussion about public library funding issues.

II. Funding Formats

Since the beginning of organized civilizations, governing bodies have levied taxes to raise revenue. There is no doubt that paying taxes has never been, is not now, and will never be popular. In the United States, taxes have been raised and distributed in order to satisfy a number of goals. Free public education through schools and libraries has been a top priority.

From their inception, public libraries were considered a public good similar to other essential services (e.g., public safety, public schools, roads, etc.). Unlike many other developed nations in the world, the United States has not developed a state or national system of support for public libraries.

Public libraries were and are institutions governed and sustained by local governments, typically with a heavy dependence on the property tax.

Relative to other local governmental programs and to their alleged importance to society, public libraries received a minuscule share of local tax revenues, about 1%. Local governments generally provide from 85% to 90% of public library funding needs through direct appropriations from the general fund. State governments provide 10% to 12%, and 1% to 2% is received from the federal government. Depending on the community, fundraising, grants, and fees have provided some level of support ranging from almost nothing to 10% to 15% ($4.9 bil. for public libraries . . . , 1993). The historic dependence of public libraries on tax revenues may no longer be viable. There is a high level of interest in examining the interplay of private and public funding of public libraries ($37,950 Wilson grant . . . , 1993).

Malcolm Getz notes that the twists and turns of public library budgets do not reflect shifts in the use, value, or cost of library services. "Rather, the sharp turns may reflect the small size of libraries relative to total city budgets, the fact that the deterioration of library services does not pose an immediate threat to public health or safety, and the fact that political support for libraries may not coalesce until a crisis is at hand" (Reynolds, 1986, p. 29). Getz wrote those words in 1980 and now, certainly, a crisis is at hand.

Public library funding in the past has been largely determined by the fiscal climate affecting local, state, and federal governments. As local taxes increased with the economy and/or inflation, so did the public library budget. State funding accrued through matching fund formulas and grants, more often to regional cooperatives than to individual libraries. Federal government dollars flowed to public libraries almost exclusively through various titles of the Library Services & Construction Act (LSCA).

Beginning in the 1970s, changing relationships among these three levels of government have had both direct and indirect effects on public library budgets. Unfunded and underfunded mandates proliferated. The federal government began to delegate more responsibility for programs to the states but gave them less money. State governments did the same thing to local governments. Tax revolts and economic recession made matters worse. In these fiscal wars, public libraries were early casualties. In just 1 year (1987–1988), the federal government's contribution to public libraries declined 25%. State and local governments had to share an increasing burden (Selsky, 1990).

There is much evidence that public confidence in government at all levels is eroding and that the fiscal crisis in many areas is as much political as it is economic. Many local governmental services, including public libraries, have depended on the property tax. Property taxes have been consistently voted the least popular tax in opinion polls (Reynolds, 1986) and may no longer be a viable source of local revenues for public libraries.

At the state level, the era of innovative programs for public libraries may be over. In California, current efforts focus on gaining cost of living adjustments or matching fiscal appropriations with authorized funding levels. Almost no attention is given to increasing existing state aid programs or generating new state legislation.

Analyzing the state role in funding public libraries nationally is not easy; the only comprehensive source is *American Library Laws*, last published by the ALA in 1988. It is a compilation of legal statutes relating to libraries, state-by-state, but it contains no analysis. In Hawaii, public libraries are an arm of state government. Ohio public libraries "stand out from the crowd."

Until 1986, Ohio public libraries statewide had first claim on a portion of the proceeds of the intangible property tax, which local communities could supplement if they wished (Summers, 1980). Since 1986, public libraries in Ohio have received 6.3% of statewide personal income tax collections. Public libraries apply to the local budget commission, and funds are received from the state's Department of Taxation. Although funding levels are subject to various formulas, funds are disbursed to public libraries "with no strings attached" (Susan Thomas, Ohio Deputy State Librarian for Administrative Services, personal communication, November 1993). Of the 1993 to 1994 budget of the Toledo and Lucas County Library, 63.8% is state funding and 26.4% is local property tax (Library concerts, 1993).

The federal role in support of public libraries began in 1956 with the creation of the Library Services Act. Expanded in the 1960s to the LSCA, this act has helped public libraries in a number of ways, by providing competitive grants to expand public library service to unserved populations, create demonstration projects, encourage cooperation, and build library facilities. In recent years, LSCA has also promoted services to special populations such as Native Americans and new adult readers.

Despite the alleged importance to the United States of a literate, informed citizenry, the federal role in helping public libraries do their job remains minimal. Indeed, the last two Republican administrations and the current Democratic administration have not only downplayed the importance of public libraries but also actively sought to underfund or eliminate LSCA.

The current administration in the White House is promoting a National Information Infrastructure (NII). Librarians nationwide are hopeful federal funding of library programs will be revitalized and included in NII. The editors of *Library Journal* published An Open Letter to the President and Vice President recommending five major areas that should receive attention at the federal level, including service equity, pricing of federal information, and the electronic superhighways envisioned by NII (Dear President Clinton . . . , 1993). Nonetheless, it is likely that efforts at the federal level today and in the future will emphasize preservation of existing levels of funding, not creation of new programs.

III. Cost Control

For a number of reasons, cost control in public libraries is now a major issue. This was not always so. The environment public libraries operated in was relatively stable. Public libraries had the reputation of being frugal operations, almost by definition. Compared to other governmental services, they did not absorb much tax revenue.

Public libraries generally returned many times the value back to the public per tax dollar invested. They were popular, valued institutions that, in most cases, had their budgets approved without much scrutiny. It is true that annual cost inflation of library materials tended to be higher than the general consumer price index, but until recently these costs were absorbed.

The first step into cost control is to examine the budget. As entities of local government, public library budgets generally fall into the line-item, incremental format. Special projects and programs, usually funded by categorical grants, often operate under program budgets. Budget innovations of the late 1970s and early 1980s, such as performance and zero-based budgets, except in rare cases, were not significant factors in reducing cost or in increasing performance (Reynolds, 1986).

With the advent of total quality management (TQM), the concept of multiyear budgets, lump sum budgets, innovation funds, and Peter Drucker's opportunity budgets has gained renewed interest. Although not related directly to cost control, these budgets encourage a shift in thinking from short to long term and away from the tradition of "if we don't spend it this year we won't get it next year."

Innovative, longer-term budgeting has the potential for several positive effects: discovering multiyear true costs over the life of the service or product, identifying potential crises or decision points for future planning, and encouraging cost savings in the present for future allocation. One result of multiyear budget planning can be political courage: based on information about the future, local governing bodies can afford to make decisions today about tomorrow. Without this futuristic focus, such decisions would either be perceived as controversial at best or nonsensical at worst.

Because many public librarians operate today in such an unstable environment, with so many imponderables and pressures beyond their direct control, innovative budgeting is not as powerful a tool as it might otherwise be. Cost control possibilities will be found instead within the four major library budget categories: personnel, materials, operating expenses, and capital projects and purchases.

Personnel costs—public library salaries and benefits—generally comprise the majority of the budget. Personnel costs are, therefore, the most important factor in overall cost control. The challenge is to minimize these costs over time, while also maintaining and/or increasing productivity. Thomas Ballard suggests that productivity increases—especially in an economic recession—will be a key element in sustaining public library funding. Because public libraries are a service industry and thus labor intensive, productivity increases will be difficult to achieve. This may be one reason why allegedly nonessential services like public libraries are viewed by the public with increasing cynicism (Reynolds, 1986). Not only must public libraries begin to produce services more efficiently and effectively, but the public must also be made aware of progress.

Human resources are also the most significant long-term investment in public libraries. To preserve this investment, public library budget cutting generally follows this pattern: trim discretionary costs-programs (e.g., building expansion and maintenance); cut library materials; reduce or lay off staff. Staff is the last to go, yet budget reductions of any magnitude almost always require cuts in personnel.

Operating expenses, such as office supplies, utilities, rent, and so forth, are not fruitful sources for reducing revenue for several reasons: they are a relatively small portion of the budget; they are not subject to discretionary manipulation (often being fixed costs such as a proportionate share of overhead charges by other departments of local government); and they tend to be driven by the total level of service to the public (i.e., hours open determines the utility bill). Other ways to control costs should be explored.

The rapid onset of technology in public libraries is certainly allowing existing staff to be more productive. Technical services and cataloging—traditionally allocated to higher-paid professionals—is now staffed in many libraries by paraprofessionals due to the widespread use of computerized copy-cataloging provided by bibliographic utilities and other vendors.

Volunteers work in many public libraries as support staff and even, in some cases, replace staff who have been moved to other duties or who have been laid off. Public library volunteerism is a controversial issue with many ramifications beyond the scope of this essay. Cost control by having volunteers complement, rather than replace, existing staff is the preferred option.

Health insurance, the most costly employee benefit by far, is being contained through a variety of means: wellness programs, health maintenance organizations, and public/private brokering for reduced medical procedure rates. Health premium costs have also been minimized by discouraging job sharing and promoting the use of temporary, part-time help.

Continuing education is a consideration. Through continuing education existing staff can keep up to date in their skills, leading to better morale and higher productivity. The need to hire new employees and reinvest in obligatory training with longer learning curves can be reduced. In public libraries the payment of costs for continuing education is almost always seen as a positive investment. These courses are now less expensive through distance learning, which is often facilitated by video and other telecommunications technology. Yet, a recent Urban Libraries Council (ULC) study shows a dearth of continuing education programs. ULC President Joey Rodger stated, "While our professional attention has been on this fairly small proportion of workers in librarianship [recipients of the MLS degree], we have no sustained programs for keeping current or upgrading skills for everyone else" (St. Lifer and Rogers, 1993, p. 113). Continuing education is a cost control factor that is being underused.

As noted earlier, automation of library procedures has allowed lower paid staff to work in technical processing. When it makes economic sense, libraries are contracting with outside vendors for ongoing cataloging, as well as retrospective conversion projects. Vendors such as Baker & Taylor are providing customized, value-added services, which libraries with reduced staff find appealing (Annichiarico, 1993). Automation has allowed cost savings in several other areas: automated versus manual circulation and overdues of library materials. Automated telephone equipment is being used to save money (examples include receive renewals, materials holds, notify patrons of hold status, and overdues) in libraries like the Fort Vancouver Regional Library in Washington, the Springfield-Greene County Library in Missouri, and the Mississauga Library System in Ontario (Voice Processing, 1993).

Innovations in library automation can also create more work for a finite or reduced staff. Self-checkout units are being introduced in libraries in hopes of stretching existing circulation staff further. In at least one library environment, self-checkout units are not saving staff time (Dennis Walter, Circulation Supervisor, University of South Australia, personal communication, October 1993). Reference librarians discovered early that automated catalogs and databases often require more frequent and lengthy interactions with users than traditional print sources. Added to the needed training time, librarians must often spend time explaining to frustrated customers why the machine cannot deliver the full text document as easily as it delivered the citations. This is especially true in a public library environment where the customer base is constantly changing.

Public library materials expenditures generally comprise 10% to 20% of the budget. In response to changing customer needs and the influence of technology, a not-so-quiet revolution is taking place in the ways public libraries acquire, process, and distribute their materials. When public library collections were largely print-related and delivered at the library site, the equation was simpler. Costs were easily tracked, and economies could be gained by using regional processing centers and material jobbers' discounts. Acquisition and processing of materials were one-time costs, except for binding and repair. Putting aside issues of lost or damaged materials, an item could be bought once and used multiple times with no added cost. Electronic storage and delivery of library materials has altered this equation, creating new cost centers and the need to make cost-allocation decisions in different ways.

Print resources have been described in the literature as a "prison," and librarians are urged to "shed the mantle of compromises developed under the print paradigm" (Shed print . . . , 1993). The traditional goal of ownership is being replaced by the goal of access. Patron access to materials has long been an issue in the literature and formerly revolved around facility size, location, and collection development. Now, the issue is document delivery: What materials should a library own and what resources should be accessed remotely via technology? Desires to better serve the customer and the reality of limited resources are paramount issues in this discussion, as are copyright and pricing (Bluh, 1993).

In California, telecommunications networking to facilitate sharing of resources while reducing costs is receiving statewide attention. Depending on the level of telecommunications needed, services and costs vary to suit the needs of the individual library (Smith Automation Systems, 1992). According to Raymond Kurzweil, "New means of paying for access to information will evolve to reflect the ease of communicating and sharing electronic information. Today, libraries pay for books by the copy . . . With electronic books, it might make more sense to pay for person-minutes" (Kurzweil, 1993). Kurzweil (1993) recognizes how library budget limitations might affect public libraries' equitable distribution of information without charge. He proposes that: "In the virtual world, the limitation could be reflected in a finite number of lending minutes, which would be equitably distributed to a library's patrons . . . but a reasonable means of restricting access while still fulfilling the democratic goals of the library system will need to be found" (p. 55).

Decisions affecting materials management and costs are probably the most volatile and complicated aspect of public library management today. More study is needed to help public library staff decide issues of print versus electronic, onsite access versus remote, and offline versus online. For example, in the online environment, costs and results can vary dramatically depending on which databases are used and whether the user is a novice or experienced searcher. Cost control and budgeting in this arena will be a complex equation involving equity, pricing, and staff allocation. Some questions to consider include: What should the mix of print, offline, and online services be? Should electronic services be free to the user? If not, how will the price structure be developed and still preserve user equity? How and when should staff be allocated as expert searchers versus giving customers direct access to remote databases?

Library automation has created new, more intimate relationships among personnel costs, collection development, and service delivery. Efficiency, effectiveness, and accountability to customers should be the top priority. "Things we should all be planning for in the hardware arena are networking, graphics, and full text. . . . Interconnectivity and multiple purpose machines are where we all should be heading. Getting the most use from every subscription, every resource, and every bit of equipment is an economic necessity" (Tenopir, 1993, p. 156).

Cost control in public libraries is a necessary activity and a major challenge. Personnel costs will be controlled through technology, continuing education, volunteerism, scheduling, and economical benefit packages. Smaller savings will occur in operating expense, maintenance of equipment and buildings, and in capital projects. Operating expense is largely driven by decisions in personnel and materials. Deferring maintenance and capital projects only shifts costs to the future and increases costs overall. Acquiring goods and services cooperatively, with parent jurisdictions or with regional library cooperatives and networks, should be maximized. Purchasing value-added services (formerly performed in-house) from vendors and bibliographic utilities may save money. Savings from energy efficiency and building retrofits should be a concern. Ultimately, the changing shape of information delivery will allow the huge cost of library buildings to drop because the warehouse building concept will be at least partially replaced with the virtual library concept.

Expenses for library materials in various formats will be harder to predict, will be more interrelated with personnel allocations, and will require altogether new management paradigms. Public libraries must also contend with the need to budget for electronic equipment and software, which become obsolete at an ever-accelerating pace.

IV. Entrepreneurship

In addition to controlling and allocating costs, public librarians must approach their work with more businesslike attitudes. Public libraries of today must be considered nonprofit businesses. Yet, it is simplistic to suggest a one-to-one relationship between the for-profit world and the nonprofit world; the rules, guidelines, and expectations are not identical.

The bulk of public library revenues will most likely continue to derive from tax dollars. Nonetheless, the way public libraries design, distribute, and price their services must be revised. Entrepreneurship, public-private partnerships, marketing, business plans, fees, contracts, and fundraising must all be considered. Public librarians must understand how to develop, nurture, and allocate resources (human, material, fiscal) and do so in a fashion that makes economic sense (Carrigan, 1988). It is extremely likely that *until* all these preliminary steps are taken success in sustaining and/or increasing public library tax revenues will not occur. Public libraries need a business plan.

How we see ourselves and how others see us will help answer the question, What business are we in? I attended a meeting in October 1993, joining almost 40 other public library directors and the California State Librarian to discuss ways to promote a sustainable future for public libraries in California. Many ideas were generated, including a consensus that some sort of statewide solution would be necessary, perhaps involving a statewide initiative submitted to the voters. At the end of the day one library director commented that public libraries might need a change of identity. Rather than considering these libraries as departments of local government, we should consider ourselves as nonprofit corporations that happen to receive tax funds as part of our revenue. This could be an important nuance, connoting an entirely new approach to public library service and fiscal support.

A few issues in the past that have hindered thinking of public libraries as nonprofit businesses include stable funding, a major dependence on tax revenue versus other sources, reactive attitudes, shyness about political activity, lack of attention to marketing and business techniques in the nonprofit environment, lack of training in public or business administration, an orientation to distribute products (print and audiovisual materials) rather than create targeted services, the public library paradigm of "being all things to all people," and the challenge of not being able to segment services or control service levels in a public service environment. These barriers must be recognized and overcome if public libraries are to remain viable.

A first step is to develop a marketing plan. Public library managers need to know how and why people seek information. What are the barriers that keep more people from using public libraries more regularly? Library consultant Lowell Martin's (1983) famous theory of concentrate and strengthen is a fine beginning, but which services should be strengthened? A well-known joke about advertising illustrates this dilemma: A business executive complained to a friend: "I spent a million dollars on advertising last year and wasted half of it!" The sympathetic friend answered, "That's terrible!" The executive concluded: "It's even worse—I don't know *which* half I wasted!" Public librarians must begin to think of their customers not as a totality but as an aggregate of market segments, each of which needs targeted resources, services, and appropriate public relations techniques.

Public librarians should look both inward and outward in order to market their services properly. Who are we and what business are we in? Do we define ourselves by the information packages we distribute or the value-added services we provide? Are we information providers or knowledge creators? Within librarianship today, there are even debates about whether the term *library* remains pertinent. For example, the graduate school of librarianship at the University of California at Berkeley recently decided to remove the word *library* from the name of their school. The lack of consensus on professional image and focus help push libraries further into the background (Foster, 1993).

Segmenting current and potential customers and studying them using market research is a valuable exercise. User surveys are now more sophisticated than in the past: they ask customers for likes *and* dislikes, to describe barriers and suggest improvements (User opinion . . . , 1993). Nonusers are an especially revealing group. Nancy Van House and others have long recognized that convenience and timeliness of service delivery is valued greatly by consumers. In the past, public libraries have not performed well in this regard (Reynolds, 1986). Service priorities must be marketed and delivered to match the expressed user demands more than theoretical needs (Reynolds, 1986). "Marketing and public relations are not in any sense charged with restructuring a library, but . . . with divining and creating the image required by the ambitions of that library" (Reynolds, 1986, p. 51).

A number of progressive public libraries are engaged in successful marketing activities. The Palatine Public Library in Illinois has reorganized its services into a Popular Services Department and an Information Services Department (A new organizational structure, 1993). Rural public libraries are anticipating new kinds of customers (and better support) as middle- and upper-income urbanites move to rural areas (90's Focus . . . , 1993). The Toledo and Lucas County in Ohio—with a 1993 to 1994 budget of more than $17 million, almost two thirds of which is guaranteed by the state—is developing a strategic marketing plan (Library concerts . . . , 1993). The Charlotte & Mecklenburg County Library in North Carolina has used a comprehensive marketing and fundraising program to convert a "sagging entity" into a thriving, visible force in the community (Fleming, 1993).

Thinking of public library customers in market segments can also promote much-needed community partnerships—partnerships that can lead to goodwill, political support, and revenue as well. Explicitly linking public libraries to economic development, cooperation with businesses, and business support groups can reap many benefits. This partnering is distinct from traditional fundraising through grants; it involves give and take as well as mutual benefits accruing to all participating groups.

In the 1980s a nonprofit group called Partners for Livable Places planned and implemented economic development projects across the United States, in cities like Richmond, Virginia. The purpose of these projects was unique: the cultural "signature" of a community was identified and then local amenities (museums, parks, art programs, libraries, etc.) were enhanced and fine-tuned to recognize a given theme. In the sluggish Richmond economy, the rundown, downtown wharf on the James River was converted into a vital community center, with tours of ships, theme-oriented shops, and an aquarium. Public and private partnerships were forged between the white and black communities, using fiscal resources from Richmond as well as community block grants. The idea was to create an area that showcased unique local attributes and attracted residents, tourists, and business investment. The Partners group claims that no other economic package is as attractive to long-term business investment as a carefully planned, vigorous array of cultural amenities (Penne, 1986). A recent study by Cognetics, Inc., confirms this research: that local amenities, including libraries, have long been recognized as an economic development tool (A view from elsewhere, 1993).

Other community partnerships between the public library and other agencies—both private and public—are blossoming everywhere. Some subject areas include interagency committees on youth at risk, serving the homeless, and counseling resources for displaced workers. At the Carnegie Library in Pittsburgh, director Bob Croneberger says that "[the library's] activities have helped boost political support . . . and prevent further [budget] reductions . . . and the interest stirred up has created a whole climate of political advocates for libraries" (Gurwitt, 1992).

In other examples, the state of California is trying to reduce recidivism in its overcrowded prisons by awarding the Riverside City and County Public Library a state grant for a unique program to educate prerelease inmates on the Library as a Resource ($104,000 for prisoner class . . . , 1993). Thirty-two New Jersey public and academic libraries are joining two "Baby Bell" companies to provide public library customers with 24-hour access to the Internet ("NJ libs. join Internet . . . , 1993). The Wendy's fast-food chain is supporting a 3-year "Wendy's Connection" to the Internet in Montana with a gift of $150,000 (Wendy's $150,000 gift . . . , 1993). Staff at the Free Library of Philadelphia are considering creative ways to provide staff training, including private sector funding, resource sharing with the city, and using existing staff to train their peers (St. Lifer and Rogers, 1993).

As described earlier, thinking and acting in businesslike ways can produce multiple benefits. Marketing allows public library staff to consider important subsets or services—subsets that are more easily manipulated and measured. Marketed services when combined with community partnerships create and nourish linkages with outside groups. These relationships can lead not only to enhanced community awareness of the public library and political support but also to a diversified revenue stream.

Because of the public library's traditional passive role in the community, an aggressive campaign of outreach is perceived by local residents as a pleasant surprise. Since most everyone supports the concept of a public library (at least in the abstract), the partnerships initiated by the library are even more potent and primed for success: they give local people a relatively easy and low-cost way to help the library, the community at large, and, not coincidentally, themselves or their company in the bargain.

Public libraries cannot function on goodwill alone, and the techniques noted earlier should also direct planning toward a positive cash flow. Public libraries are a tax-supported service industry whose budgets involve year-after-year expenses in areas like personnel, materials, and technology. Marketing should reveal community partners for whom public libraries can create customized, value-added services on a contractual, for-pay basis.

Contractual library services are often performed by individual information brokers but also include major urban libraries like the County of Los Angeles Public Library and the Milwaukee Public Library. Enhanced public relations and positive cash flow are two advantages, but some of these services have also attracted lawsuits and have actually lost money (Smith, 1993).

Much of this contractual, fee-based activity is new, and one must draw conclusions with caution. Most public libraries are not going to have the resources to produce, price, and sell services on the level of public libraries like those in Los Angeles or Milwaukee. Fee-based relationships with local businesses and individuals make sense, as do contractual relationships with cities and schools.

Fee-based contracts between public libraries and education—school districts, colleges, and universities—may be an area worth exploration. Most citizens and educators recognize—while they won't admit it publicly—a crisis in education. Even with the best resources and curriculum, education provided in the classroom is incomplete, doesn't address individual needs, and in a fast-changing world is soon obsolete. Public libraries have always performed a support role for active students as well as for the out-of-school adult. This role has been taken for granted and seldom has money flowed from schools to public libraries in recognition of this relationship.

That public libraries are expected to pick up where school libraries leave off is all too evident. As a cost-cutting measure, New York Governor Mario Cuomo has proposed lifting a 67-year-old education mandate requiring junior and senior high schools to employ certified librarians (N.Y. governor proposes . . . , 1993). In 1992, California school libraries (ranked 50 in per capita funding) were recognized by the American Library Association as the "worst of the worst." The Oakland school district has responded by starting library clubs; giving students badges bearing slogans like I Love Libraries, and taking them on trips to public libraries (School libraries struggle . . . , 1993).

Today, the crisis in school and public libraries can serve as a catalyst to better serve students and gain financial support for struggling public libraries.

CLASP, the DeWitt Wallace-Reader's Digest Connecting Libraries and Schools Project of the New York Public Library, is an outstanding example (Del Vecchio, 1993). Homework assistance centers for middle school students have been established through partnerships including the Riverside City and County Public Library, the Riverside Unified School District, and corporate sponsors (including a local shopping mall) (Baird and Plessner, 1993).

As library director for the Siskiyou County Library, I coordinated a 2-year homework center for elementary school students during 1990 to 1992. The library provided staff, materials, and added hours of service to the community. The city of Dunsmuir provided the facility and a share of utility costs. The school district paid under contract for added public library staff and also arranged for partnerships among teachers, students, and parents to ensure project success.

Rather than bickering or complaining, everyone benefits from public library and school cooperation, and this outreach is now more important than ever, as discussed eloquently by Anitra Steele and Kathleen Horning in a recent article (Steele and Horning, 1993). The education of children, whether during times of economic boom or bust, remains a top priority with voters and taxpayers. Public librarians should recognize this and take action.

Lillian Gerhardt wrote in a recent editorial that librarians have not mastered the art of "CashSpeak—the only language that taxpayers in revolt wish to use or hear." She argues that children's librarians should communicate more aggressively about the actual expenses involved in providing library service, comparing the cost of library resources used in the preparation of a typical C-grade term paper ($4000) versus an A + term paper ($8000) (Practice CashSpeak . . . , 1993).

In York, Pennsylvania, William H. Schell directs the Martin Memorial Library. The Martin Library has adopted an entrepreneurial vision that includes all aspects of what a public library should be to survive and prosper:

Mission: York's preeminent public library, Martin is a comfortable place to meet people or enjoy solitude. Martin offers readers of all ages what they want with personal service and a carefully chosen inventory. We understand that computers and video are changing customer needs and demands. A nexus for information in our community, Martin measures return on investment by the use of our products and services.

Vision: We are reinventing Martin into a more active supplier of knowledge and inspiration. Martin is gearing up to respond to customers by using today's technology and tomorrow's ideas. We are taking assertive action required by the rapidly changing marketplace. We are building relationships through new products and delivery systems. Innovative thinking and flexibility are our hallmarks.

Marketing Plan: Our Marketing Plan articulates a vision, delineates roles, and targets market(s) to be served. We deliver imaginative products, and price them effectively. We promote our products by building relationships with customers.

Library revenue categories	
Endowments/trusts	24%
Contracts (state)	20%
Donations	15%
State library funding	10%
Contracts (local schools)	8%
County funding	7%
Service fee	7%
Municipal & school district funding	5%
Sales	4%
TOTAL	100%

(William H. Schell, personal communication, October 1993)

Mr. Schell notes that no single aspect of his library program (planning, marketing, outreach, and revenue enhancement) is a panacea and progress is often painfully slow (William H. Schell, personal communication, October 1993). Nonetheless, public libraries throughout the United States would do well to look at this shining example.

An exciting partnership is about to occur in the library that I direct, the San Luis Obispo City-County Library. California Polytechnic State University, San Luis Obispo, operates a Small Business Institute, funded by the U.S. Small Business Administration. The institute performs consulting for small businesses, including the development of marketing and business plans, promotional strategies, cash flow management, and so forth. The services provided are free to the client. I asked if our library could become a client of the institute and they agreed; research began January 1994. Our library business plan should help guide our decisions and could serve as a model for other public libraries interested in a similar process.

V. Fees and Fundraising

The role of fees in public libraries has been controversial for some time. Two major pressures have intensified the discussion over fees in recent years: public library budget cuts and the array of new services made possible by technology. Most likely, the argument over fees (whether to institute, who should pay, how much to charge, and what should be charged for) will never be resolved. About the only thing on which most librarians can agree is that fees will never raise substantial amounts of money.

A consideration of public library fees touches on the fundamental philosophy of service: that public library service should be free to the user. That is, public libraries are supported by taxes, not user fees. Public libraries have always charged fees for abuses of the system: overdue fines, damaged or lost materials, and lost library cards. Since the advent of photocopying technology, public libraries have charged for photocopies and microform printing. The perceived need to develop new revenue sources and to offer new services—which are often more expensive than traditional services and/or whose cost patterns are unpredictable—has made public library fees much more common than in years past.

In addition to overdue fines, fees are charged for a variety of other reasons: raising more revenue, cost recovery, limiting use of certain materials, political equity, and limiting workload. As public library budgets are cut, fees can add to and diversify the revenue stream if fee revenue exceeds the cost of collection. Fees may be charged to recover costs associated with a new service or to pay for a traditional service that is valued but in danger of elimination due to budget cutbacks. Costs for certain services (e.g., best-sellers, videocassettes, books on tape, online database searches, etc.) may limit collection size and service levels, and fees can be used to limit use and/or to expand these services.

Residents of neighboring jurisdictions may be charged a nonresident fee to address questions of funding equity. This is especially prevalent where neighboring public libraries have dramatically different per capita funding levels, whether due to historic levels or recent cutbacks. Though not readily admitted, probably the most common reason for charging fees is to control or reduce the workload of library staff.

One reason the argument over fees is complicated relates to public perceptions. Recognizing the funding difficulties affecting their public library, many customers have expressed the opinion that public library user fees should be charged, even for services as basic as obtaining a library card or attending a story hour. They often do not understand the ethical and legal constraints that limit fee choices. More fundamentally, they do not comprehend the fact that even widespread use of fees will not begin to "pay the freight" of a public library budget (Turner, 1993).

A more serious reason why the fee question has become so contentious is that public librarians create an artificial dichotomy. The either/or choice is described as: don't charge fees, which will drastically limit the service array; or do charge fees, and offer a dramatically enhanced service array. Charging fees is politically attractive but not particularly practical (White, 1993).

Fees at the Milwaukee Public Library were studied by the Public Policy Forum. The study was a response to widespread beliefs among area businesses and public officials that substantial nontax revenue could be realized through fees and that library administration was not looking closely enough at fees as a revenue source. The results of the study indicated that a very limited number of services could be supported by fees, partly due to legal constraints but also because of economic cost-benefit analysis (DeCandido, 1989). Susan DiMattia claims that "Libraries are beginning to admit that you can't make money on fees—if you go into this thinking it's going to add to your bottom line, forget it" (Smith, 1993, p. 43).

Ronald Dubberly (1986) believes that public library services are not profitable, nor are they intended to be. The discussion over fees has both philosophical and practical aspects, but it is the philosophy that should guide decision making. He describes four alternative strategies to user fees: (1) increasing revenue at the institutional level, (2) increasing efficiency of existing resources, (3) limiting service, and (4) restructuring service priorities while reallocating existing resources. Dubberly (1986) feels that fees should and can be avoided.

Charging fees in a public library may or may not make sense politically or strategically. The political pressure to charge fees is there. A recent poll of 467 Illinois residents asked what they would favor as a library funding solution—50% chose user fees and only one third favored increasing taxes (Half OK library fees . . . , 1993). In a recent Urban Libraries Council survey, 43% of responding libraries reported feeling pressured to charge fees, yet 61% of them had not previously developed policy guidelines for charging fees (Charging of fees, 1993).

Public library fundraising looms as a larger issue than fees, if only because the amounts of money involved are vastly different. The job title of library development officer is now common, often joined with a public relations function. Larger libraries tend to hire specialists, while in smaller libraries the task usually falls to the director and/or to Friends of the Library groups.

There is no argument about the importance of public library fundraising as a supplement to traditional revenue sources. Friends of the Library probably have been raising money via book sales and other means since the creation of public libraries in the United States. Today, the issues are more urgent and complex.

As the economy has declined and demands for accountability increased, more groups are fundraising. Competition for public goodwill and philanthropic dollars has intensified. Volunteer fundraisers often work hard for relatively few dollars; burnout is not uncommon. Library development officers must bring enough outside dollars in to sustain their salaries as well as add to the communal coffers.

Because the main cost center in a public library is the ongoing cost of personnel, philanthropic donors (whether community members or foundations) almost never pay for staff costs. Exceptions are made for special, limited-time projects. Most fundraising dollars are aimed at one-time expenditures—expenses central to the mission of the library or extras the basic budget cannot afford. Books, equipment, furniture, shelving, and buildings fall into this category.

In the area of grantsmanship, perennial challenges include acquiring the expertise, personnel, and resources to research, apply for, and administer grants; making sure that resources expended are outweighed by grant revenue gained; and designing a good fit between institutional goals and individual grant requirements and expectations. If grant-funded activities are a failure, the image of the public library in the community can be damaged. If a grant-funded program is successful, then care must be taken either to plan on continuing the program with other sources of revenue or to explain to angry or disappointed stakeholders why the program is no longer available.

Fundraising activities in public libraries range from the simple to the sophisticated, from normal to unusual. One is tempted to say that everything has been tried, but surprises are constant.

The Queens Library in New York has hired the lobbying firm of Davidoff and Malito to obtain additional funds from state and local officials. In the past 3 years, the firm has secured revenues at twice the level of what it charges the library for services rendered (Retaining a lobbyist, 1993). In California, the Kings County Library and Tulare County Library are including a solicitation for donations mailed with property tax bills. Already sustained by a very high per capita spending level, the Berkeley Public Library is selling "years" (the year you were born, fell in love, etc.) and placing certificates with donors' names in the library. The supply is inexhaustible, since the library will sell the same year to more than one person (Buy a year for the library, 1993). In Kansas, Great Bend Public Library Director James Swan bakes gourmet bread at $50 per loaf to pay for library operating expenses (Library fundraiser showcases . . . , 1993). No newcomer to fundraising, Mr. Swan wrote a short "cookbook" of recipes for successful fundraising for small public libraries in 1989 (Swan, 1989).

Many public libraries now benefit from having their own foundation. A library foundation lends credibility, shifts workload from staff to library supporters, and forges valuable links with community leaders. Very often, though, these foundations are associated with only the largest libraries.

Fees and fundraising perform important, and often misunderstood, roles in public libraries. They are sometimes controversial and, without careful planning and implementation, can do more harm than good. Herbert White correctly notes that the purpose of outside fundraising must be carefully delineated. Outside funding destined to enrich and diversify what could not otherwise be accomplished is a good idea. Outside funding designed to cover the failure of library administrators or funding authorities to do their jobs is an extremely bad idea (White, 1992).

VI. Political Action

Public library budgets have traditionally depended on tax revenues for the bulk of their financing. Taxes will continue at the core of public library funding. Tax support for public libraries, historically speaking, has never been exorbitant or even adequate in many cases. Tax support for public libraries may have been based upon a philosophy of benign neglect, but at least the sources, schedules, and amounts of funding were more or less predictable.

Today, nothing about government funding is predictable. Since California's Proposition 13 passed in 1978, a fundamentally new political paradigm rules the land. California's tax-cutting fever did not subsequently infect the nation, but antitax sentiments certainly did. It is rare to find anyone inside or outside government who will publicly support new or higher taxes.

We are taught that a major purpose for fighting the Revolutionary War was to gain freedom from taxation without representation. Since the 1970s, we have gone a step further. Today, voters in many states have a direct role in approving new or higher taxes—in some cases, by a supermajority. In bypassing our elected representatives on tax issues, a new political era has been created.

Voter expectations of government are high and voter confidence in government is low. Voter-taxpayer participation in the system of raising, manipulating, and spending public revenue is difficult because the system is complex and changes daily. Fiscal decisions are made constantly and not just at election time. Bringing the fiscal needs of public libraries into this equation is a major challenge.

Budget support of service delivery in public libraries often depends on more than one funding source and/or level of government. Sometimes, lines of authority, responsibility, and accountability are not readily apparent. Customizing, or even explaining, program deliverables to local users can be problematic. Library users want to hear that they can get the services they need when they want them, how they want them, and at the right price; they do not want excuses. They want to believe the decisions and choices affecting their daily lives are made by them or local representatives accountable to local voters. It is disconcerting to all concerned that public library funding issues are often pawns in a larger game.

Public librarians and their supporters must become proactive and imagine a world in which libraries and schools are growing faster than prisons and welfare rolls. Political action is a vital component in beginning to create this better world.

Political action by librarians and library supporters is a relatively recent phenomenon and is now seen as essential to the survival of public libraries. Some people believe that fiscal scarcity for programs like public libraries is a law of nature, that political action is either inappropriate or useless, or both. *Library Journal* publisher Fred Ciporen refutes this notion and urges involvement in the process: "Since politics determines how we allocate resources, politics determines whether we will continue to have illiteracy and starving libraries" (Ciporen, 1991).

Former Baker & Taylor CEO Gerald Garbacz believes that libraries are in trouble because they are not competing effectively for scarce dollars. His proposals include: marketing the library to the public at large in order to convince politicians to move libraries up the ladder of priorities; combining all resources to focus on political action in a unified way; and vigorously entering politics to get friends of libraries elected to policymaking posts, thus ensuring libraries a piece of the fiscal pie. On a national scale, Garbacz suggests a coalition of librarians, library associations, and vendors plus publishers, distributors, and others leading to creation of political action committees for libraries (Garbacz, 1993).

Part of getting ready for political action relates to geography. At what level of government will the decision or election take place: local, state, or federal? Each level of government requires a different approach and different expectations.

Experience shows that local voters have the strongest commitment to, and will work hardest for, library outlets serving their community. Whether governed by a city, county, or citizens' board, customers are bonded to the library or libraries they use regularly. A political campaign must be couched in terms of benefit to a particular library outlet while also explaining the relationship of that branch library to libraries elsewhere—other branches of the same system and beyond.

Local funding priorities are often determined at the state level through mandates (often unfunded or underfunded), matching funds, maintenance of effort clauses, and other legal and fiscal controls. In this scenario, local needs may not be met. Political action at the state level often requires a different set of strategies and a statewide organization. Most statewide campaigning for libraries will be directed at legislatures.

Only a minority of the fifty states allow direct democracy by popular vote: voter initiative to change the constitution (16 states); voter initiative to change statutes (18 states); voter referendum on existing legislation (24 states) (*The Book of the States*, 1992). Only 2 states out of 50 require a two-thirds supermajority of voters to win tax elections: Missouri and California (Pete

Sepp, Public Relations Director, National Taxpayers' Union, personal communication, November 1993). A peculiarity of California's Proposition 13 is that new taxes must be approved in *local* elections by a two-thirds supermajority but can pass in a *state* election by a 51% simple majority.

Public librarians in California are now examining the potential for a statewide initiative for public libraries. Assuming new or higher taxes are not likely, one possibility would be earmarking a percentage of the state budget for public libraries. Many librarians and library supporters in California believe that a vote of the people statewide offers the best hope for a long-term solution.

At the federal level, the political focus has been on sustaining LSCA. A new area for federal involvement has been recognized, due to the development of the National Research and Education Network (NREN) and the National Information Infrastructure (NII). LSCA, NII, and other federal programs such as the government documents depository program are of national concern to public libraries but do not play a large role in basic funding issues.

Public spending and public policy control are inexorably linked. It follows that if public libraries are to continue being responsive to local needs then the majority of public library funds should derive from local sources. Funds sought and gained from outside sources—whether from other levels of government or from philanthropic agencies—almost always bring their own "baggage" and do not fit as well into the local service pattern. In most areas of the United States, at least where a simple majority is allowed, political action at the local level is recommended. A local focus also allows the benefits of marketing, partnerships, and outreach to be used as a foundation for political success.

Public librarians and their supporters have discovered that the political process is anything but predictable. Library issues unrelated to funding (e.g., censorship) can sway an election (Ft. Vancouver PL passes levy . . . , 1993). The presence or lack of other complex issues (especially those involving taxes) sharing a ballot with a library measure can affect the outcome.

How to plan for, implement, and win a library political campaign would be a best-seller. Unfortunately, there is no magic formula. Library elections have been won by landslides and lost by a few votes. Research and analysis into library bond elections for capital projects is fairly well studied. The analysis and research into winning a library election for ongoing operating expenses is much less clear. Anyone contemplating a library funding election should first contact others who have tried this. In California, since the passage of Proposition 13, only a handful of libraries have succeeded with the needed two-thirds supermajority. A recent success story comes from the Pasadena Public Library, which won a 5-year property tax levy in June 1993 with a 79.5% yes vote (Pasadena library tax hikes win . . . , 1993).

The process of organizing a library funding election is deceptively straightforward. The library must be a valued community agency used regularly by a substantial segment of the community and a priority even for those who don't use the library often or at all. A library support group—often coalescing around a Friends of the Library organization but not always—is essential. In areas where serial levies must be won periodically, these support groups have an ongoing task. In many communities, library support groups only get political when a funding crisis looms or when capital projects are needed. In all cases, public library services must be matched to community needs and public library leaders should be well connected to influential people or groups in the local area.

A library vision must be articulated, including a description of service patterns and levels targeted at expressed community needs. Simple logos, catchphrases, and graphics can build from this vision. The vision should be developed in cooperation with library supporters and community opinion gatekeepers using a variety of methods: surveys, telephone interviews, and focus groups. The opinions of nonusers as to why they *do not* use the library should be carefully scrutinized. Public opinion about why a particular public library service is *not* valued is often a more dependable guide than positive comments (Reynolds, 1986). In larger communities (more than 50,000 population and/or where the campaign needs to be conducted over a broad geographic area) engaging professional polling or public relations experts may be helpful.

The general library vision and detailed service patterns must be priced and funding mechanisms explored. When new taxes are needed and require validation by voters, different options should be researched and presented to the community for opinions. No tax will ever be, in any sense, popular, but taxes can be discovered that are the most equitable and the least unpopular. Taxing mechanisms vary greatly by area, but common ones used for libraries include: property, sales, dwelling, utility, benefit assessments, and income taxes. More exotic taxes such as luxury, vehicle license fees, tobacco and alcohol, and gasoline taxes are often confined by statute to thematically related programs such as highway construction and substance abuse avoidance. Tax ideas now being discussed in California include "sin taxes" (e.g., taxes on videocassette rentals) and supply-side taxes (taxes on products libraries purchase and on telephone bills).

The design of a taxing mechanism should be carefully adjusted to build on historic levels of support from the parent jurisdiction and guarantee, if possible, some level of continued fiscal support from that jurisdiction. Without that commitment, the public will perceive the new tax as a way for the city, county, or library board to evade an ongoing responsibility to sustain the library at least at some reduced level.

A key challenge in winning a library taxing election is the relationship of the library to its parent jurisdiction and the relationship of that jurisdiction to the community. If the library has a positive community image and the parent jurisdiction does not, then care must be taken to distance the library and potential new tax revenues from that parent agency. Library districts that are politically and fiscally separate from government are becoming increasingly attractive (Brawner, 1993).

After polling the community, developing a library vision, and designing a taxing structure, the issue must be put on the ballot—usually by a voter petition or through action by a city council or board of supervisors or commissioners. A voter petition drive can be helpful because it serves as a rehearsal for the political campaign. Once an election date has been determined, a timeline of campaign activities must be scheduled.

When to hold an election and the decision to hold a special versus general election are important factors, but no definitive conclusions may be drawn. Special elections in a small, compact community may be helpful, while sharing the ballot with other issues in a general election may be better for a larger and/or spread-out jurisdiction (Regina Minudri, Library Director, Berkeley Public Library, personal communication, December 1991). Without extenuating circumstances, special elections can serve as magnets for bringing out the no votes en masse—votes that can be diluted in a general (especially presidential) election. At least for bond referenda, any time of the year but spring seems to favor a yes vote for library elections (Hall, 1991).

Once an election timeline has been established, elements of the library election campaign can be delineated and implemented. Successful political action involves: media releases, informational flyers, posters and signs, speakers' bureaus, endorsements by important individuals and groups, volunteer recruitment, public meetings, periodic opinion polls during the campaign, and a get-out-the-vote effort on election day. A decision must be made early about how to make contact with the public. Door-to-door is ideal, if enough volunteers can be recruited. Personal contacts may also be made over the telephone and by having booths at shopping malls, county fairs, and other community events.

Careful attention to community demographics is essential. If a library election must be won in only one community, it is easier to feel the community pulse and to campaign. In regional elections—large cities, counties, or multi-county systems—the political environment varies greatly. Decisions need to be made early as to the boundaries of a library election. A library tax election may have heavy political support in rural areas, where voters are few, and low support in urban areas, where voters are concentrated; the reverse may also be true. Potential yes voters may be concentrated areas served by a library from another jurisdiction.

Where library budget cuts are already an unhappy fact of life, communities formerly served by one agency tend to pull apart. Statements such as these will be heard: Why can't our community withdraw from the (city or county) system and establish our own independent library? We never got our fair share of service even in the best of times. We'd be happy to establish a fund for new books, or lobby for votes, but only for our own branch library. We know you have had to cut the budget, which has reduced staff and open hours. We'll replace staff with unpaid volunteers. Communities that have lost their branch libraries in previous budget cuts can be a large source of no votes in a subsequent election. Many of the questions noted here can come from people who will vote no. Political experience also demonstrates that yes voters in polls often vote no in the election booth and that a lack of organized opposition to a library tax measure is not a bellwether for success.

Most political campaigns deemphasize swaying no voters. A strong effort is made to sway or better inform maybe voters, and to get all yes voters to the polls on election day. Regardless of the issue, yes votes are harder to get than no votes (Reynolds, 1986). No votes tend to predominate if ballot measures are complex, misunderstood, or controversial, or if higher levels of taxes are proposed or the measure involves taking existing tax revenues away from popular programs. For whatever reasons, no voters tend to go to the polls more dependably than yes voters. This is a phenomenon commonly seen by election clerks. Absentee voters often vote much more conservatively and negatively than the general population on election day.

When voters in a library election are not citizens but legislators a slightly different strategy is employed. Often, legislative staff—rather than the legislators themselves—can be the key contact points. Politicians tend to like libraries and are often willing to support library issues if library supporters do their homework. The most important task is to get the library issues to the table, with an identified funding source. Benefits provided by the proposed legislation should be linked, as far as possible, to those paying for the service. The focus of benefits should be tied to economic development issues, especially during recessionary times. Library campaigners should recognize that politicians are cautious by nature: they have to be convinced, they don't like to make mistakes, and they often do not commit until "late in the game" (Rodger, 1993).

VII. Conclusion

Adequate funding for public libraries has been, is, and will continue to be important to the fate of the democratic culture of the United States. Strong public libraries will not operate as they have in the past. Public library services will not be sustained by reactive, traditional attitudes. Although some people consider tax support of public libraries to be an anachronism, taxes will probably continue to be the main ingredient.

Supporters of public library service should begin their work by studying the past: Why and how were public libraries created in the United States? How did those libraries adapt to changes and build support in the last 160 years?

Present conditions show some public libraries dying and others flourishing; this is nothing new. Even before Proposition 13 and economic recession there were public libraries in California with annual per capita spending levels below $5 and close to $100. What are the factors that make such varied levels of support possible or tolerable?

Cutting-edge issues in public library funding include cost control, marketing, community partnerships, revenue diversification, revenue enhancement, and political action. Public librarians and public library supporters are confronting radically new issues, in different ways, with attitudes that would have been unthinkable in the past. How public librarians and their supporters plan today will determine how—or even whether—public libraries will be providing services tomorrow. The future of public libraries in the United States is ours to create.

References

'90's focus on rural community. (1993). *Library Administrator's Digest* **28**, 44.

$104,000 for prisoner class to Riverside CA PL branch. (1993). *Library Hotline* **22**, 7.

$37,950 Wilson grant for ULC funding study. (1993). *Library Hotline* **22**, 2.

$4.9 bil. for public libraries in '91, federal study shows. (1993). *Library Hotline* **22**, 2–4.

Annichiarico, M. (1993). Baker & Taylor's coup de grace. *Library Journal* **118**, 44–46.

Baird, J., and Plessner, J. (1993). Homework assistance centers. *California Libraries* **3**, 13.

Berry, J. (1986). All you can read (& more) for $11.14. *Library Journal* **111**, 112.

Bluh, P. (1993). Document delivery 2000: Will it change the nature of librarianship? *Wilson Library Bulletin* **67**, 49–51, 112.

The Book of the States, 1992–93, ed. (1992). The Council of State Governments, Lexington, Kentucky.

Brawner, L. B. (1993). The people's choice: Public library districts. *Library Journal* **118**, 59–62.

Butler, O. E. (1993). Free libraries: Are they becoming extinct? *Omni* **15**, 4.

Buy a year for the library. (1993). *Library Administrator's Digest* **28**, 69.

Carrigan, D. P. (1988). Librarians and the "dismal science." *Library Journal* **113**, 22–25.

Charging of fees. (1993). *Library Administrator's Digest* **28**, 52.

Ciporen, F. (1991). The politics of scarcity. *Library Journal* **116**, 6.

Curley, A. (1990). Funding for public libraries in the 1990s. *Library Journal* **115**, 65–67.

Curley, A. (1993). Statement by Arthur Curley, candidate for ALA president. *American Libraries* **24**, 278.

Dear President Clinton and Vice President Gore. (1993). *Library Journal* **118**, 6.

DeCandido, G. A. (1989). New Limited fee plan for Milwaukee PL. *Library Journal* **114**, 18.

Del Vecchio, S. (1993). Connecting libraries and schools with CLASP. *Wilson Library Bulletin* **68**, 38–40.

Dickson, P. (1986). *The Library In America: A Celebration in Words and Pictures.* Facts on File, New York.

Dubberly, R. A. (1986). Managing NOT to charge fees. *American Libraries* **17**, 670–676.

Fleming, H. R. (1993). Library CPR: Savvy marketing can save your library. *Library Journal* **118**, 32–35.

Foster, S. (1993). Information literacy: Some misgivings. *American Libraries* **24**, 344.

Ft. Vancouver PL passes levy, overrides censorship challenge. (1993). *Library Hotline* **22**, 1.

Garbacz, G. G. (1993). Library politics: A manifesto for change. *Library Journal* **118**, 46.

Goldhor, H. (1986). Public library spending jumps 9.7%; Circulation up 1.8%. *American Libraries* **17**, 54.

Goldhor, H. (1987). Public library spending makes biggest jump in decade. *American Libraries* **18**, 566.

Gurwitt, R. (1992). Shelving tradition in the library. *Governing* **5**, 24–26.

Half OK library user fees in Illinois user survey. (1993). *Libary Hotline* **22**, 1.

Hall, R. B. (1991). Still a boom for bonds? *Library Journal* **116**, 48–53.

Kurzweil, R. (1993). The virtual library. *Library Journal* **118**, 54–55.

La Ganga, M. L. (1993). Merced County to close its public libraries. *Los Angeles Times* (November 24), A-3.

Library concerts. (1993). *Library Administrator's Digest* **28**, 71.

Library fundraiser showcases director's culinary talents. (1993). *Library Hotline* **22**, 9.

Marquand, B. K. (1990). Library's future uncertain as county faces bankruptcy. *American Libraries* **21**, 709.

Martin, L. A. (1983). The public library: Middle-age crisis or old age? *Library Journal* **108**, 18–22.

A new organizational structure. (1993). *Library Administrator's Digest* **28**, 53.

New York governor proposes lifting school librarian mandate. (1993). *American Libraries* **24**, 206.

NJ libs. join Internet venture. (1993). *Library Journal* **118**, 16.

Pasadena library tax hikes win 79.5 percent of vote. (1993). *Library Hotline* **22**, 1.

Penne, R. L. (1986). *The Return of the Livable City: Learning from America's Best.* Acropolis Books, Washington, DC.

Plight of public libraries featured on ABC network. (1993). *Library Hotline* **22**, 1.

Practice "CashSpeak" Gerhardt urges librarians. (1993). *Library Hotline* **22**, 4.

Public wants increased support. (1993). *Library Administrator's Digest* **28**, 61.

Quinn, J., and Rogers, M. (1992). Library budgets survey '91: Hard times continue. *Library Journal* **117**, 14–28.

Retaining a lobbyist. (1993). *Library Administrator's Digest* **28**, 66.

Reynolds, B. A. (1986). Proactive management in public libraries—in California and in the nation. In *Advances in Library Administration and Organization* (G. B. McCabe and B. Kreissman, eds.), pp. 1–78. JAI Press, Greenwich, Connecticut.

Rodger, E. J. (1993). *High Tech. High Touch: Perspectives on Future Libraries.* Program presented at the 1993 California Library Association conference in Oakland, California; from notes taken by the author.

Schilling, E. (1993). The state's libraries struggle to do more with less. *California Journal* **24**, 25–27.

School libraries struggle in Calif. (1993). *Library Administrator's Digest* **28**, 51.

Selsky, D. (1990). Government spending on libraries increased 3.8 percent in 1988. *Library Journal* **115**, 42.

Shed print paradigm, federal librarians told. (1993). *Library Hotline* **22**, 1–2.

Smith, Wendy. (1993). Fee-based services: Are they worth it? *Library Journal* **118**, 40–43.

Smith Automation Systems, Inc. (1992). *California Library Telecommunications Study Project, Report #1*. California State Library, Sacramento.

St. Lifer, E., and Rogers, M. (1993). ULC study finds libs. invest little in staff development. *Library Journal* **118**, 112–113.

Starr, K. (1993). How books helped build Los Angeles. *Los Angeles Times* (special LAPL supplement, Oct. 1), 3–4, 11.

Steele, A. T., and Horning, K. T. (1993). Shifting the burden. *Wilson Library Bulletin* **68**, 63–65.

Summers, F. W. (1980). Finance and budget. In *Local Public Library Administration* (E. Altman, ed.), pp. 130–140. American Library Association, Chicago.

Swan, J. (1989). Fund-raising for the small public library. *Wilson Library Bulletin* **63**, 46–48.

Tenopir, C. (1993). Forces shaping electronic access. *Library Journal* **118**, 155–156.

Turner, A. (1993). They just don't get it. *California Libraries* **3**, 3, 13.

User opinion on services surveyed by two libraries. (1993). *Library Hotline* **22**, 5–6.

A view from elsewhere. (1993). *San Luis Obispo County Telegram-Tribune* (September 30), B-6.

Vogel, N. (1993). As closings mount, California called the "Sarajevo" of public libraries. *San Luis Obispo County Telegram-Tribune* (November 25), A-5.

Voice processing. (1993). *Library Administrator's Digest* **28**, 42.

Wendy's $150,000 gift supports Internet connection in Montana. (1993). *Library Hotline* **22**, 4–5.

White, H. S. (1992). Seeking outside funding: The right and wrong reasons. *Library Journal* **117**, 48–49.

White, H. S. (1993). Fee vs. free: A catchy but not very meaningful option. *Library Journal* **118**, 55–56.

Romania and United States Library Connections

Opritsa D. Popa and Sandra J. Lamprecht
Shields Library
University of California
Davis, California 95616

I. Overview of Romanian Librarianship to 1989: A Legacy of Despair

The winter of 1989 will be remembered in the pages of Romanian history for the fall of communism and as a time of renewal and hope. By spring of 1990, however, the euphoria of freedom had gradually subsided and the damages inflicted by 45 years of repression became all too visible. "One of the main consequences of the communist rule and the idiosyncratic economic and social policies of the Ceausescu regime is that Romania is entering its postcommunist era as a country with one of the most impoverished populations in Eastern and Central Europe, except for Albania. According to the United Nations Human Development Report published in 1992, Romania has the lowest rating among the European countries in the Human Development Index—0.733 (calculated on the basis of most recent data on income, literacy, years of schooling, and life expectancy as measures of quality of life in a particular country) . . . this statistical ranking well illustrates the sheer size and scope of the need for Romania's social and economic development" (Sadlak, 1993).

In the months following the Romanian "revolution," several international library teams visited Romania to assess the library situation and determine needs. Their reports reflected appalling conditions of deterioration and neglect: outdated collections, antiquated equipment, inadequate building structures, a dearth of educational opportunities. Romania, a country with a library tradition reaching back several centuries, had been systematically starved of information and forced to produce, collect, and preserve works extolling the "superiority" of the communist system. Fact-finding missions concluded that extensive international assistance may eventually bring Romanian libraries to the level of libraries in Poland (Hojsgaard, 1990).

ADVANCES IN LIBRARIANSHIP, VOL. 18

Until World War II Romania's libraries had kept pace with developments in Europe. The end of the nineteenth century and the first decades of the twentieth century had been marked by accelerated economic, social, and educational developments and had led to a strong demand for information. Research libraries and a strong public library system came into existence. The roots of decline can be traced back to 1948. This is when the newly established communist state nationalized all means of production, including publishing, and redefined the role of libraries to fit within a socialist cultural framework. Under the control of the Communist Party and the ideological straitjacket of Marxism-Leninism, libraries became propaganda tools responsible for remolding a bourgeois mentality into that of the "new socialist citizen." Early on the communist dictatorship recognized libraries as one of "its most formidable ideological pillars" (Kuzmin, 1993, p. 570). Paradoxically, the party's incessant rhetoric on the educational and ideological importance of libraries did not translate into tangible financial and professional support. Quite to the contrary, so-called communist special attention and care for culture and libraries meant nothing more than a progressive loss of book funds, a perennial elimination of professional positions, and a constant reduction in library space (Bercan, 1990).

During this time, library acquisitions shifted to materials depicting the "glorious, historical forward march of socialism and communism." Emphasis on acquiring marginal literature stifled the growth of library collections and coincided with a policy of neglect of valuable archival materials and with deliberate acts of vandalism.

> The rounding up of manuscripts for deposit elsewhere was frequently undertaken in a crude and reckless manner. . . . Local practices often added to injury. In the Transylvanian city of Brasov, medieval charters were still in 1988 displayed on the walls of the local museum with the help of pins pushed through the parchment. . . . According to a regulation in force during the 1980s, manuscripts which were more than 50% damaged were ineligible for any sort of repair. (Rady, 1991, p. 125)

The long-term consequences of decline of research collections and the outright destruction of many valuable manuscripts and rare books are only now coming to light. Today thousands upon thousands of rare books remain in a critical state of deterioration (Hermina Anghelescu, personal communication, 1993).

The last 15 years of the Ceausescu regime were marked by particularly adverse conditions for the knowledge sector. In order to cope with a growing economic crisis and accelerate the repayment of the country's foreign debt, the state imposed a severe austerity program on its population. In 1980, hardcover books disappeared from the market; the quality of paper and binding registered progressive deterioration. In 1989 Romanian book publishing dropped from 5000 to a mere 1000 titles. As only one 40-watt light bulb was allowed per household under strict penalties, reading and writing became a luxury. Light and heat in library buildings were drastically curtailed. One librarian remembers that the glass of water left on her desk in the morning was frozen solid by midday. Memberships to international library organizations were discontinued; permission to attend international conferences was routinely denied; outdated library equipment was no longer replaced. In 1989 the National Library had only one functioning microfilm reader with no printer. Acquisition budgets for foreign materials were totally eliminated. All foreign subscriptions and book acquisitions from abroad were canceled. The barely existing information trickle from the West dried up altogether. Romania became completely isolated from Western information and thought.

In March 1990, 3 months after the "revolution," an assessment of conditions by an international library team concluded that Romania's libraries resembled those of Western Europe at the beginning of the 1950s (i.e., scarce photocopying facilities, no automation, and interlibrary cooperation based solely on printed sources) (Hojsgaard, 1990). The same report, however, gives credit to Romanian librarians, who in spite of hardships, kept their libraries open and functioning: "It is necessary to try to understand how much libraries have suffered, how much harm has been done through the total isolation from the international library community, the financial starvation, and the constant political control. The persistence and dedication with which librarians have been able to carry on their work calls for admiration" (Hojsgaard, 1990, p. 2).

A. Brief Overview of Libraries and Collections

Romania has two national libraries, as well as well-developed academic and public library systems. A lesser developed special libraries network also exists. The Library of the Academy and the National Library (formerly known as the Central State Library), with individual collections exceeding 8 million volumes, are the two national libraries of Romania. Three university libraries (Bucharest, Cluj, and Iasi) serve the academic community and coordinate the activities of branch libraries, which function in colleges and academic departments. The public library system, made up of county, city, and communal libraries, functions under the aegis of the National Library.

The Library of the Romanian Academy is the principal research library of the country. With an extensive collection, emphasizing the social sciences, humanities, and the arts, and especially strong in Romanian history and culture, this library is open by special permit to researchers. The library has jurisdiction over various research institutes. The National Library strives for comprehensive coverage of foreign materials in all fields but excels mostly in the humanities and social sciences. The flagship of the public library system, the National Library publishes the current national bibliography, provides central cataloging for Romanian books, offers methodological support, and distributes duplicate materials within the public library system. The university libraries (Bucharest, Cluj, and Iasi) serve as research and support libraries for their respective institutions of higher learning. In addition, numerous special libraries and documentation centers support the information needs of government agencies, businesses, research units, museums, and so on.

B. Library Facilities

Major urban libraries are housed in fin de siècle style buildings that are not well suited to library operations. The National Library, for instance, occupies the former Stock Exchange building and has long outgrown its stacks, office, and reading room space. At the height of the communist dictatorship a large new structure was being erected to house its rich collections. Ceausescu, who, like Hitler, had artistic ambitions, personally designed and redesigned the plans for the library. The "revolution" put a halt to the project and the construction remains unfinished. Danish–Swedish report expresses shock over existing and planned library facilities. "A monstrosity of a new library, designed as a monument to serve Ceausescu's ambitions, is more than half-built, but totally unsuited for library purposes . . . The Bucharest Municipal Library is housed in a beautiful but not very well suited house built around 1900 as an abode for the mistress of a tycoon" (Hojsgaard, 1990, pp. 5–6). Many of these buildings suffered extensive structural damages during a devastating earthquake in 1977 and were left in disrepair. While pursuing an aggressive policy of urban development, the Ceausescu regime constructed few libraries to serve these new areas. Far from augmenting the number of public libraries, the regime abolished all village libraries in 1974, thus depriving rural population of direct access to information (Schifirnet, 1990).

In most research libraries, shelving space is scarce and infrequently used books are relegated to remote storage. Deselected books from the National Library collection were transported to storage facilities by open truck, with no regard for the fragile state of some older materials. No adequate inventories of collections stored at remote sites exist and access to deposited materials is virtually impossible (Hermina Anghelescu, personal communication, 1993).

Environmental controls, such as air conditioning or humidity control systems, are nonexistent. In Bucharest the damp, hot summer months, compounded by dust, air pollution, and automobile exhaust fumes, turn books into microfungi breeders. This situation is particularly disastrous for the National Library and the Library of the Academy, which house irreplaceable national and international treasures.

C. Library Organization

Generally, collections are organized by the Universal Decimal Classification System. Card catalogs are organized by author, title, and classified subject approach and are at best incomplete. This is due in part to the existence of the Collections with Special Circulation (i.e., censored books). Traditionally, public service work consisted of circulation, bibliographic work, and library tours, with no dedicated reference services. Large libraries maintained and still maintain closed stacks and allow only a certain number of books to be requested at a time.

D. Library Education

Academic education in librarianship, initiated in the 1940s, was discontinued during World War II. Until the 1970s, however, undergraduate programs in technical services and basic library management continued to be offered. Although inadequate for existing demand, this coursework provided new library workers with the rudimentary theoretical and practical knowledge that kept libraries functioning. Since there was no dedicated library school, graduate and postgraduate training in "bibliology" was possible only by attending library-related courses offered through such university departments as history or Romanian literature. Nevertheless, interest in library science existed as demonstrated by the first Ph.D. degree, which was awarded in 1973.

For rank-and-file academic and public librarians, continuing education, however, was a question of personal initiative and perseverance. With limited library literature at hand, few national meetings, and scarcely any international contacts, remaining professionally up to date was a challenge (Mihaela Parus, personal correspondence, 1993).

E. Neglect and Censorship

In Ceausescu's Romania, active censorship was omnipresent and began with the act of independent thinking and free expression, both considered manifestations of insubordination. At the publishing level, works deemed inimical to the party never reached the printing presses. In the 1950s, library collections underwent ideological purification (i.e., books were purged and publicly burned). The Council of Culture and Education was directly responsible for book censorship. Existing collections were segregated into materials for general use and materials with special circulation—the notorious S Collections. These consisted of works deemed to be of a sensitive nature that were kept in separate rooms, with their records in separate card catalogs. Taboo subjects included anticommunist and antiparty literature, historical writing disputing marxist assumptions, Hungarian and German periodicals of the nineteenth century (Hategan, 1990), literature of the extreme right, writings critical of Ceausescu, all works by dissidents, and contributions of Romanian writers in the diaspora (Emil Cioran, Eugene Ionesco, Mircea Eliade, etc.). Hermina Anghelescu, Fulbright Scholar at the University of Texas at Austin (1992–1994), recalls that the National Library received the *Encyclopedia of Philosophy* from France, a work in 20 volumes. Eleven of those were sequestered in the S Collection, as they included definitions of communism, doctrine, or dictatorship (Hermina Anghelescu, personal correspondence, 1993). At the height of the Ceausescu personality cult, the S Collections were bulging with books that had irreverent remarks or allusions less than complementary to Ceausescu. Among these, for example, was a bedtime story by Ana Blandiana describing a megalomaniac tomcat. It was banned to the S Collection because it reminded censors of the nation's leader (Campeanu, 1990).

Aside from special lists of "reactionary authors" supplied by the secret police, no specific guidelines existed for removal of materials considered to undermine the social order. It was expected that a librarian with a revolutionary conscience would know the difference between a wholesome and a subversive book (Hategan, 1990). Such vague and threatening directives caused much apprehension and fear. Romanian and foreign researchers interested in historical sources or otherwise needing to consult these sensitive materials were requested to file for permission with the Council of Culture, who then sent their applications to the secret police (Campeanu, 1990). Few dared risk their position for the freedom to read.

F. Appointments, Promotions, and Working Conditions

Appointments to librarian positions were offered on a competitive basis. University graduates were eligible to apply and were ranked after a test. Training in technical or public services was done on the job. Librarian salaries were at the low end of the national payscale. Opportunities for advancement were limited to a one-step merit from librarian to principal librarian and were awarded on the basis of professional longevity. Administrative positions were most often reserved for political appointees. A family member residing abroad or correspondence with people in capitalist countries automatically disqualified any candidate from a position of leadership (Mihaela Parus, personal correspondence, 1993). "The systematic promoting of mediocrity and opportunism by the regime achieved the expected results: fear of initiative and decision-making, lack of responsibility, non-critical acceptance of official judgment" (Schifirnet, 1990, p. 14).

Under the communist centralized system, the publishing industry automatically deposited copies of all printed materials in the principal libraries. Although this ensured the existence of most published materials in library collections, the concepts of selection and collection development had no real meaning. Librarians were not at liberty to reject Romanian books coming on deposit. However, they were eager to accept any foreign publication through international exchanges (Hermina Anghelescu, personal correspondence, 1993).

In order to discharge their responsibility as propaganda dispensers, librarians were forced to spend endless hours preparing book exhibits on current socialist successes, organizing tightly controlled book discussions where no spontaneous dialogue or criticism was permitted, or compiling useless sociopolitical bibliographies. In smaller libraries, this activity was conducted to the detriment of routine library work (Mihaela Parus, personal correspondence, 1993).

G. Professional Life and Publications

The Association of Romanian Librarians, founded in 1956, was a political organization that functioned in name only. The association was monopolized early by the leadership of the Central State Library, who, with the blessing of the party, used it to control all international contacts, especially IFLA activities. Results of international meetings, at which only communist leadership participated, were not communicated to the membership (Regneala, 1990). For academic and research librarians, international book exchanges became the only way to maintain a lifeline to libraries in the Western world. Public librarians had even less opportunities for international contacts.

Among professional publications, the most important periodicals were *Probleme de Informare si Documentare*, *Studii si Cercetari Documentare*, and the irregular *Biblioteca*. In general, editors favored political articles. Yet librarians struggled over the years to maintain a professional profile and succeeded in publishing an important body of professional literature. Dominant topics were bibliographic control, library education, the use of microformats, library history, bibliographic instruction, and automation. "It can be admired that despite restrictions, control, and dismal physical resources, there has been any genuine academic work at all. This kind of encouraging 'surprise' had actually been confirmed in a bibliometric survey carried out in 1988 by the Institute for Scientific Information" (Sadlak, 1993, p. 92).

II. Crisis and Transition

On December 22, 1989, the fundamental condition of Romanian librarianship and the isolated state of its libraries were shattered and transformed literally overnight. On that fateful day Romania exploded in a bloody revolution against communism and its oppressive dictator. Nicolae Ceausescu and his wife, Elena, were executed after a brief trial. From December 22 through

December 24, the Central University Library in downtown Bucharest was caught in the crossfire between warring factions: fire ravaged the beautiful neoclassical building and destroyed a quarter of the library's collection— more than 500,000 volumes. The dramatic plight of the Central University Library caused the deplorable condition of Romania's libraries and its woefully inadequate information systems to come into the world's spotlight. With the sudden overthrow of Ceausescu, now, for the first time in four decades Romania was open to the West. Several countries and organizations came to the aid of Romania's libraries; notable among these were the United States, the Netherlands, Great Britain, France, and the International Federation of Library Associations (IFLA).

A. America Responds to Romanian Library Crisis

U.S. librarians initiated several book drives to aid Romanians. On May 21, 1990, the *New York Times* had an editorial entitled "Starved for Books: Another Hunger in Eastern Europe." The author noted that the old regime had banned all types of books from the West—medical and scientific works, social science and literary books, and applauded the efforts of one of the larger book drives, Books for Romania (USA) (Sigal, 1990).

B. Books for Romania (USA)

Books for Romania (USA) was initiated just after the Christmas Revolution at the 1990 Midwinter meeting of the American Library Association (ALA). A resolution to help restore library services in Romania was unanimously passed by the ALA Council. The U.S. Information Agency (USIA) offered, via a grant, to cover all transportation expenses of library-related materials from the USIA warehouse in Brooklyn, New York, to Constanta, Romania.

Press releases announcing this Romanian library relief effort were issued by ALA and the USIA and disseminated to professional journals. The authors, assisted by Doina Farkas (University of Florida), coordinated the book drive, Books for Romania (USA). Among those who responded to the call for books and equipment were university presses, trade publishers, and libraries who wished to donate duplicates to their counterparts within Romania. Individual professors and private individuals also made donations.

As offers of books and journals were made, it became apparent that some items were not suitable for Romania. In any book drive it is important not to waste energy or money collecting and transporting books that will not be used; otherwise recipients may find themselves deluged with crates of books that cannot be incorporated into their existing collections. To avoid this, potential donors were told that only current, substantive, scholarly materials that corresponded to the guidelines received from Romanian libraries could be accepted; other material was politely and firmly rejected (Popa and Lamprecht, 1991). Examples of rejected material included cookbooks, travel books, incomplete sets of periodicals, popular fiction, and seriously outdated reference books.

The book drive lasted 1 year. During that time over 240,000 books and journals were sent to Bucharest for distribution to many libraries according to interest and need. The estimated value of the materials sent exceeded $4 million. Robert Doyle, ALA liaison to the project, noted, "Reaction in Bucharest was especially appreciative for the quality of the ALA donations" (Doyle, 1991, p. 106).

Lessons learned during the Books for Romania (USA) drive may be useful for future book relief programs. Namely, the endorsement and support of a professional organization is extremely beneficial. In the case of Books for Romania (USA), ALA referred potential donors to the coordinators, issued press releases, and informed the library and general public of the progress of the project. A connection with a government agency such as the USIA, who had direct ties to Romania, was vital. The USIA and the staff in the American Library in Bucharest helped the relief effort by taking charge once the books arrived by containerized cargo. They were able to cut through bureaucratic red tape, arrange contacts with Romanian officials, and hire English-speaking students to sort incoming books. Its staff members had an intimate knowledge of which Romanian libraries and institutes specialized in particular areas; thus they were able to send subject specific books to the appropriate libraries. Too often book drives result in books collecting dust in an out-of-the-way warehouse or, as can happen in a country desperate for knowledge and currency, sold on the black market. For Books for Romania (USA) the American Library in Bucharest was the appropriate distribution point.

Continuous media coverage during the span of the drive is essential. In the United States, the library media carried numerous announcements and articles on the book drive, which in turn generated a continuous flow of donations. In Romania, radio, television, and newspapers covered the book relief story. The American ambassador to Romania, who occasionally helped in the effort by presenting donated books, lent additional prestige to the project.

C. Other U.S. Book Drives

Gordon Aamot, head of the Business Administration Library at the University of Washington, traveled to Romania on a U.S. Agency for International Development (AID) funded grant entitled Management Training and Economics Education in Romania. (The University of Washington, School of

Business and the Washington State University College of Business coauthored the grant to promote business education within Romania after the overthrow of Ceausescu.) The two recipient institutions in Bucharest were the Academy of Economic Studies (AES) and the Polytechnic Institute of Bucharest (PIB). As part of the overall grant, two librarians, Aamot and Alice Spitzer of Washington State University, were responsible for the library development component. Their duties entailed a visit to Romania to assess the needs of the institutions. This was completed in November 1991. After returning to the United States, they ordered scholarly books for the two academic libraries as well as for the newly established Small Business Development Centers. A total of $30,000 was allocated for books: 745 books plus several hundred gift books were shipped to Romania during 1991 and 1992. Essentials such as business dictionaries, introductory textbooks and journals (e.g., the *Harvard Business Review*) were desperately needed and wanted. The Romanian librarians even requested the *Seattle Yellow Pages* as an example of a business information source. "There is a hunger for Western business information that is almost physical," Aamot noted (Mudrock, 1992).

Another donation project arose from a plea for scholarly journals made by an Eastern European visiting professor to Arien Mack, editor of *Social Research*. Without any outside financial aid, Mack responded to this plea by organizing a project to provide free journal subscriptions. She got the project off the ground by writing to friends who edited journals; she was later joined by the American Council of Learned Societies. Today, over 363 journals in all disciplines are being sent on a regular basis to Romania, as well as to 150 other university libraries in Eastern Europe. Janet Greenberg, an ACLS program officer, observed that "this is a program run by scholars for scholars and this fact has made the program highly successful" (Desruisseaux, 1993).

Aside from these key book drives, other efforts, individual and institutional, have no doubt come into being as well. At the time of this writing, these combined efforts have resulted in better and richer Romanian library collections.

D. International Book Drives

Although this article concentrates on the U.S. connection with its diverse ramifications, other key international book drive efforts will also be briefly highlighted.

Several other countries have come to the aid of Romania, notably those in Western Europe, as would be expected given their close geographic proximity. One of the larger campaigns was the English Books for Romania project coordinated by Professor R. J. Crampton, of the University of Kent, Canterbury and three of his colleagues. The British team was able to issue a widespread appeal in the press asking the public for books and periodicals in any language that would be useful for the Central University Library in Bucharest. Donations were solicited and the British Council agreed to pay for transportation costs. Requests for books and donations appeared in the *Manchester Guardian Weekly* (Kinsey, 1990) and in the prestigious *Economist*. Their results were amazingly successful: at the conclusion of the drive over half a million books were sent to Romania from England.

The Scottish appeal for books was coordinated by Sally Wood at Edinburgh University Library. More than 20,000 academic books and journals donated by Scottish universities, booksellers, and publishers were sent to Romania in February 1990, in a convoy of 23 trucks carrying aid of various kinds. The books were sent to four separate university libraries: Bucharest, Cluj, Tirgu-Mures, and Timisoara, plus the Theological College of the Romanian Reformed Protestant Church in Oradea (Wood, 1990).

The French National Library launched a 1-day book donation campaign targeting the general library public. It was entitled Operation Springtime for Romanian Libraries and was held on March 20, 1990. People were asked to donate the money equivalent of one book to help restore the devastated libraries. Proceeds were sent to the Romanian Ministry of Culture earmarked for restoration of book collections. The International Federation of Library Associations (IFLA) and UNESCO also were involved in relief efforts or publicity. Their donations were made primarily to public libraries and included fiction, nonfiction and children's books.

Sandor Fazakas, a pastor from Romania who escorted the Scottish book donations, eloquently sums up the spirit of those involved in book drives: "Clothes and food are short term and quickly finished, but the books are our passport to Western education to bring us up-to-date with a world we have been cut off from for 30 odd years. The books are our future" (Wood, 1990, p. 918).

III. In Search of New Paradigms: Romania's Libraries and U.S. Models

The new social, political and economic reality of the postcommunist era caused many problems in the Romanian library world. Under immense pressure to democratize and modernize library operations, library decision makers had to assess needs and balance them with fiscal realities and set priorities for short- and long-term goals. The euphoria of freedom was quickly overshadowed by the sobering realization that self-governance has its price and that the transition to market economy demanded that librarians learn a new set of survival skills (i.e., how to compete for scarce funding sources). "Currently there are 43 university-level libraries, 41 pedagogical libraries, and 10,000 school libraries in a country of 23 million people. Every library is fighting just to exist" (Moldovan, 1993, p. 5).

The search for new paradigms was evident from the first postrevolutionary issues of the professional journal *Biblioteca*. In it, editor-in-chief Ioana Lupu emotionally greeted the new era and the newfound freedom from censorship: "A new library world is emerging, brimming with new thoughts, new models, new expressions—we are rethinking the role of the librarian" (Ioana Lupu, personal correspondence, 1993). A new section called "Library Meridian" was dedicated to articles on international librarianship and U.S. librarians were invited to contribute. Discussions focused on library management (Chapman, 1992), personnel issues (Chapman, 1993), children's libraries (Miller, 1992), and reference services in academic and public library settings (Popa, 1991). However, while democracy brought with it freedom of expression, the newly unleashed market forces imposed new difficulties on the publishing industry as well.

> The current economic crisis is particularly harsh on non-productive sectors, such as culture and the press. Professional library journals are going through very difficult times due to lack of funding, lack of paper or both. For months in a row reporters, editors, and typesetters work without a salary, as payroll payments cannot be met. While the revolution has allowed for freedom of expression the current financial difficulties are even harsher than before. Yesteryear, there was censorship of contents, and today we are facing financial censorship. (Ioana Lupu, personal correspondence, 1993)

Romanian contributors to *Biblioteca* focused on neglected areas in library organization and management, reviewed advances in Western librarianship dealing with technical and public service and new library equipment. Of particular interest was automation, interlibrary cooperation, the creation of democratic library associations, articulation of a domestic and foreign acquisition plan, blueprints for library construction, and education in librarianship.

The international library community responded with an avalanche of enthusiastic suggestions as well as a perplexing array of options for improvement and change. Postrevolutionary Romanian library literature reflects Romanian interest in Western models and concepts. Dutch, French, British, Scandinavian, and U.S. policies, practices, or novel library equipment, developed in the free world during Romania's long absence from the international library forum, are described, analyzed, admired, and their potential application to Romanian circumstances hotly debated. For the first time in years, Romanian librarians traveled to Western Europe to observe and discuss with colleagues modern library trends and technological advances. Their views and recommendations for Romanian libraries are recorded in the pages of *Biblioteca*.

In this new environment assuming responsibility for one direction, choosing one model or one system over another became a library administrator's daunting task. American library literature is replete with warnings against librarians' natural impulse to tell others how to emulate our efforts. "This type of attitude toward international involvement is not only inappropriate, but in no way helpful . . . one should refrain from offering solutions from one's own experience as the obvious answer to international or regional library and information problems, without a realization that those solutions may be . . . in need of extensive modification to suit a particular situation" (Segal, 1992, p. 100). The resolve for change and the choice of direction had to emanate from Romania. One way of assisting administrators was to expose them to a large array of models and allow them the opportunity to select appropriate solutions for their unique situation.

A. U.S. Models and Romanian Decision Makers

A number of U.S. library models appeared to have potential relevance to Romanian conditions. From 1991 to 1992, several U.S. government agencies and private foundations recognized the need to facilitate firsthand observation of the U.S. library scene and extended invitations to a group of Romanian librarians. These travel and study grants were a welcome beginning in United States–Romanian library cooperations. Prominent among the organizations sponsoring such study visits were the USIA, U.S. Department of Agriculture, Soros Foundation, International Research & Exchanges Board (IREX), and Mortenson Center for International Librarianship (University of Illinois, Urbana-Champaign). Romanian decision makers and key library personnel were invited to spend up to 1 month in the United States. Among these first visitors were Ion Stoica, Director of the Central University Library in Bucharest; Gheorghe Bercan, Director of the National Library of Romania; Doru Radosav, Director of the Lucian Blaga University Library in Cluj; principal catalogers; and heads of special libraries. Although visits were tailored to individual information needs, the many similarities in goals, experiences, and impact allow analyses in general terms.

For each person, objectives were identified in advance of arrival and site visits and appointments with key people were prearranged. Most Romanian decision makers were interested in organization and function of large libraries and library networks, library administration and personnel management (organizational charts, work flow, training methods, ways to evaluate and motivate library employees), models of outreach to special populations, and delivery of special services to minority groups. (Romania has a large Hungarian population, as well as smaller numbers of Germans, Serbs, Jews, and gypsies.) Other aspects included library automation, library education, professional development and continuing education, trends in modern library architecture, and finally, the role of the democratic professional library associations in the life of librarians.

Itineraries included visits to the Library of Congress, meetings with officers of ALA, visits to Columbus, Ohio, and the OnLine Computer Library Center (OCLC), and tours of prominent academic, public, and state libraries. After visiting several countries in Western Europe, Bercan stated upon return, "I am convinced that the United States has the best library system in the world. Impressions accumulated during my visit to the U.S. are so overwhelming, that I can hardly express myself in objective terms" (Bercan, personal correspondence, 1993). U.S. library study tours play an important role in the posttotalitarian reorganization of libraries in Eastern Europe. The large variety of models, ideas, and programs observed and the productive discussions conducted with American library colleagues have opened new vistas for East European library life and have helped illustrate and define international professional standards.

The first group of visitors also paid special attention to library school organization and curricula as models for Romanian library education. Immediately after the fall of communism, a new library school within the Faculty of Letters in Bucharest opened its doors, and today a first class of professional librarians is entering the work force. As a direct result of the study visits to the United States and with the encouragement of the Mortenson Center, a School of Library and Information Sciences and an American Studies Center were created in Cluj (Transylvania).

Study visits have also allowed librarians to establish and/or renew book exchange programs, a method that still constitutes a major acquisition venue for international publications. In the field of electronics, visitors have been offered a unique possibility to study a variety of OPACs (such as the University of California's Melvyl system), automated library systems, a large array of software applications, and CD-ROMs. They have also facilitated direct negotiations with U.S. business representatives.

Administrators studied contemporary library architectural designs. As the National Library and the Central University Library in Bucharest are scheduled to move into new quarters, visits to new American libraries, such as the Chicago Public Library or the new addition to the Library at the University of California, Davis, allowed for a better understanding of modern architectural concepts. It goes without saying that functional space interaction, comfortable, well-designed furnishings, modular offices, walls and windows treatment, lighting and climate control, security systems, compact shelving, clear signage, and so on can be best understood and appreciated when seen, used, and experienced.

Discussions with ALA and USIA representatives have led to proposals for the posting of a second ALA Library fellow to Romania in the spring of

1994, as well as to requests for Fulbright Scholars to teach at the newly created library schools. On request ALA has provided a series of ALA documents (e.g., the Library Bill of Rights) that reflect our democratic experience, documents that may be used as models to help shape the philosophy of the new professional associations in Romania. Finally, these visits allowed for personal contacts and for professional friendships to develop, which help bring about a better understanding of common problems and common achievements on both sides.

B. Education: Romanians Studying in the United States

In their reports on Romania, the IFLA Deputy Secretary General (1990) as well as the Danish–Swedish fact-finding team (1990) identified the availability of scholarships to study abroad as one of the most urgent needs in Romanian librarianship: "The isolation from the international library community is deeply felt and renewed contact is seen as one of the most important means of future professional development" (Hojsgaard, 1990). Current U.S. economic conditions as well as the enormous difficulties experienced by Eastern European countries in their transition to market economies have made U.S. educational grants and scholarships in library science very competitive. In Romania, rampant inflation has made international travel prohibitive. Low librarians' salaries and scarce governmental funding opportunities have impeded the development of meaningful opportunities for advanced training or research in the United States. As a result, only a few Romanian librarians have been able to work and study in American libraries. Nonetheless, the fact that some educational trips to Western Europe and the United States have taken place is a gigantic step forward from the isolation of yesteryear. The acquired knowledge, experience, and the broad understanding of Western library life gained by all participants are already starting to make a positive impact on Romanian libraries and will continue to contribute to their democratic transformation and modernization.

Several organizations have joined forces to provide international librarians with opportunities for work-study visits to the United States. Among the leaders are once again the Mortenson and Soros Fellows Program, the Fulbright Program, various USIA programs, the International Research and Exchanges Board (IREX), and the ALA Library Fellows Program.

Although most of these organizations are well known to librarians involved in East European affairs, the Mortenson Center is definitely a newcomer. The Mortenson Center for International Librarianship was created in 1988 by a generous gift from C. Walter and Gerda B. Mortenson, longtime book lovers and friends of the University of Illinois, Urbana-Champaign Library. The Mortenson Center is a unique forum promoting international understanding and intellectual freedom. It is the purpose of the center "to foster international tolerance and peace by strengthening ties among the world's research libraries and librarians in an effort to ensure access to knowledge throughout the world" (Mortenson Center for International Librarianship, 1993). International librarians come to the University of Illinois to observe and learn first-hand about the workings of a major U.S. library and to share their own experiences with American librarians.

For Romanian librarians, U.S. educational opportunities have ranged from short-term professional invitations to participate at national meetings or specialty conferences to extended fellowships to attend library school. As the following representative examples illustrate, each type of educational sojourn is valuable on its own merits. The presence of international colleagues in our libraries benefits visitors and hosts alike. International relations serve as a reminder of the global context of our profession and should be approached with "humility in terms of acknowledging the dauntless efforts of our colleagues in developing areas of the world who have, with minimal resources and support, created libraries and information systems for their institutions and countries" (Segal, 1992, p. 100).

Since the fall of communism, ALA has played a leadership role in spearheading professional programs for Eastern bloc countries, including Romania. In 1991 and again in 1992, ALA welcomed two Romanian colleagues to its annual meetings. Participation at annual meetings can give international librarians an insight into our professional life and an understanding of the role of a professional organization. Of interest to East European librarians are our committee business meetings, where they can observe parliamentary proceedings in action and our programs, which contribute to professional growth. The exhibits offer an opportunity to review in one place a variety of new print and nonprint materials and formats, technologies, or library furniture.

In 1991 and again in 1993, two other Romanian librarians were invited to attend U.S. professional conferences. One of these was Laura Demetrovici, head librarian at the Library of the Banat University of Agricultural Sciences, who was invited by the U.S. Department of Agriculture and the National Library of Agriculture to present a paper entitled "Information Transfer in a Global Economy." The conference brought together representatives of Central Europe and was aimed at strengthening organizational links, cooperation, communication, and coordination among the United States and Central European libraries. For Romania, known before World War II as the breadbasket of Europe, agricultural information is of vital importance. With her Central European counterparts, Laura Demetrovici searched for better and faster ways to provide current agricultural information to educators, students, researchers, and farmers. The visit offered an introduction to a variety of new technologies from online searching to OPACs and CD-ROMs.

You ask me about my impressions? What can I say? In one word: amazing! It had such a strong impact on me that ever since I have been asking myself over and over again, how did we survive all those years in such darkness? Before 1989 my library was practically starved for information. We made do with what could be acquired on exchanges, but even exchange books did not always reach the intended university. Now, more than ever, I am aware that we MUST update our working methods, that we MUST introduce new technology. How can we achieve these goals, in financially difficult times? Our goodwill, while not enough to bring about real change, will certainly help us find a way! (Laura Demetrovici, personal correspondence, 1993)

Short-term study fellowships are another venue of professional development that contribute to the development of special skills. A two-month fellowship to the Mortenson Center for International Librarianship was awarded, for instance, to Christina Voichita Dragomir, a systems librarian at the Central University Library in Bucharest. Dragomir arrived at Mortenson Center in March 1993 to study automation and electronic mail. A self-starting, energetic, and enthusiastic librarian, Dragomir was soon conversant with systems and networks, and at the time of her departure, she was ready and eager to share her knowledge and contacts with her colleagues. Her acquired skills were timely indeed: last fall Romania became a member of the Internet family. The Romanian ROEARN node was put into operation at the end of November 1992. Before leaving for Romania, Dragomir planned to get electronic mail addresses for all her colleagues.

In 1992, James H. Billington, Librarian of Congress, and George Soros, President of the Soros Foundation, announced the launching of the Library of Congress–Soros Foundation Visiting Fellows Program for Librarians and information specialists from Eastern Europe and the Soviet Union. Through a competitive application process, 14 visiting fellows, representing different countries and types of libraries, were selected for the 1992 program. Among these was Ana Maria Capalneanu from the Lucian Blaga University Library in Cluj. The 3-month program introduced Capalneanu to the mission, organization, and operations of the Library of Congress. This orientation was followed by a specific work assignment within the library.

Although the experience and knowledge acquired during study visits in the United States contribute substantially in shaping library life in Romania, there is no substitute for a total immersion into the American library culture. "Less developed nations look to the United States to fulfill more than a basic educational role for international personnel by virtue of the continued reputation of the United States for excellence in the development of information technologies, theory and principles of library and information science, and the service tradition of the profession in the United States" (Bearman, et al., 1992, pp. 117–118). Being a student in an American library school has offered a young reference librarian this full range of educational perspectives. Hermina Anghelescu, the first Fulbright Fellow in library science from Romania, arrived at the University of Texas, Austin, in fall 1992. Excellent English language skills have allowed Anghelescu to hit the ground running. She is particularly interested in library administration and is determined to implement American principles of democratic management in Romania. Another area where her American experience could make a difference is preservation. "Romania is very rich in old and rare books. Many of them are in great need of restoration. Here is where I hope to be able upon return to bring my modest contribution of knowledge and advice" (Anghelescu, personal correspondence, 1993).

IV. U.S. Librarians in Romania

American librarians have also been active and have initiated a series of educational programs within Romania meant to assist in the rebuilding of Romanian library systems. Among these were the ALA Colloquium on Library Science and extended stays in Romania by an ALA Library Fellow and Fulbright Scholar-librarians.

A. ALA Colloquium on Library Science

The Colloquium on Library Science held in Brasov, Romania, on August 10–12, 1991, was sponsored by ALA and supported by grants from the International Research and Exchange (IREX) Board and the National Library of Romania. The objective was to provide Romanian librarians with an overview of American library and information science concepts and tools as a basis for further scholarly interaction, to promote the adoption of international library standards, and increase international understanding and scholarly cooperation through the establishment of professional relationships (IREX, 1992). The ALA Colloquium was an outgrowth of the successful Books for Romania (USA) project. Thirteen nationally known librarians and educators, under the leadership of then ALA President-Elect Marilyn Miller, traveled to Romania and lectured on a wide range of topics. More than 100 Romanian academic and public librarians, administrators, and library school educators attended the colloquium. Topics discussed included library organization and management, automation, library education, public and technical services, computer searching and CD-ROM technology, and the mission and role of library associations. On-site visits to Romanian libraries and roundtable discussion groups rounded off the participants' agenda.

The Romanian librarians in attendance were enthusiastic in their welcome.

> The American specialists tried to give us an image of how librarianship looked like in the United States. Our librarians, shy at first, dared more and more to participate in a dialogue

with the American team. This direct contact, the invitation to communicate, the confidence and optimism of the Americans were for us a bridge, a link between librarians in the two countries. (Clinca, 1991, p. 11)

Perhaps one of the more important legacies of the ALA Colloquium was its emphasis on democratic concepts of library services. Information and referral services, children's services, and literacy programs arising out of expressed community needs were exciting new concepts and evoked a passionate response from the Romanian participants (Popa and Doyle, 1992). It is hoped that those concepts will become part of everyday library practice in a democratic Romania.

B. ALA Library Fellows to Romania

The ALA Library Fellows program, which began in 1986, is funded by a grant from the USIA. Through this program U.S. Library Fellows are provided with the opportunity to travel abroad and share their expertise with librarians in other countries. From 1991 to 1992, the first American Fellow was sent to Romania. James Moldovan spent 6 months in Bucharest. Moldovan is fluent in Romanian and already knew the country and its libraries; hence he was especially well prepared to begin his assignment immediately upon arrival. Some of Moldovan's actual duties included preparing for an online catalog network installation at the Central University Library, answering cataloging questions on a one-to-one basis, and helping staff to adapt to the idea of automation. On March 1, 1992, the installation was completed and the first Romanian library online network was underway. Seeing a need for written documentation, Moldovan also wrote an introduction to resource sharing and OCLC in Romanian and, with American colleague Patricia Larsen, participated in a joint National Library–University Library Romanian project to translate the 1987 edition of the IFLA *Unimarc Manual*. The manual has been published and constitutes a fundamental text in online cataloging.

Many libraries vied for Moldovan's expertise and he wished he had the time to help them. Nonetheless Moldovan felt that he had achieved the goals and objectives of his visit.

The contribution of a fundamental translation that serves as the basis for on-line cataloging in [Romania] changes the history of Romanian librarianship. It also makes for some much needed cooperation between major library institutions. On a larger scale, it constitutes a real contribution to building library infrastructure, so desperately needed in Romania. (Moldovan, personal correspondence, 1993)

Concerning Moldovan's personal, overall impression of his stay in Romania and any hardships he may have endured while there, he replied that he would repeat the exact experience in spite of physical discomforts. Moldovan went knowing that it would be a rewarding, but spartan, 6 months.

C. Fulbright Scholars

Three librarians have traveled to Romania on Fulbright grants within the recent past. From September 1991 to March 1992, Anita Breland lectured at the University of Cluj on the principles of librarianship and technology. Ronald Chapman, Director of Honolulu Community College Library, taught at the University of Bucharest Library School from September 1991 through mid-August 1992. Patricia Larsen, Assistant Director for Access Services at the University of Northern Iowa, taught at the University of Bucharest Library School from mid-September 1992 to mid-June 1993.

Ms. Breland's goals focused on assisting Cluj librarians in maximizing their current resources, introducing them to computer technology, and teaching them how to plan for future development. She found that some library administrators in Romania were not yet convinced of the relevance of technology for overall library management. This in turn made introduction of technology somewhat of a challenge for Breland. Other challenges included unreliable telephone service and inadequate electrical power, which made connections with libraries outside of Cluj or Bucharest difficult. Running personal computers became problematic at times. In spite of challenges and setbacks, Breland taught a series entitled "Frontier Librarianship: An American Perspective" to 70 students. The three modules of this course included Introduction to Librarianship, Introduction to Library Management and Administration, and Introduction to Library Automation. She also offered a short course in personal computing, as well as tutoring in English and a class in how to use a file management package (ProCite). When asked about her personal experiences, Breland commented that she wouldn't trade this experience for anything, except perhaps the opportunity to repeat it once again (Breland, personal correspondence, 1993).

Ronald Chapman, while on Fulbright assignment at the University of Bucharest from 1991 to 1992, found that some of his teaching goals could not be achieved due to factors beyond his control. He had been told, for example, that students would be able to understand lectures in English. This was not the case, and Chapman was required to use an interpreter. Because class attendance was not mandatory, student participation steadily declined; oral examinations were not conducted because Chapman did not speak Romanian. In addition to classes at the University of Bucharest, Chapman initiated lectures and consultations at the National Library of Romania. He also gave speeches that were published in the Romanian library journals and made television appearances. When queried what further work needs to be done in Romania, Chapman commented that a common philosophy toward access to information, cataloging, collection development, and lending policies should be developed. He found vast conceptual differences in all these areas (Chapman, personal correspondence, 1993).

Patricia Larsen taught two courses at the Bucharest Library School: one on planning and implementing library computerized systems and networks and another on online cataloging with Unimarc. In addition to teaching, Larsen collaborated on the translation of the IFLA *Unimarc Manual* and on a dictionary of computer terms. The dictionary, published by *Biblioteca* in 1993, offers the first compilation of terms used in library automation in the Romanian language. Larsen believes that, beyond their practical applications, the *Unimarc Manual* and the dictionary are important, as they allow Romanian librarians to think in terms of standardization and thus begin connecting with each other and the world. Larsen is eager to return to Bucharest and continue her work on behalf of Romania. On her recommendation, another Fulbright scholar has been selected for Romania: Margaret Guccioni from St. Lawrence University, New York, had a teaching appointment at the University of Bucharest Library School from September 1993 to spring 1994 and continued to build on Chapman's and Larsen's work.

V. The Road Ahead

Despite the problems of its inherited past and current chaotic economic and social conditions, Romanian librarianship is moving rapidly and decisively forward, seeking to regain its place in the international library community. Although observers of Romanian affairs criticize current ambiguous political developments, libraries show many signs that allow us to be cautiously optimistic. It is true, that each new day asks for a new miracle. Some of those miracles have been, are, and will be achieved in collaboration with U.S. colleagues.

Books for Romania (USA), together with other book drives, were important first programs, expressions of professional solidarity and goodwill. They replenished empty shelves and hungry minds with a bounty of new and liberating ideas. However, no book drive can rebuild national collections. To help support and expand foreign literature collecting efforts, American university and public libraries, with Romanian vernacular collections or interest in Romanian area studies should seek to establish and/or broaden gift and exchange agreements. For its part, Romania needs to formulate cooperative multilibrary collection development plans to avoid costly duplication of foreign materials, and maximize each purchase. For multilibrary collection development agreements to work, they must be backed up by functional interlibrary loan policies and systems. Various prototypes of cooperative collection development and lending agreements already exist in the United States and may be adaptable to local conditions.

Preservation remains an important priority. Although we realistically cannot expect Romania to remodel its library buildings to conform to modern American library environmental standards, one of the priorities of study in the United States, should concentrate on preservation. "The importance of preserving those national and international treasures which are decaying beyond repair needs to be recognized and urgently acted upon" (Aman and Khan, 1992, p. 74). Aman goes even further to suggest that after restoration these documents ought to be reproduced on optical disks and the disks deposited with research libraries around the world. This could be an international effort, similar to UNESCO's International Microfilming Project of the 1960s. The Library of Congress Preservation Program would be well suited to take a leadership role in organizing this worthwhile activity.

The importance of technological transfer to Romania need not be stressed. However, transplanting the latest hardware and software, without developing local expertise and infrastructural support is, in the long run, counterproductive. Technological transfer goes hand in hand with training, practice, and continuing education. It demands a national commitment to financial and human resources and to stable policies that actively support the free flow of information. As a leader in information science and technology, American librarians can act as facilitator and help Romanian colleagues identify the best suited systems for Romanian libraries.

The philosophy of American librarianship, placing not the book but the patron in the center of all activities, is an American trademark. The majority of European librarians see their role as preservers of cultural materials. Our emphasis on service is what makes our libraries democratic institutions and active players in the life of our communities. "Shifting the focus of the Eastern European library community from information for the sake of information to information for the sake of the end-user will require a profound change in the philosophy of library education. . . . The shift must be from a policy of control and manipulation of information to an emphasis of gathering and providing access to accurate information" (Emmolo, 1992, p. 9). In Romania, residues of the old totalitarian society still exist. While dismantling the S Collections, for instance, some Romanian librarians argued in favor of restrictive circulation policies for books that were labeled as inciting anarchy, promoting pornography, or as right-wing literature (Hategan, 1990; Simion, 1990). Our affirmed opposition to censorship or governmental intimidation, and our support for free expression of ideas makes ours a noble profession. This is a model worth exporting.

Only days after the fall of the Ceausescu regime, Romania moved to create democratic library associations. In January 1990, the Association of Librarians in Public Libraries and the Association of Academic Librarians came into being. Letters of introduction were sent to major professional associations of the Western world. At the same time affiliations to IFLA and other international organizations were reinstated. Romanian associations are currently acting as pressure groups, pushing for recognition and advancement of the profession, lobbying for national legislation for libraries, better working conditions and salaries, and improved educational opportunities. It would be useful if ALA were to continue to lend its support actively to these incipient professional bodies. Participation of Romanian librarians in international associations needs to be further encouraged and supported. Our landmark achievements against censorship, for freedom of speech and free flow of information can stand as an example for others to follow. The political role played by American librarians in promoting the importance of information, lobbying for access to government publications, and inclusion on communication networks could serve as a model of civic and professional duty to be studied and possibly emulated.

As demonstrated by the Books for Romania drive, the Colloquium on Library Science, or by hosting Romanian librarians at national meetings, the ALA has moved quickly and decisively to end the isolation of Romanian librarians. Continuity in educational programs for Romania would consolidate advances already achieved and provide new growth and development. "Continuity is the key in rebuilding the information infrastructure of Romania. Time and political convenience often intervene, and quickly our attention (and money) can pass from one cause to another in a different part of the globe. The American Library Association should be congratulated for its long-term vision on Romanian librarianship" (Moldovan, 1993, p. 10).

Rebuilding an information infrastructure extends far beyond collection development, technology, or professional organizations. It requires a concentrated long-term focus on library education and an effort to educate capable library professionals to carry the work into the twenty-first century.

> The education of librarians and information scientists from developing countries can be one of the great contributions that library and information science programs in the United States can make to our profession worldwide. Those students who return to become leaders in their libraries and information systems as well as the many who become educators will themselves contribute to the internationalization of library and information services. Our profession can play a leading role in building our global interdependency toward improving the quality of life around the world. (Bearman et al., 1992, pp. 143–144)

American library schools need to find ways to allow Romanian librarians to partake in our educational opportunities. Exchanges, sister-library connections, fellowships, and study tours all contribute to endow Romanian libraries with the knowledge and quality personnel they desperately need. Romania's ultimate success in becoming a full-fledged member of the international library community once again, will rely heavily upon a new generation of well-trained, informed, and internationally minded library professionals.

References

Aman, M. M., and Khan, A. R. (1992). Information technology, transfer and use in developing countries. In *The Role of the American Academic Library in International Programs* (B. D Bonta and J. G. Neal, eds.), pp. 59–83. JAI Press, Greenwich, Connecticut.

Bearman, T. C., Josey, E. J., Tallman, J., and Wools, E. B. (1992). Education of librarians from developing countries. In *The Role of the American Academic Library in International Programs* (B. D. Bonta and J.G . Neal, eds.), pp. 117–146. JAI Press, Greenwich, Connecticut.

Bercan, G. (1990). How the Central State Library is rethinking its structures and functions. *Biblioteca* 1, 10 (in Romanian).

Books for Romania. (1990). *Economist* 314 (7641), 95.

Campeanu, F. (1990). Library life. *Biblioteca* 1, 7 (in Romanian).

Chapman, R. F. (1992). Library management. *Biblioteca* 3, 30–31 (in Romanian).

Chapman, R. F. (1993). Personnel development in U.S. libraries. *Biblioteca* 4, 60–62 (in Romanian).

Clinca, G. (1991). Brasov, 10–12 August: a connecting bridge. *Revista Biblioteca* 2, 10–11 (in Romanian).

Desruisseaux, P. (1993). Scholar's remark leads to journal donation for Eastern Europe. *Chronicle of Higher Education* June 23, A28.

Doyle, R. P. (1991). Books for Romania program concludes with $4 million. *American Libraries* 22, 106.

Emmolo, L. M. (1992). Lending a hand to Eastern and Central European libraries. *SpeciaList* 15, 1–9.

Hategan, I. (1990). Is there still an "S" Collection? *Biblioteca* 1, 26 (in Romanian).

Hojsgaard, U. (1990). *Assistance to Romanian Libraries: Results From a Danish-Swedish Visit to Bucharest, March 11–18, 1990, and Suggestions for Action.* Danish National Library Authority, Copenhagen.

International Research and Exchanges Board (IREX). (1992). *Romanian Summer Institute on Library Science Colocvii de Bibliologie, August 10–12, 1991. Brasov, Romania.* IREX, Princeton, New Jersey.

Kinsey, A. (1990). Books for Romania. *Manchester Guardian Weekly* January 14, 2.

Kuzmin, E. (1993). From totalitarianism to democracy: Russian libraries in transition. *American Libraries* 24, 568–570.

Miller, M. (1992). An indirect invitation to reflect on children's libraries. *Biblioteca* 4, 61–62 (in Romanian).

Moldovan, J. (1993). *Interview with a Vampire: Ceausescu, Libraries and Romania.* Unpublished manuscript.

Mortenson Center for International Librarianship. (1993). *International Leads* 7, 6–8.

Mudrock, T. (1992). Business librarian reaches out to Romania. *Library Directions: A Newsletter of the University of Washington Libraries* 2, 2–3.

Popa, O. D. (1991). Reference services: Academic and utilitarian functions. *Biblioteca* 2, 69-75 (in Romanian).

Popa, O. D., and Doyle, R. P. (1992). Journey to Transylvania: The 1991 ALA Colloquium on Library Science. *C & RL News* **53,** 174.

Popa, O. D., and Lamprecht, S. J. (1991). Western campaigns to provide scholarly materials to East Europe require care and quality control. *Chronicle of Higher Education* **July 3,** B1–B2.

Rady, M. (1991). Transylvanian libraries and archives in contemporary Romania. *Journal of the Society of Archivists* **12,** 123–126.

Regneala, M. (1990). Association or federation? *Biblioteca* **1,** 6–7 (in Romanian).

Sadlak, J. (1993). Legacy and change: Higher education and restoration of academic work in Romania. *Technology in Society* **15,** 92.

Schifirnet, C. (1990). Book, reader, library. *Biblioteca* **1,** 14 (in Romanian).

Segal, J. S. (1992). American academic librarians and international library organizations. In *The Role of the American Academic Library in International Programs* (B. D. Bonta and J. G. Neal, eds.), pp. 85–103. JAI Press, Greenwich, Connecticut.

Sigal, L. V. (1990). Starved for books: Another hunger in Eastern Europe. *New York Times* **May 21,** A18.

Simion, I. (1990). Library life. *Biblioteca* **1,** 8 (in Romanian).

Wood, S. (1990). Books for Romania: The Scottish appeal. *Library Association Record* **92,** 917–919.

Indoor Air Quality: Planning and Managing Library Buildings

Carmel C. Bush and Halcyon R. Enssle
Morgan Library
Colorado State University
Fort Collins, Colorado 80523

I. Introduction

"I experience a bad taste and stinging eyes." "There seems to be a lack of consistent airflow—it is extremely stuffy." "The odors, dust, and wax removal around me are causing breathing problems." "I have a scratchy throat, hoarseness, and a burning sensation on my face. There is a strange odor. However, when I was out of the building at noon I was fine." These reports from library staff about problems experienced at work alert library building managers to possible indoor air quality (IAQ) problems; these problems are a concern for 25% of the work force and for libraries (Clark, 1985; Goldberg, 1992; Larue and Larue, 1991; National Institute for Occupational Safety and Health, 1991; Silberman, 1993; Simon, 1990; Yocum, Clink, and Cole, 1971).

People in the United States spend an estimated 90% of their time indoors, and the air indoors is a growing cause for concern. The Environmental Protection Agency (EPA) ranks indoor air pollution as one of the top five environmental health risks (U.S. Environmental Protection Agency, 1991). Once developed in a building it may be extremely costly in terms of staff absenteeism, the service of experts in the field to identify causes, building renovations to eliminate these causes, and litigation. Medical charges and lost productivity in the United States annually cost $50 to $60 billion due to indoor air problems according to EPA's estimates (Girman, 1993). Library building managers need to be aware of the probable causes of IAQ problems and factor them into consideration when planning for space and the use of space. Knowledge and awareness are key to maintaining a healthy building and avoiding problems in remodeling and renovating.

A. Problems

A variety of labels have been given to the health problems associated with indoor air. Health problems with a defined etiology are grouped under "building-related illness." These illnesses include infectious syndromes such as Legionnaires' disease, dermatitis, hypersensitivity pneumonitis, toxic syndromes, asthma, and allergic rhinitis. Symptoms with unknown etiology are commonly referred to as sick building syndrome (SBS). SBS is used to describe a building in which a substantial percentage of occupants complain of a variety of subjective symptoms. Common symptoms include eye, nose, or throat irritation; skin irritation; neurotoxic symptoms; hyperreactions; and odor or taste complaints. Symptoms usually progress during the day and disappear when the worker leaves the building (Samet and Spengler, 1991; U.S. Environmental Protection Agency, 1991a).

B. Sources

Contamination of indoor air can originate from activity of the occupants, outdoor air, or building construction and operation. Toombs (1991) describes the evolution of library architecture to include central air conditioning, modular construction, freestanding bookcases in open environments, suspended ceilings with fluorescent lighting, and carpeting. Each change has attendant potential for contributing to the indoor air environment.

Since 1965 many buildings have been constructed with an internal support structure surrounded by a thin, continuous outer shell (Samet, Marbury, and Spengler, 1988). This envelope creates a barrier for the filtration of air to and from the building and can contribute to the buildup of pollutants when air flow and ventilation are not properly managed. Building construction materials themselves can contain contaminants.

In addition to building design changes, changes in building system operations occurred in the early 1970s. Conservation measures were introduced as a response to the oil embargo and concern over energy consumption. Although the embargo was lifted and the immediate crisis passed, energy conservation became a part of the cultural consciousness (Turiel, 1985). Among voluntary and mandatory measures that may have an impact on indoor air are the following:

1. Reduction of outdoor air to a minimum in supply systems coupled with increased recirculation of indoor air
2. Reduction in airflow rate to occupied space to minimum value
3. Use of caulks and other sealants to prevent infiltration of air
4. Periodic shutdown of ventilation system components
5. Decreased use of humidifier and dehumidifier systems

6. Regulated thermostat settings for heating and cooling in public buildings so that temperatures in summer are warmer and those in winter are cooler
7. Design of buildings to heat the air by internal sources such as machines, lights, and people in which air delivery rates are varied to maintain temperatures (Hughes and O'Brien, 1986; Samet and Spengler, 1991)

Several of these factors can contribute to inadequate ventilation, which appears as a leading contributor to indoor air problems. Seitz (1989) reports that 529 investigations conducted through 1988 by the National Institute of Occupational Safety and Health (NIOSH) showed that 53% of the buildings had inadequate ventilation resulting from improper design or operational problems. These may be inadequate air supply capability, exceeding initial system design in renovation, locating supply and return diffusers in proximity to each other, using 100% recirculated air as an energy conservation measure, or having an imbalance in ventilation when some space receives more than others.

In addition to ventilation, humidity and temperature can contribute to adverse health effects. A review of studies indicates that health problems are associated with too high and too low levels of relative humidity—less than 40% and greater than 60% (Arundel et al., 1986). The rate of off-gassing of building materials and the level of water vapor available to interact with chemicals in the air are related to relative humidity. High relative humidity combined with increased temperature causes discomfort through reduction of evaporative cooling of the body, exhaustion, and other potentially more serious effects. Turiel (1985) notes that increased formaldehyde off-gassing can occur when relative humidity and temperature increase.

The literature suggests that when these energy conserving practices are associated with imbalances in operational design and/or contaminants are present, effects on indoor air quality can result. Levin (1993) agrees that reduction in ventilation and use of sealants contribute to contaminant concentrations but disputes other energy conservation measures as causative.

What contaminants can be present in indoor air? Major pollutants are volatile organic compounds (VOCs), hazardous chemicals, respirable suspended particulates, bioaerosols, and outdoor contaminants. Their sources are many. (See Table I for selective sources of contaminants.) Complicating the issue is the difficulty in establishing measurable levels of chemicals that might be causing problems with air quality. "It is important to note that IAQ complaints in nonindustrial environments usually are triggered by chemical levels 100- to 1000-fold below published TLVs" (Threshold Limit Values) (Brooks and Davis, 1992, 7). Volatile organic compounds (VOCs) are sub-

Table I   Selective Sources of Contaminants

Contaminants	Sources
Volatile organic compounds	Adhesives, cleaning products, caulking compounds, floor wax, carbonless forms, printers, computers/video display terminals, carpeting, floor and wall coverings, particle board, paints, plastics, acrylics, preservatives
Ozone	Photocopy machines, outdoor air
Dust	Books, paper, furniture, improperly working HVAC systems, maintenance or remodeling activities
Particulates (respirable)	Tobacco smoke, paper shuffling
Carbon monoxide	Vehicle exhaust, tobacco smoke
Carbon dioxide	People
Airborne bioaerosols	Molds, mildew, bird droppings, dust, plants (conveyed by ventilation systems, sweeping, etc.)
Radon	Soil or rocks under buildings, building materials
Inorganic gases	Photocopy machines, laser printers, outflow air, emissions from other facilities

stances that contain carbon that tend to evaporate quickly. They can irritate mucous membranes of eye, nose, and throat and can have respiratory effects. Examples of VOCs are aldehydes, which may be used in book manufacture, and trichlorethylene, which may be found in cleaning compounds. The most notorious VOC is formaldehyde, a gas with a pungent odor that may be emitted from a wide array of items ranging from personal products to building materials (Gammage and Kaye, 1985; National Institute for Occupational Safety and Health, 1989; National Research Council, 1981; Turiel, 1985).

People are the most common source of carbon dioxide, a by-product of metabolic activity. Carbon dioxide can be a problem in too high concentrations, leading to headaches and respiratory problems, but primarily it serves as an indicator for ventilation problems. Carbon monoxide, nitrogen oxide, and other gases are emitted from combustion. Diesel exhaust, in particular, is the subject of research that suggests that exposure to unfiltered diesel exhaust has the potential to cause damage (Hobbs and Mauderly, 1991). Intake vents located at ground level near traffic can draw in these chemicals from vehicle emissions. Another pungent hazardous chemical is ozone. Although ozone is generally considered an outdoor pollutant resulting from photochemical reactions, it can be emitted from equipment found in libraries.

Respirable particulates chiefly result as products of combustion from tobacco smoking. Recognition of the potent health effects of smoking has been most recently noted in a report regarding secondary smoke (U.S. Environmental Protection Agency, 1993).

Bioaerosols are airborne contaminants from bacteria, molds, pollen, viruses, or other biological particulates such as bird droppings. Their growth indoors is dependent on a moisture source. They can become airborne through HVAC (heating, ventilation, and air conditioning) systems, air circulation, and by cleaning activities such as sweeping. Although NIOSH attributed only 5% of its indoor air quality investigations to bioaerosols (Seitz, 1989), the impact on health could be serious if Legionnaires' disease is diagnosed.

Proximity to sites that emit contaminants or the site itself could contribute to indoor air quality problems. Radon may be found in soils and rocks under a building or may be in building materials. Risk projection modules indicate an association of radon with lung cancer (Samet and Spengler, 1991). Vehicle emissions, atmospheric dust and fugitive emissions from other buildings can be entrained or transferred into a building and have health effects.

Confounding factors associated with health effects of indoor air quality include those of psychogenic origins, ergonomics, and stress. Illness occurring simultaneously in a group of individuals is termed mass psychogenic illness. The cause is unknown but appears to involve a trigger. Subjects become ill when they see or hear that others have become ill (Shearer, 1991). It is distinguished from SBS in that the "symptom pattern of the sick building syndrome is not very typical for mass psychogenic illness" (Skov, Valbjørn, and Pedersen, 1989). In order to understand and solve IAQ problems successfully, it is important to understand that emotion and perception are as important to the issue as scientific measurement and overt disease (Brooks and Davis, 1992).

Ergonomics, or lack thereof, can be a confounding factor for indoor air quality problems. Staff experiencing a generalized feeling of unwellness because of hours spent in a poorly fitting chair or who suffer from a painful and sometimes crippling ailment such as carpal tunnel syndrome, may be more apt to react to reports of illness in others around them. Symptoms resulting from poor ergonomic work conditions can also mimic those experienced as a result of air contaminants. These include mental fatigue and irritation of the eyes, both of which can be caused by poorly designed workstations. Stress can also contribute to this generalized feeling of unwellness.

Lighting is an ergonomic factor that can create visual stress. Inappropriate lighting may cause eye irritation and headaches (Brooks et al., 1991). "Good lighting and a comfortable chair were the highest ranking factors which affected comfort in the minds of the participants" of a study on productivity and office comfort (Isacco, 1985). Although research has been done on the influence of personal characteristics, job-related factors and the influence of psychosocial factors on SBS (Skov, Valbjørn, and Pedersen 1989), research into the corollaries between indoor air pollution and ergonomics is lacking.

II. Planning for New Buildings

For those planning new facilities care should be taken to avoid past mistakes that have led to the development of indoor air quality problems. For those planning to renovate or remodel, actions can be taken to rectify existing poor conditions and also to avoid creating situations that might facilitate development of problems. Every librarian involved in space planning or building management needs to incorporate indoor air considerations into their thinking.

Librarians have many sources of information available on the development of building plans. Notably, the American Library Association and its Library Administration and Management Section have published several items (Dahlgren and Beck, 1990; Martin, 1992; Metcalf, 1986; Sannwald, 1982; Smith, 1986) describing the process of developing a building plan through to its implementation and occupation. The growing literature on indoor air augments these valuable publications and suggests expansion of the role of the library building manager engaged in building planning. The library building manager should present library staff concerns regarding indoor air, assist architects and designers in considering healthy building materials and furnishings, question building plans for their impact on indoor air, document actions regarding indoor air, and communicate with library staff concerning actions.

An approach to building design that considers the building occupants, the exterior environment and their interrelationship with the building as a dynamic system can be a significant contribution to improvement of IAQ. Consideration of IAQ begins with actual selection of the building site and continues throughout the process up to and including final inhabitation of the building.

Early in the planning stages a building checklist should be compiled, incorporating strategies for achieving good IAQ and allowing for input from the library building manager and others involved in the planning of the building (Levin, 1992).

A. Site Selection

Factors that should be addressed at the point of site selection include soil analysis for possible sources of radon and soil contaminants; sources of pollutants from industrial processes in the nearby area or from agricultural activities;

exhaust from combustion such as automobiles and public transport; and prevailing wind patterns. Building designers can design for control of such factors. For example, if the outdoor air quality requires that the air is cleaned prior to pumping through the building, the designers can specify this requirement in the design.

B. Design

Woods (1991) advocates incorporating building diagnostics into the design of a building. His approach to healthy building design includes establishing basic performance criteria according to applicable legal and regulatory requirements; translating these performance criteria to preventive criteria for construction; evaluating the performance in the commissioning (testing phase to ensure that the building is ready for occupancy) phase by an independent evaluator; scheduling periodic reevaluations of performance, especially when building modifications are planned; and ongoing shared responsibility with building managers and occupants for performance (i.e., no inappropriate activities in the space or tampering with the system).

Design assumptions and the building systems descriptions must be stated clearly and with sufficient detail (Levin, 1992). This documentation is then used to ensure that all phases of the design have been completed according to specifications during the development of the project and in the commissioning period. Successful design can be achieved by assuring that the indoor air satisfies three basic requirements: acceptable temperature ranges, normal concentrations of respiratory gases, and acceptable levels of contaminants and pollutants. Temperature quality was highlighted as one of the nine issues directly affecting job satisfaction among library workers[1] (Isacco, 1985).

Keeping the requirements in mind, important considerations to incorporate into a design include:

1. Air intakes must be carefully planned to avoid entraining contaminants from potential sources such as vehicle exhaust from loading docks or street traffic, local pollutants from dumpsters and other fugitive sources, and reintroduction of air being exhausted from the building itself.

2. Exhaust locations must be located with the same considerations in mind. Locating exhaust downwind from intakes will prevent reentrainment.

3. Interior pollution generating operations such as preservation activities and on-site binding and repair should be identified and planned for in the design phase. Common office supplies such as "green bar" computer paper, correction fluids, and carbonless copy forms, which can be sources

[1] The nine issues identified were floor area, temperature and air quality, lighting, safety and security, noise, ease of communication, comfort, participation, and flexibility.

of VOC emissions, should be stored in ventilated areas (Brooks and Davis, 1992).

4. If smoking is to be permitted in the building, areas identified as allowing smoking must be designed in such a way that smoke does not intrude into nonsmoking areas.

5. Copy machines have proliferated along with computer technology. These machines can be sources of indoor pollution unless well vented and maintained. "Machines that are not externally vented can release ozone, trinitrofluorenone, and methyl alcohol into the work space" (Simon, 1990). Plans should include enclosing copiers in separate rooms with their own air exhaust to avoid the spread of such pollutants and others, which can include ammonia, benzene, carbon black, and ozone (Brooks and Davis, 1992; Simon, 1990).

6. The envelope of the building and structural materials used within the envelope should be chosen for low pollution emission characteristics. The same effort should be made to minimize potential pollutants from furnishings, and so on, which will be brought into the building prior to occupancy (see section on Preventive Installation Procedures).

7. If external sources of pollution have been identified, building entrances should be located so that they do not permit contaminants to enter.

8. Maintenance of internal positive pressure within occupied areas of the building is necessary to avoid entrainment of pollutants. Care must also be taken to ensure that areas of the building such as mechanical or equipment rooms are designed with a negative pressure to contain the flow of air and keep possible contaminants from venting into occupied areas.

9. Revisions in the American Society of Heating Refrigeration and Air Conditioning Engineers (ASHRAE) standard attest to a movement toward bringing more fresh air into buildings as a way to improve ventilation and hence air quality for building occupants. However, a recent article in the *New England Journal of Medicine* disputes this. "In this study, increasing the supply of outdoor air in mechanically ventilated office buildings was not associated with either improved environmental ratings or a reduction in the number of symptoms reported by the participants" (Menzies et al. 1993, p. 824). The buildings studied, however, were not selected because they had been identified as sick but because they had characteristics similar to buildings in which the Sick Building Syndrome had been described (Menzies et al., 1993). Although this study has questioned the value of increased levels of outdoor air in improving IAQ, it did not address whether more outside air would help buildings with the poorest ventilation (Kreiss, 1993).

10. Additional ventilation options include occupant control of window openings, a move away from sealed environments usually associated with large buildings. Workstations can also be equipped with individual fresh air

outlets (vents built into furniture panels) subject to occupant adjustment (Levin, 1992). Environmentally responsive workstations (ERW) such as Personal Environments (manufactured by Johnson Controls, Milwaukee, Wisconsin) are available in which the ergonomic needs of the staff are melded with the environmental needs. These workstations allow employees to control lighting, ventilation, and heat according to their personal comfort levels (Beck, 1993).

11. Carbon dioxide detectors control ventilating fans and may be considered for large buildings. The sensor makes the adjustment according to percentage of carbon dioxide in the air (Mattill, 1993).

12. Lighting should be varied according to the task, the space involved, and the service being provided (Michaels and Michaels, 1992).

13. Depending on geographical location and proposed design, basement dehumidification may need to be considered to control microbial contamination.

14. If a centralized computer facility is planned, special environmental conditions must be incorporated into this area (Price, 1989).

15. Configuration of OPAC and CD-ROM stations need to keep in mind such considerations as space and ventilation needed for printers, external drives, and so on (Michaels and Michaels, 1992).

C. Ventilation and Climate Control

Ventilation and climate control are key to having good indoor air quality. A correctly balanced, clean, and properly maintained HVAC system will help prevent conditions that lead to problems. Elements in developing such a system are described in the ASHRAE 62-1989 standard.

Air cleaning and filtration are essential components of a properly designed HVAC system. Filtration is used to filter air coming into the building as well as to remove indoor contaminants from air that is mixed with outdoor air for recirculation. "Air cleaner effectiveness is a function of the pollutant collection efficiency of the cleaner and of the air circulation through the cleaner" (ASHRAE, 1989). In order for air cleaning to be effective, the air handling system must be on at all times (Sparks, 1988). If contaminants are known, designers can specify the types of filters specific to the type of particulate that must be filtered.

Gaseous contaminants are receiving more attention in recent years, and more effective adsorbents are being specified to improve indoor air quality.

Three types of filters are employed to remove gaseous contaminants: (1) activated charcoal; (2) porous pellets impregnated with reactive chemicals; and (3) air washers. Most filtration systems adsorb high molecular weight compounds in preference to low molecular weight substances. Temperature and humidity often affect performance of filtration systems. Furthermore, charcoal filters can release previously adsorbed substances as they begin to load. Air wash systems are notorious for their ability to serve as bioamplification sites.

Knowledgeable maintenance, by replacement, regeneration, or cleaning, is essential to the performance of all three types of filtration strategies. (Brooks and Davis, 1992, p. 45)

Particle collection "is achieved by either fibrous filtration, electrostatic precipitation, or electrostatically augmented filtration. Organic vapors are usually adsorbed by activated carbon filters . . . " (Sparks, 1988, p. 45). Absorbents can be tuned to specific compounds or regenerated, as in the case of charcoal, but these are expensive alternatives. Efficiency rates of filters depend on the type of pollutant present. Studies have shown that for particulate air cleaners even low efficiency filters (30% or less) improve air quality and that the "relative difference between a 70% filter and a 95% efficient filter is small due to the high air circulation rate normal for HVAC systems" (Sparks, 1988, p. 45). Depending on the local situation, designers can specify filters or air cleaners to provide a proper level of cleansing.

More attention is being given by designers to how air mixes in and moves through space. The distribution of air at varying levels within spaces rather than through traditional ceiling vents is being used to assure good space and air distribution. Planners need also to consider the placement of interior design features such as office landscaping, which might interfere with the distribution of air.

ASHRAE 62-1989 standard gives a procedure to determine a ventilation rate that is related to the quantity and quality of outside air, occupant density, and space. It is important to remember that *all* standards are minimums and must be adjusted to fit the size of the space being planned and the uses to which the space will be put. As libraries have variable occupancies, factoring on the maximum peak load is suggested. It is important to track building occupancy data for calculating ventilation rate. A review of the ASHRAE 62-1989 standard has begun with a view toward increasing the quantity of outside air mixed with indoor air. When a new standard is issued it should be reviewed vis-à-vis current operating parameters.

Plans should incorporate accessibility of the HVAC system for easy inspection and cleaning. The potential for future upgrading should also be factored into the planning process.

Geographic and climatological local influences must also be taken into account. A building in a densely populated, high pollution, high humidity, urban area will have different requirements relative to ventilation than one in a more rural, arid, or semiarid setting.

D. Microbial Control

The minimizing of potential microbial amplification within ventilation systems (Levin, 1992) warrants attention. Fibrous materials used as insulation, both acoustic and thermal, should receive careful installation (such as placing insulation outside of ductwork or eliminating insulation completely) and its protection from dirt and moisture. Any fibrous material, such as fiberglass, rock wool, or glass wool, can be potent media for microbes should it become wet. The San Francisco main public library building was specifically designed to be a healthy building and it was specified for this building that

> Exposed fiberglass (porous insulation) within the HVAC system has been encapsulated to eliminate amplification sites for fungal and bacterial microorganisms with only minimum impact on sound attenuation. (Bernheim, 1993)

Improvements are being made in the design of air systems—ductwork, plenums, cooling systems and humidification systems are all being designed to minimize the possibility of microbial growth and contamination. Librarians planning new facilities should be aware of these factors and specify that they be addressed in the design of the building.

E. Materials Selection and Specification

"Materials selection plays a crucial role in reducing the risk of indoor air pollution" (Gantenbein, 1990). Librarians working with architects and designers should share concerns regarding products. One type of material that has been identified as a source of off-gassing of formaldehyde is particleboard; specifications should be written specifically to exclude its use (Bernheim, 1993).

Another material that should receive close attention is carpeting, particularly if large areas are to be carpeted. The binder should not generate detectable emissions of 4-phenylcyclohexene (4-PC). Specifically, styrene butadiene rubber (SBR), a latex binder, is not acceptable (Bernheim, 1993). The mill should comply with EPA Carpet Policy Dialogue as well as participate in the Carpet and Rug Institute's Indoor Air Quality Carpet Testing Program (Carpet and Rug Institute, 1992).

Other products that must be investigated for off-gassing potential are adhesives, stains, caulking compounds, ceiling tiles, chipboard and particleboard, draperies, floor and wall coverings, upholstery, and paint. Most contain VOCs; manufacturers should be queried as to the potential for off-gassing and hazardous emissions. Nonsolvent-based adhesives, stains, caulks, and paints that do not emit high VOC levels are preferred. Carpeting, tiles, and insulation materials can absorb large quantities of VOC as well as provide a fertile ground for microbial growth if they become wet (Brooks and Davis, 1992).

F. Low Emitting Materials

Manufacturers are becoming aware of the dangers of construction materials that emit high levels of VOCs. Finding out what hazardous materials manufacturers use in their products requires a review of Material Safety Data Sheets (MSDS). Although the information in a sheet is not comprehensive, it provides a start that can be followed up by searching toxicological databases and other pertinent literature (Raimodo, 1992) and contacting environmental specialists.

G. Preventive Installation Procedures

Every effort should be made to minimize the potential pollutants that are brought into a new building. Whenever possible, furniture and equipment that might be subject to off-gassing should be unpacked away from the actual building and allowed to off-gas prior to installation (Bosco, 1993). If possible, even carpeting should be unrolled off-site and allowed to off-gas. Any finishing that can be done off-site should be encouraged so that a minimum of pollutants and contaminants are brought into the new building.

Work should be checked against design documentation for compliance with performance requirements. Making sure that the construction itself does not result in contamination in or outside the building requires instructions regarding cleanup of the site.

H. Commissioning

Commissioning involves a complete inspection of the building and check of indoor air requirements. Operation and maintenance manuals should be deposited with libraries as well as facilities units.

During the commissioning phase, there are several steps that can be taken to minimize air problems after occupancy. Special ventilation, with more air being vented into the building, can be specified before and during initial occupancy. "All outside-air, 24-hours-per day, ventilation is used to minimize occupant exposure to emissions from new materials and furnishings" (Levin, 1992, TOPIC.VI.B. 10-11). Ventilation should be operated at the maximum outside air for several weeks (up to eight) after occupancy, and the building should be reflushed after any period of closure.

In-place curing (also referred to as bake-out) is also a possible method of assuring that emissions have thoroughly off-gassed prior to occupancy. This involves heating the building to a high (120° to 130° Fahrenheit) temperature so that the solvents, dyes, adhesives, etc., will off-gas more rapidly. Until recently, little hard data was available to demonstrate this or to define the optimum duration, temperature, and ventilation rates needed to accomplish successful bake-out. However, recent studies conducted by the California Indoor Air Quality Program of five office buildings show that "a large decrease (approximately 94%) in total VOC concentration was observed inside the most intensely baked-out building" (Girman, 1993, p. 710), leading to the conclusion that "bake-out is a promising technique for reducing exposures to VOCs in new office buildings" (Girman, 1993, p. 711). This study indicates that the process shows promise and lends support to this method of reducing VOCs. However, it is one study, and the results need to be replicated before this process can receive complete endorsement.

III. Planning for Existing Buildings

A. Remodeling and Renovation

In an era of tightening funds, renovation may be the option of choice. The *American Libraries* annual survey of building projects reflects the numerous projects involving renovations. Even in the absence of formal renovation, introduction of new technologies and the attendant equipment are forcing librarians and managers to squeeze more into existing space. "When modifications are made in libraries, they should be examined in light of potential health hazards. Library building managers should question new building plans with health and safety concerns in mind" (Clark, 1985, p. 334). Indoor air quality should be a major consideration in the operation of a library facility, whether the plan is for a formal renovation or the addition of an online catalog with many terminals and peripherals.

Some of the same areas that need to be considered in designing a new building are also appropriate to remodeling or renovation planning. These include (1) operation and maintenance of the building including such factors as the ventilation system and operational routines and schedules, housekeeping and cleaning, and equipment maintenance; (2) occupants of the building, including the types of activities engaged in by the occupants and their personal hygiene; and (3) building contents—equipment, materials, furnishings, and appliances.

B. Operations and Maintenance

"Predictive maintenance is the wave of the future for ensuring good indoor air quality" (Bosco, 1993, p. 46). Literally a case of "a stitch in time" may make the difference between a building that remains healthy and one that develops SBS.

Maintenance questions that library building managers should ask are listed here.

1. Is there a regular maintenance check of the system? For example, faulty operation of a closed HVAC system using biocides to control microbiologicals can allow the biocides to be introduced into the interior air.

2. Is the system clean? Dirty air exchange systems can harbor irritants or bacterial contaminants that can contribute to indoor air quality problems. Preventive maintenance should "include annual heating, ventilating, and air conditioning (HVAC) equipment inspection, changing filters, washing coils, cleaning condensation pans and ductwork" (Bosco, 1993, p. 46), although annual cleaning of the ductwork may be unnecessary if filtering mechanisms are operating effectively. Regular inspection should reveal if duct cleaning is necessary. A more important consideration is to determine the source of the dust and dirt if it is being introduced into the ductwork.

3. Is the building properly balanced so that a negative pressure is not drawing in exterior pollutants and so that mechanical rooms are not allowing air to leak into occupied areas?

4. Does the system at least meet the ASHRAE 62-1989 standard for air movement based on occupancy? It is important for library building managers to stay abreast of current guidelines and to work in conjunction with facilities personnel to keep their buildings up to date. Having the newer standard implemented, which calls for higher minimum amounts of air per occupant, may avoid problems or improve a building already identified with IAQ problems.

5. Is the design of the system adequate for new technologies that may have been introduced? In the past ten years libraries have been automating at an ever increasing pace. Online circulation systems have expanded into online public access catalogs; acquisitions and serials systems have been brought online; CD-ROM products have exploded onto the scene; staff workstations are increasing, and laser printers are being added. Existing systems may be adequate for the increased load but, if the capability is inadequate to support the additional heating brought into them by introduction of this technology, ventilation problems can be created.

C. Occupants and Their Activities

"The mere presence of people in a building or residence can significantly alter indoor air quality" (Brooks and Davis, 1992, p. 27). In addition, libraries are notorious producers of dust. Attention should be paid to the level, frequency, and effectiveness of cleaning. The library building manager should work with facilities managers to form partnerships in the effective and proper cleaning of both the physical facility and the materials housed within the facility. Cleaning must be coordinated with the custodial staff to ensure that the work areas, public areas, and stacks are maintained in a condition that will not contribute to irritants. Dust can be a contributor to allergies and other medical conditions.

Cleaning products should be examined. "Emissions from aerosol spray devices can include fluorocarbons, ammonia, and vinyl chloride, which can contaminate air in the workplace. Dried detergent residue left in carpets after they have been shampooed with underdiluted carpet shampoo has been known to cause respiratory irritation" (Clark, 1985, p. 331). Many toxin-containing products can be replaced by "green" products that will not contribute irritants into the environment. Use of nontoxic cleaning compounds should be standard in the library environment. Vacuuming instead of dust mops or brooms should be used whenever possible. Use of high efficiency filter vacuums prevents dust and dirt from reentering the indoor atmosphere. A damp dust cloth can be an effective cleaner (Clark, 1985).

Copy machines can be sources of indoor pollution unless well vented and maintained. Care needs to be taken in the handling of toners, as respirable particulates can be released into the air unless handled carefully. When planning a renovation consider if it is possible to provide separate space for copiers, as suggested in planning for new buildings.

Rearrangements of workspace and use of office landscaping mandate review. Do new office landscape panels interfere with air flow patterns designed for a more traditional office arrangement? Are air diffusers and returns being blocked by furniture added to accommodate terminals, personal computers, etc.? Are rooms being constructed in former study space without adequate modifications to HVAC systems, temperature controls, etc.? These are important considerations in designing new work areas within existing space.

D. Materials, Furnishings, and Appliances

The composition of the walls, flooring, and furniture should be investigated. Many products have a toxic component. During renovations and remodeling, library building managers need to be aware of such things as adhesives used in laying carpet or in the fiber content of office landscaping, dyes in fabrics, composition of paneling, emissions from paint and adhesives, and other materials that may be introduced into the library atmosphere during renovation or remodeling. Planning should include working with purchasing departments to make sure that environmentally safe or low polluting products are specified in purchasing documents.

For installations, the library building manager should make every effort to schedule work that may introduce VOCs into the atmosphere during a period when the building is unoccupied. If this is impossible, notification to the staff of upcoming work will allow staff to make other arrangements, such as working in another area of the building or working at home during the installation.

Placement of plants in the workplace for air cleansing is mentioned in the literature. Key research on the pollution control properties of plants has been done by a NASA group led by Wolverton (1989). The work centered on individual plant species and their effectiveness on specific pollutants in controlled conditions. With identified pollutants, a mix of plant species may be beneficial. Consideration should be given to installing plants with substitutes for soil-based media to avoid possible complications. Room dimensions will guide the number of plants required for installation. Overall, the better strategy is ventilation and climate control.

If sources of potential contamination are present in the outdoor environment, remodeling and renovation may provide the opportunity to correct potential problems. Considerations outlined in the earlier section on new buildings can also be applied to renovations.

IV. Establishing a Baseline

What if you are not about to plan for a new building or renovation? Library building managers should develop a "snapshot" of their building as it exists currently, even if there are no immediate plans for changes. Knowing the current condition of your building—its heating, ventilation, and cooling system; the current ventilation rates; occupancy rate; the amount of humidity present in the building during various seasons; sources of indoor pollution; etc.,—can provide invaluable information for future planning. The planning checklist in Table II, while designed for those actively planning new buildings or remodels or renovations, can serve as a starting point for determining the current condition of an existing building as well. If library building managers are familiar with current conditions of their buildings, they can be more effective in dealing with future modifications.

V. Summary

The field of indoor air quality has many unknowns. While much research has been done, more answers are needed. Problems with indoor air can have adverse health effects and the problems can be frustrating. The source of the complaints does not matter; unless causes are identified they cannot be eradicated.

Preventive action is the best assurance for the maintenance of good indoor air quality. Use of planning checklists will ensure that major areas needing attention are not left out of building projects. Regular inspections of the building's mechanical operations are a necessity, and a good working relation-

Table II   Air Quality Planning Considerations Checklists

I. Building program plan	
Site selection	
Soil analysis for possible contaminants	_____
Industrial pollutants in area	_____
Particulate contamination from combustion	_____
Record-keeping system	_____
Design of building	
Physical location	
Air handling units (mechanical rooms)	_____
Air intakes	_____
Air exhausts	_____
Entrances/exits	_____
Pollution generating operations	
Binding and repair	_____
Storage of supplies	_____
Copy machines	_____
Heating, ventilation, and air conditioning	
Type of HVAC system	_____
Supply of outdoor air	_____
Thermal acceptability	_____
Humidity range controls	_____
Monitoring controls	_____
Air cleaning and filtration	_____
Concentrations of respiratory gases	_____
Dilution/removal of contaminants (air exchange rate)	_____
Ease of inspection and cleaning	_____
Microbial control	_____
System documentation	_____
Air/temperature control: workplaces	
Location of temperature controls	_____
Distribution of air	_____
Ventilation rate	_____
Special needs of computer operations	_____
Materials selection and specification	
Low emitting materials for construction	
Carpeting	_____
Adhesives	_____

continues

Table II   Continued

Stains	_____
Caulking compounds	_____
Ceiling tiles	_____
Panel fabric	_____
Draperies	_____
Floor and wall coverings	_____
Upholstery	_____
Paint	_____
Materials durability	_____
Ease of maintenance	_____
Installation procedures	
Off-gassing prior to installation	_____
Construction contamination	_____
Quality control	_____
Specifications check	_____
Commissioning	
Ventilation during initial occupancy	_____
In-place curing	_____
Inspection of work performed	_____
Expert validation	_____

II. Ongoing maintenance—renovation/remodeling projects

Materials selection and specification	
Low emitting materials for construction	
Carpeting	_____
Adhesives	_____
Stains	_____
Caulking compounds	_____
Ceiling tiles	_____
Panel fabrics	_____
Draperies	_____
Floor and wall coverings	_____
Upholstery	_____
Paint	_____
Materials durability	_____
Ease of maintenance	_____
Installation procedures	
Off-gassing prior to installation	_____
Construction contamination	_____

Table II   Continued

Quality control	———
Specifications check	———
Operations and maintenance	
System check: HVAC	———
System cleaning	———
System balancing	———
ASHRAE guidelines	———
Impact of new technologies	———
Building occupancy	———
Occupant activities	
Physical plant cleaning	———
Cleaning products	———
Equipment servicing	———
Interior pollutants	
Copy machines	———
Binding activities	———
Workspace design	———
Ergonomic considerations	———
Occupant space	———
Airflow	———
Lighting	———
Temperature control	———
Scheduling	
Notification of work schedule	———
Notification of schedule changes	———
When building is unoccupied	———
Periods of low occupancy	———
Relocation of staff	———

ship with those providing cleaning and maintenance to the building must be established. Library building managers should gather information about their current building to establish a baseline of operations that will be useful for future planning or in the event problems should occur. Library building managers should also increase awareness of what affects the environment in which they work through training and education.

From a building's design to its operational use, library building managers should take an active role in working with architects, engineers, purchasing agents, and other planners to create a quality indoor air environment that supports productive and healthful working conditions for library staff members.

References

American Society of Heating Refrigeration and Air Conditioning Engineers (ASHRAE). (1989). *Standard 62-1989: Ventilation for Acceptable Indoor Air Quality.* Atlanta, Georgia.

Arundel, A. V., Sterling, E. M., Biggin, J. H., and Sterling, T. D. (1986). Indirect health effects of relative humidity in indoor environments. *Environmental Health Perspectives* **65**, 351–361.

Beck, P. E. (1993). Intelligent design passes IQ test. *Consulting-Specifying Engineer* **13(1)**, 34–38.

Bernheim, A. (1993, August 22–28). *San Francisco Main Library: A Healthy Building.* Paper presented at the 59th IFLA Council and Conference, Barcelona, Spain.

Bosco, P. (1993). Indoor air quality: Blowing in the wind? *Buildings* **87(3)**, 47–48.

Brooks, B. O., and Davis, W. F. (1992). *Understanding Indoor Air Quality.* CRC Press, Boca Raton, Florida.

Brooks, B. O., Utter, G. M., Debroy, J. A., and Schimke, R. D. (1991). Indoor air pollution: An edifice complex. *Clinical Toxicology* **29(3)**, 315–374.

Carpet and Rug Institute (CRI). (1992). *A Guide to Carpet and Your Indoor Environment.* Dalton, Georgia.

Clark, S. M. (1985). Every breath you take: Indoor air quality in the library. *Canadian Library Journal* **42**, 327–334.

Dahlgren, A., and Beck, E. (1990). *Planning Library Buildings: A Select Bibliography.* American Library Association, Chicago.

Gammage, R. B., and Kaye, S. V., eds. (1985). *Indoor Air and Human Health.* Lewis Publishers, Chelsea, Michigan.

Gantenbein, D. (1990). Indoor ecology. *Architecture* **79(6)**, 107–109.

Girman, J. R. (1989). Volatile organic compounds and building bake-out. *Occupational Medicine* **4**, 695–712.

Girman, J., panelist. (1993, March 4). Statement presented on "Healthy Buildings and Materials." *Building Connections.* A series of three national videoconferences, Program II. American Institute of Architects, Washington, DC.

Goldberg, B. (1992). Colorado library worker's malaise traced to sick building syndrome. *American Libraries* **23**, 824–826.

Hobbs, C. H., and Mauderly, J. L. (1991). Risk assessment for diesel exhaust and ozone: The data from people and animals. *Clinical Toxicology* **29(3)**, 375–384.

Hughes, R. T., and O'Brien, D. M. (1986). Evaluation of building ventilation systems. *American Industrial Hygiene Association Journal* **47(4)**, 207–213.

Isacco, J. M. (1985). Work spaces, satisfaction & productivity in libraries. *Library Journal* **110(8)**, 27–30.

Kreiss, K. (1993). The sick building syndrome in office buildings—A breath of fresh air. *The New England Journal of Medicine* **328(12)**, 877–878.

Larue, J., and Larue, S. (1991). The green librarian. *Wilson Library Bulletin* **65**, 27–33.

Levin, H. (1992). Critical building design factors for indoor air quality and climate. In *AIA Environmental Resource Guide Subscription*, Topic VI.B 1-12. American Institute of Architects, Washington, DC.

Levin, H. (1993). The myth of indoor air pollution. *Progressive Architecture* **74(3)**, 33–37.

Martin, R., ed. (1992). *Libraries for the Future: Planning Buildings that Work.* Proceedings of the Library Buildings Preconference, June 27–28, 1991, in Atlanta, Georgia. American Library Association, Chicago.

Mattill, J. (1993). To help sick buildings recover. *Technology Review* **96(4)**, 12.

Menzies, R., Tamblyn, R., Farant, J. P., Hanley, J., Nunes, F., and Tamblyn, R. (1993). The effect of varying levels of outdoor-air supply on the symptoms of sick building syndrome. *The New England Journal of Medicine* **328**, 821–827.

Metcalf, K. D. (1986). *Planning Academic and Research Library Buildings* (P. D. Leighton and D. C. Weber, eds.). American Library Association, Chicago.

Michaels, A., and Michaels, D. (1992). Designing for technology in today's libraries. *Computers in Libraries* **12**, 8–25.

National Institute for Occupational Safety and Health, U.S. Environmental Protection Agency. (1991). *Indoor Air Quality and Work Environment Study: Library of Congress Madison Building*, 3 vols.

National Institute for Occupational Safety and Health, Division of Standards Development and Technology Transfer. (1989). *Indoor Air Quality: Selected References.* Cincinnati, Ohio.

National Research Council, Committee on Indoor Pollutants. (1981). *Indoor Pollutants.* National Academy Press, Washington, DC.

Price, B. J. (1989). Computer room air conditioning. *Library Hi Tech* **7(3)**, 29–47.

Raimondo, P. G. (1992). Indoor air pollution resources. *Special Libraries* **83**, 118–126.

Samet, J. M., Marbury, M. C., and Spengler, J. D. (1988). Health effects and sources of indoor air pollution, part II. *American Review of Respiratory Diseases* **137**, 221–242.

Samet, J., and Spengler, J. D., eds. (1991). *Indoor Air Pollution: A Health Perspective.* The Johns Hopkins University Press, Baltimore.

Sannwald, W. W., ed. (1991). *Checklist of Library Building Design Considerations.* American Library Association, Chicago.

Seitz, T. A. (1989). NIOSH indoor air quality investigations: 1971 through 1988. In *The Practitioner's Approach to Indoor Air Quality Investigations: Proceedings of Indoor Air Quality International Symposium* (D. M. Weekes and R. B. Gammage, eds.). American Industrial Hygiene Association, Akron, Ohio.

Shearer, R. W. (1991). Building-associated illness. *Professional Safety* **36(12)**, 15–21.

Silberman, R. M. (1993). A mandate for change in the library environment. *Library Administration and Management* **7(3)**, 145–152.

Simon, M. J. (1990). The sick (library) building syndrome. *Library Administration and Management* **4**, 87–91.

Skov, P., Valbjørn, O., and Pedersen, B. V. (1989). Influence of personal characteristics, job-related factors and psychosocial factors in the sick building syndrome. *Scandinavian Journal of Work Environmental Health* **15**, 286–295.

Smith, L. K. (1986). *Planning Library Buildings: From Decision to Design.* American Library Association, Chicago.

Sparks, L. E. (1988). Air cleaners and indoor air quality. *ASHRAE Journal* **30(7)**, 45.

Toombs, K. E. (1991). The evolution of academic library architecture: A summary. *Journal of Library Administration* **17(4)**, 25–36.

Turiel, I. (1985). *Indoor Air Quality and Human Health.* Stanford University Press, Stanford, California.

U.S. Environmental Protection Agency. (1991). *EPA and Indoor Air Quality* (Indoor Air Facts, 1 (rev.)) U.S. Government Printing Office, Washington, DC.

U.S. Environmental Protection Agency. (1993). *Respiratory Health Effects of Passive Smoking. Fact Sheet.* U.S. Government Printing Office, Washington, DC.

U.S. Environmental Protection Agency and U.S. National Institute for Occupational Safety and Health. (1991a). *Building Air Quality: A Guide for Building Owners and Facility Managers.* U.S. Government Printing Office, Washington, DC.

Wolverton, B. C., Johnson, A., and Bounds, K. (1989). *Interior Landscape Plants for Indoor Air Pollution Abatement.* National Aeronautics and Space Administration, John C. Stennis Space Center, Stennis Space Center, Mississippi.

Woods, J. E. (1991). An engineering approach to controlling indoor air quality. *Environmental Health Perspectives* **95,** 15–21.

Yocum, J. E., Clink, W. L., and Cole, W. A. (1971). Indoor/outdoor air quality relationships. *Journal of the Air Pollution Control Association* **21,** 251–259.

Index

AAMC (Association of American Medical Colleges), 131
Academic library reference service, 73–101
  burnout and stress in, 83–84
  changing management and managing changes in, 94–96
  crises in, 74–87
  evaluation of service and personnel, 92–94
  funding and budgeting in, 77–79
  future of, 99–102
  general character of future, 97–99
  impact of technology on, 79–83
  questions of accuracy and quality in, 84–87
  reshaping, 87–96
Advisors, 65
AIDS, 120, 126–127
AIM-TWIX, 134
Air quality, library indoor, see Library indoor air quality
ALA Colloquium on Library Science in Romania, 206–207
ALA Library Fellows to Romania, 207–208
American Library Association, see ALA entries
American Medical Informatics Association (AMIA), 154
American Society of Heating, Refrigeration, and Air Conditioning Engineers (ASHRAE), 222, 223, 224
AMIA (American Medical Informatics Association), 154
Anomalous state of knowledge (ASK), 39
ASHRAE (American Society of Heating, Refrigeration, and Air Conditioning Engineers), 222, 223, 224
ASK (anomalous state of knowledge), 39
Association of American Medical Colleges (AAMC), 131

Behavioralism, 27
Belief fields, 3
Bibliographic instruction, 57
  levels of, 66
Bibliographic paradigm, 62–63
Bibliographic sector, 10
Bioaerosols, 219
Book drives for Romania, international, 198–199
  U.S., 196–198
Books for Romania (USA), 196–197
Brandeis model, 89
Breland, Anita, 208
Bunge's criteria, 3–5

CD-ROMs, 80
Censorship in Romania, 193–194
Chapman, Ronald, 208–209
Charting intervention, 70
Childhood socialization, 115
Children
  information needs of, see Information needs of children
  information-seeking behavior of, 114–115
CIS (clinical information systems), 135–137
Citation analyses, 23–24
Climate control for library indoor air quality, 223–224
Clinical information systems (CIS), 135–137
Cognitive fields, 3
Cognitive view of information science, 31–44
Cognitive viewpoint, 32–34
  critique of, 43–44
Cognitivism, 27
Collaborators, 67–68
Columbia Presbyterian Medical Center (CPMC) IAIMS site, 141

237

COM (computer-output-microfiche) catalogs, 134

Commissioning and library indoor air quality, 226–227

Communication studies, information science and, 17–23

Communication studies paradigm, 21

Composing, 71

Computer applications
in libraries, 133–134
of medicine, 135–138

Computer-output-microfiche (COM) catalogs, 134

Computer science, 13

Constructive process, 58

Continuing intervention, 68

Convergence, models of, 18–19

Conversations, 69–70

Copy machines, 222

Counselors, 66–67

CPMC (Columbia Presbyterian Medical Center) IAIMS site, 141

Crossover model, 18–19

Customer-driven library service, 111

Decision support systems (DSS), 142

Design science, 46
information science as, within policy frame, 27–28

Document retrieval system, 30

Documentation, 7
defined, 8

Domain of information science, 25–26
shaping, 44–47

Drugs, 120–121

Duke University Medical Center (DUMC), 144

Environmental Protection Agency (EPA), 215

Esteem needs, 120

55 percent rule, 85

Fee-based contracts, 174

FID (International Federation for Information and Documentation), 7

Flow paradigm, 31

Focus Group Method of self-study, 148

Fulbright scholars to Romania, 208–209

General Professional Education of the Physician (GPEP), 139–140

Generalized library-based model for information science, 11

Georgetown University IAIMS site, 141–142

Government funding, library, 180–185

GPEP (General Professional Education of the Physician), 139–140

Health Evaluation through Logical Processing (HELP) system, 143

Health services, information technology in, 133–138

HELP (Health Evaluation through Logical Processing) system, 143

Hermeneutics, 44–45

Hospital information systems (HIS), 135–138

Human communication, 17

Humanities, 15
information science relation to, 15–16

IAIMS, see Integrated Academic Information Management Systems program

IAQ, library, see Library indoor air quality

Identifiers, 65

ILS (integrated library system), 143

In-place curing, 226–227

Indoor air quality, library, see Library indoor air quality

Informatics, medical, 135

Information
defined, 112
potential, 36
about sex, 122
structural definition of, 38
term, 23, 45

Information highway, 131

Information management systems planning, 131–156

Information movement paradigm, 37
  variant of, 49–50
Information needs of children, 111–128
  conceptualized, 112
  defined, 113
  definitions concerning, 112–113
  diagnosing, 114
  hierarchy of, 119–123
  identifiable barriers to meeting, 124
  implications in, 126–127
  methodology for collecting data on,
    117–119
  methods for determining, 113–114
  multiple providers for, 123
  research on, in southern California,
    115–126
  significant unmet, 123–124
Information-quick reference service point, 89
Information retrieval (IR), 15
Information science, 2
  central conceptualizations of, 24–27
  cognitive view of, 31–44
  communication studies and, 17–23
  concerns for, 38
  conclusions about, 47–51
  content and scope of, 1–51
  definitional elements used in, 25–26
  as design science within policy frame,
    27–28
  domain of, see Domain of information science
  empirical relations of other disciplines
    and, 23–24
  as field distinct from library science, 7–8
  generalized library-based model for, 11
  institution and information movement
    paradigms in, 29–31
  relation of other sciences to, 12–24
  relation to humanities, 15–16
  relation to natural sciences, 12–15
  relation to social sciences, 16–17
  relationship between library science and,
    6–11
  subfields of, 40–41
  term, 9
  theoretical, 34
  as unifying concept, 8–11
Information search process, 57
  collection in, 60
  common patterns in, 61–62

as constructive process, 58
counselors' role in, 66–67
exploration in, 59
formulation in, 59–60
initiation of, 59
misunderstanding of tasks in, 62
model of, 58–60
preparation to write at end of, 60
selection for, 59
students and, 57–72
Information-seeking behavior of children,
  114–115
Information storage and retrieval, 19
Information studies paradigm, 21
Information technology, 13
  in health services, 133–138
Instruction model, 99–100
Instructors, 66
Integrated Academic Information
    Management Systems (IAIMS)
    program, 132
  awards, 140
  awards and common elements, 143–144
  benefits from, 154–155
  changed to two-tiered program, 140
  changes to, 150
  defining success with, 152–155
  first four sites for, 141–143
  meetings under, 154
  National Library of Medicine and,
    138–140
  phases and awards, 138
  target outcome by, 147
  Tufts University planning grant, 145–147
Integrated library system (ILS), 143
Integrated model, 101
International book drives for Romania,
  198–199
International Federation for Information and
    Documentation (FID), 7
Internet, 173
Intervention, 57
  charting, 70
  concept of diagnosing zones of, 63–64
  continuing, 68
  diagnostic chart, 65
  librarians and, 57–72
  zones of, 64–65
IR (information retrieval), 15

Knowledge
  anomalous state of (ASK), 39
  defined, 35
Knowledge structure, 35

Larsen, Patricia, 208, 209
Lecturers, 66
Librarians
  intervention and, 57–72
  public, 159
  U.S., in Romania, 206–209
Librarianship
  defined, 7
  principles of, 7
  Romanian, United States and, 189–212
Library
  academic, reference service, see Academic
    library reference service
  changing concept of, 96–97
  computer applications in, 133–134
  defined, 29
  and information science, see Information
    science
  public, funding, see Public library funding
  Romanian, overview of, 191–195
  word, 2
Library automation, 170
Library-based model for information
    science, generalized, 11
Library expenditures, 78
Library indoor air quality (IAQ)
  building design for, 221–223
  commissioning and, 226–227
  establishing baselines for, 230
  low emitting materials for, 225–226
  materials, furnishings, and appliances and,
    229–230
  materials selection and specification for,
    225
  microbial control in, 224–225
  occupants and their activities and,
    228–229
  operations and maintenance for, 227–228
  planning and managing for, 215–234
  planning considerations checklists for,
    231–233
  planning in existing buildings for,
    227–230

  planning in new buildings for, 220–227
  preventive installation procedures for, 226
  problems with, 216
  remodeling and renovation for, 227
  selective sources of contaminants of, 218
  site selection for, 220–221
  sources of problems with, 216–220
  ventilation and climate control for,
    223–224
Library science
  defined, 7, 10
  as field distinct from information science,
    7–8
  relationship between information science
    and, 6–11
Library services, current paradigm for, 111
Library services, principle of uncertainty
    for, 62–63
Linguistic theory, 24
LIS, see Information science
Locators, 65
Love and belonging needs, 120
Low emitting materials for library indoor air
    quality, 225–226

Macroevaluation, 93
MARC records, 134
Market-oriented library service, 111
Marketing plans, library, 171–172
Massachusetts General Hospital Utility
    Multi-Programming System (MUMPS),
    136
Matrix model of management, 95
Mediation, levels of, 65–66
Medical informatics, 135
Medical Library Association (MLA), 154
Medicine, computer applications of,
    135–138
MEDLINE (MEDLARS on-line), 134
Metatheoretical frameworks, 4, 6
Microbial control in library indoor air
    quality, 224–225
Microevaluation, 93
MLA (Medical Library Association), 154
MUMPS (Massachusetts General Hospital
    Utility Multi-Programming System),
    136

National Information Infrastructure (NII), 165, 182
National Institute of Occupational Safety and Health (NIOSH), 217, 219
National Library of Medicine (NLM), 131–132
 IAIMS program and, 138–140
National Research and Education Network (NREN), 182
Natural sciences, 4, 13
 information science relation to, 12–15
Networking, telecommunications, 169
NII (National Information Infrastructure), 165, 182
NIOSH (National Institute of Occupational Safety and Health), 217, 219
NLM, *see* National Library of Medicine
NREN (National Research and Education Network), 182
Nutrition needs, 121

Online public access catalogs (OPACs), 132
Organizers, 65
Orientation strategies, 4, 5–6, 32–33
 as integrators of broadening field, 47–51
Overlapping fields model, 18–19

Paradigm, term, 29
Paradigm shift model, 18–19
Paraprofessionals at reference desk, 90–92
Partners for Livable Places, 172–173
Personal construct theory, 58
Physiological needs, 120
Planning considerations checklists for library indoor air quality, 231–233
Policy frame of reference, 27
Postmodern science, 46
Potential information, 36
Preventive installation procedures for library indoor air quality, 226
Problematics, 4
Process intervention strategies, 67–71
Public librarians, 159
Public library funding, 159–186
 cost control in, 166–170
 entrepreneurship in, 170–176
 fees and fundraising for, 176–180

funding formats, 163–165
history of, 161–163
political action and, 180–185

Reference, 57
Reference desk
 abolishment of, 88–90
 paraprofessionals at, 90–92
Reference providers, 75
Reference service
 academic library, *see* Academic library reference service
 model of, 74
Research fields, 3
 characteristics of, 3–5
Retrieval system model, 49
Retrieval tools, 79–80
Romania
 ALA Colloquium on Library Science in, 206–207
 ALA Library Fellows to, 207–208
 book drives for, *see* Book drives for Romania
 Books for (USA), 196–197
 censorship in, 193–194
 Fulbright scholars to, 208–209
 U.S. book drives for, 196–198
 U.S. librarians, 206–209
Romanian librarianship, United States and, 189–212
Romanian libraries, 191–195
Romanians studying in United States, 203–206

Safety needs, 120
SCAMCI (Symposium on Computer Applications in Medical Care), 154
Sciences, 4
Self-actualization needs, 120
Sex, information about, 122
Sick building syndrome (SBS), 216, 219, 222
Social construction theory, 116–117
Social sciences, 17
 information science relation to, 16–17
Socialization, childhood, 115

Students, information search process and, 57–72
Symposium on Computer Applications in Medical Care (SCAMCI), 154
Systems viewpoint, 32

Telecommunications networking, 169
Text, 38
Theoretical activity, types of, 5–6
Theoretical information science, 34
Theories, defining, 14
Theory-dependent meanings of concepts, 36
THSC (Tufts Health Science Campus), 145
Total quality management (TQM), 166
Tufts Health Science Campus (THSC), 145
Tufts University IAIMS planning grant, 145–147
Tufts University School of Medicine (TUSM), 145–147, 150–151
Tutors, 66

ULC (Urban Libraries Council), 168
UMAB (University of Maryland at Baltimore) IAIMS site, 142–143
Unit theories, 4
United States
    book drives for Romania in, 196–198
    Romanian librarianship and, 189–212
    Romanians studying in, 203–206
University of Maryland at Baltimore (UMAB) IAIMS site, 142–143
University of Utah IAIMS site, 143
Urban Libraries Council (ULC), 168
User-centered services, 98

Value-added services, 98
Ventilation for library indoor air quality, 223–224
Volatile organic compounds (VOCs), 217–218

Zones of intervention, 64–65

ISBN 0-12-024618-X

90040

9 780120 246182